# THE FAT TAIL

# THE

# FAT TAIL

### The Power of Political Knowledge for Strategic Investing

## IAN BREMMER
## AND
## PRESTON KEAT

OXFORD
UNIVERSITY PRESS
2009

# OXFORD
## UNIVERSITY PRESS

Oxford University Press, Inc., publishes works that further
Oxford University's objective of excellence
in research, scholarship, and education.

Oxford  New York
Auckland  Cape Town  Dar es Salaam  Hong Kong  Karachi
Kuala Lumpur  Madrid  Melbourne  Mexico City  Nairobi
New Delhi  Shanghai  Taipei  Toronto

With offices in
Argentina  Austria  Brazil  Chile  Czech Republic  France  Greece
Guatemala  Hungary  Italy  Japan  Poland  Portugal  Singapore
South Korea  Switzerland  Thailand  Turkey  Ukraine  Vietnam

Published by Oxford University Press, Inc.
198 Madison Avenue, New York, New York 10016

www.oup.com

Oxford is a registered trademark of Oxford University Press

Library of Congress Cataloging-in-Publication Data

Bremmer, Ian, [date]
The fat tail : the power of political knowledge
for strategic investing / Ian Bremmer and Preston Keat.
p.  cm.
Includes bibliographical references and index.
ISBN 978-0-19-532855-4
1. Risk management—Political aspects.  2. Investments—Political aspects.
3. Country risk—Management.  4. Political stability—Evaluation.
I. Keat, Preston.  II. Title.
HD61.B685 2009
332.6—dc22      2008048632

1 3 5 7 9 8 6 4 2

Printed in the United States of America
on acid-free paper

# Contents

# Acknowledgments

Political risk matters. That was clear when we started out as political scientists, clearer when we developed our company, and clearer still today.

There are a number of reasons for this. The world's energy supply increasingly comes from parts of the world that are politically unstable. The world's economic growth is increasingly driven by emerging markets—countries with less defined rule of law, less well-developed institutions, and greater political volatility. Dangerous technologies, from improvised explosive devices to ballistic missile componentry, are becoming more widely available, making rogue states and organizations a greater threat to global markets. And all of this is occurring at a moment when the United States, the world's only superpower, increasingly lacks both the political capital and the political will to promote and protect the security and prosperity of the global marketplace.

These emerging trends require a serious shift in how companies go about their business. Executives need to understand and assess political risk—how politics affects the markets where they operate or want to operate—if their businesses are to thrive. The business world isn't yet well placed to handle this challenge.

Truth be told, the private sector has a lousy record of hiring political scientists. Wall Street hires economists, strategists, and people with business backgrounds. A growing number of physicists, computer scientists, engineers, and mathematicians have joined their ranks. Yet for the questions that will increasingly determine the wisdom of their investment decisions, well, they need us.

We've talked about doing this book for years. The idea began to take shape when friends, colleagues, and clients asked us for recommendations on what to read as an introduction to political risk...and we ended up scratching our heads. As two folks with day jobs, though, it's taken some time.

We've incurred a number of debts along the way. First, at Columbia University, to Dean John H. Coatsworth and Associate Deans Patrick Bohan, Dan McIntyre, and Rob Garris at the School of International and Public Affairs (SIPA) for supporting our work and giving us the platform to teach for the past five years to some of the finest (and most eclectic groups of) graduate students on international affairs. They proved a sounding board for many of our ideas.

Second, to our colleagues at Eurasia Group. Over the years, dozens of analysts have helped us build a laboratory for understanding all aspects of political risk. They've made us broader analysts and sharper thinkers, and this book is much the better for it. A few deserve particular credit here. Ross Schaap gave very insightful comments on many of the chapters. Harry Harding, Abraham Kim, and Willis Sparks were extremely supportive and provided significant input. A number of others were very important in the research process, including Erasto Almeida, Irmak Bademli, David Bender, Heather Berkman, Enrique Bravo, Alex Brideau, Tiffany Chan, Nick Consonery, Tanya Costello, Philippe de Pontet, Mike Davies, Seema Desai, Patrick Esteruelas, Iku Fujimatsu, Chris Garman, John Green, Bob Herrera-Lim, Jonas Horner, Ana Jelenkovic, Robert Johnston, Daniel Kerner, Alex Kliment, Cliff Kupchan, Maria Kuusisto, Jon Levy, Damien Ma, Jun Okumura, Will Pearson, Wolfango Piccoli, Geoff Porter, Greg Priddy, Divya Reddy, Courtney Rickert, Scott Rosenstein, Hani Sabra, Sebastian Spio-Garbrah, Shari Stein, Sean West, and Rochdi Younsi.

In terms of production, we have been extremely fortunate to have a team we're very proud of. Our thanks to Mariah Kunkel, Alex Lloyd, and Amanda Remus, without whom our heads might well explode.

By far the most valuable contributor from Eurasia Group has been Dan Alamariu. His remarkable ability to simultaneously juggle dozens of inputs and fragments of information, combined with a knack for outstanding synthetic and historical analysis, has been essential to this project. We're grateful to have the opportunity to work with him.

We have also benefited from the intellectual contributions of a number of friends and colleagues outside the firm. We would like to mention Jon Benjamin, Matt Bishop, Pat Canavan, Vint Cerf, Robert Coolbrith, Ho Ching, Dan Dresner, Mark Franklin, David Fromkin, David Gordon, Ken Griffin, Nikolas Gvosdev, Enrique Hidalgo, Zachary Karabell, Justin Keat, Parag Khanna, Jill Lally, David Martinez, Vitali Meschoulam, Ed Morse, Bijan Mossavar-Rahmani, Tom Pickering, Juan Pujadas, Joel Rosenthal, Nouriel Roubini, Tom Stewart, and Fareed Zakaria. We're particularly grateful for the analytical rigor and coherence of Marci Shore.

At Oxford University Press, Niko Pfund is that rarest of publishers, a pragmatic intellectual visionary. Surely that's oxymoronic. And yet there he is. David McBride, our editor, is an outstanding social scientist, and has a clear eye for the big picture. Kirsten Sandberg (at Harvard Business Press, of all places) originally introduced us to the good folks at Oxford. We sent her flowers (two dozen!), but want to say thanks again here. Purdy is our publicist. He's been tremendous to work with thus far, and his name is very easy to remember. How could he not be a great publicist? Time will tell.

And to you, our reader, we hope you find this useful.

THE FAT TAIL

# Introduction | ONE

As a general rule, the most successful man in life is the man
who has the best information.
—Benjamin Disraeli

August 15, 1998, was a rough day for bankers. Leading economists were reassuring the leaders of Western financial institutions that Russia had both the ability and willingness to make payments on bonds held by international investors. With the 1997 Asian financial crisis still fresh in their minds, investors needed the reassurance, especially since Russian stock, bond, and currency markets had weakened substantially in recent days. Still, the advice of these economists seemed to make sense, and nobody panicked. Two days later, the Russian government devalued the ruble and defaulted on its debt. The fallout for investors was immediate and dramatic.

How did the experts get it so wrong? They missed a number of important political factors: Russia's weak and unfocused leadership, the pervasiveness of its corruption, poor market regulation, and the fact that a handful of well-placed Russian officials would actually benefit personally from a devaluation. In sovereign credit models used by banks, all these factors were absent or stuck in the "error term." They were considered too difficult to measure or to manage. But they were vitally important.

*What do we mean by a "fat tail?" Fat tails are the unexpectedly thick "tails"—or bulges—that we find on the tail ends of distribution curves that measure risks and their impact.*[1] *They represent the risk that a particular event will occur that appears so catastrophically damaging, unlikely to happen, and difficult to predict, that many of us choose to simply ignore it. Until it happens.* Russia's 1998 financial meltdown represents a quintessential fat tail, one much worse than anyone's risk model considered possible at the time. We generally expect that dramatic, high-impact events occur only rarely, appearing as "thin tails" on a curve. Yet, history shows that they happen with surprising frequency.

Russia's financial crisis offers one of many cases in which a better understanding of a fat tail would have made a big difference for both investors and policy makers. The world of politics is dynamic and complex. It is not incomprehensible. Political risk can be understood and managed with much more success than most of us think.

Investors and corporate decision makers tend to approach the political risks they face in unfamiliar markets in one of three ways. There is the "We are all doomed" approach. We'll simply ignore the risks, because they're too scary and too complex, and what can we do about them anyway? There is the "Let the big guys lead" philosophy. We'll ride along in the wake of the companies that have more resources and are better equipped to deal with the risks. If the big boys are safe there, so are we. Finally, there is the "We have our expert" strategy. We've already got a guy in-house who lived in that country for more than a year. His wife went to school there. He used to vacation there. He seems like he knows what's going on.

None of these strategies are effective. To succeed in the current global environment, decision makers must acknowledge the limitations—and serious pitfalls—of these approaches. Management of political risk requires a dynamic worldview that includes a combination of flexibility, creativity, and demonstrated expert knowledge.

There is no single formula for understanding and managing political risk. In Brazil, monitoring and evaluating the behavior of political parties and politicians in the National Congress are crucial for the accurate forecast of policy outcomes. In China, analysis of the personal power dynamics within an opaque Communist Party and among elite factions is vitally important. But the tools most helpful in evaluating political risk in Brazil or China are almost useless in Saudi Arabia, where politics are a family matter.

A growing number of investors and policy makers understand the importance of political risk. Yet, they also know that they lack a comprehensive and systematic set of tools for evaluating these risks. Most corporations actively manage enterprise risks that directly affect business organizations, such as credit, market, and operational risks. Credit risk, for example, has become an enormous industry—in 2008, banks will likely spend $8 billion on credit risk software alone.[2]

Yet, most businesses spend far less energy on the assessment and management of political risk. A recent survey of executives on risk management in the financial services industry[3] revealed that political risk was considered *the least* likely of all risk categories to be managed well. Geopolitical risk was also perceived as *least* likely to impact a corporation—and thus *least* likely to be included in a company's risk management planning. Business decision makers, investors, and risk managers tend to ignore political risk until it produces a crisis—like the one that roiled Russian markets in 1998.[4]

Why do intelligent policy makers and corporate decision makers so often ignore these types of risk? First, they view political risk as too complex and too difficult to forecast. Perhaps some changes are simply not foreseeable. Second, risk managers like data, and they haven't yet found much hard data on political risk. Many of the risk analysts working in the private sector have backgrounds in economics or finance. "How do we quantify political instability?" they ask. When it comes to data-driven forecasts, politics is too difficult to deal with. Third, companies often manage risks, such as credit or market risks, because the law says they have to. But there are no regulatory or legal requirements that corporations and financial institutions must manage political risk.

Yet, the dramatic increases in global economic integration, trade, and capital mobility in recent decades, combined with growing political instability and government intervention in markets, have created a climate in which political risk is more relevant than ever for companies and governments. This book will illustrate how political risks can be identified, analyzed, and mitigated—just like any other risks.

Political risk matters both at the macro (national and transnational) level and at the micro (local, regional) level. Geopolitical strategies drawn up in Moscow, Beijing, Tehran, and Washington will shape and reshape the international investment environment over the coming decades. So will efforts to enact market-friendly pension reforms in Ankara and Budapest that influence market sentiment on currency, bond, and equity prices. So will decisions made by local politicians and interest groups in the provinces, towns, and villages of the Brazilian and Indian countrysides.

In addition, investors' time horizons vary substantially. In the near term, currency strategists and bond and equity traders manage the impact of today's political developments on their market positions. Over the intermediate term, more strategic capital market participants take "long" views on country risk dynamics. Company managers cope with underlying local political and social stability. In the long term, corporations with substantial fixed capital assets on the ground and strategic planners for companies and governments must plan for a broad range of future scenarios.

Politics matter even in "safe" places. In the most politically stable markets like the United States, the European Union, or Japan, regulatory issues, often driven by politics, can have a dramatic impact on the business environment. The global banking crisis of 2008 exposed a number of serious flaws in companies' risk management systems and highlighted the importance of effective regulation. Governments in the United States and Europe intervened with massive infusions of capital and vowed to dramatically overhaul the regulatory frameworks governing the financial system. In addition, consider the growing anxiety in the United States over foreign investment in politically sensitive U.S. assets. The Committee on Foreign Investments in the United States (CFIUS) has become a political football following the controversies over the aborted bid by a Chinese oil company (CNOOC) to acquire the assets of U.S. oil firm Unocal and the failed attempt by a state-owned Arab firm (Dubai Ports World) to operate several major U.S. ports. Concern is growing among EU member states that have faced off with the European Commission over energy policy and financial market deregulation. Germany recently passed a law to regulate investments by sovereign wealth funds (SWFs) in "strategic" domestic companies. External financial and corporate interests have been unhappy with Tokyo over regulatory constraints that both suppress merger and acquisition activity and favor domestic firms. Taken together, these regulatory changes in developed world governments intensify concerns among international investors that "backdoor" protectionism is on the rise.

**Risk and Political Risk**

Risk is the probability that any event will turn into a measurable loss.[5] It is composed of two factors, probability and impact. How likely is the risk to occur? If it does occur, how big an impact will it have? Yet, in some cases it can be extremely difficult to answer either of those questions—or to determine what has created a particular risk.[6]

A relatively straightforward risk comes with smoking. For Canadian men who smoke, the lifetime probability of developing lung cancer is 17.2%. For male nonsmokers, it's just 1.3%. Data from medical research and life insurance companies allow us to establish a clear connection between smoking and cancer—and to accurately predict the consequences of smoking. Male nonsmokers in Canada have a life expectancy of 80.5 years. Male smokers can expect to live to about 73.[7]

Any "risk event" is part of a causal chain. A certain cause (or causes) can increase the chances that a specific event will occur. Once it does—whether it's a market crash, a terrorist attack, or a change in government—it will have consequences. The consequences of an event depend on who is exposed to it.

Political risk is the probability that a particular political action will produce changes in economic outcomes. It is quite different from the risk of disasters, like earthquakes, disease outbreaks, and droughts. It is also distinct from economic risks, such as inflation or sovereign credit risk. Most political risks are much harder to quantify than the risk of smoking. Yet, on a fundamental level, political risk is no different than any other form of risk

### The Complexity of Political Risk

Often, it is not easy to deconstruct political risk in terms of its causes, probability, and impact. That does not mean that the process of analyzing difficult issues is not valuable. Take the Bolshevik Revolution of 1917.[8] In October, after months of confusion and competition for political power following the abdication of the czar, Vladimir Lenin and other leading Bolsheviks overthrew Russia's Provisional Government. They set in motion a series of momentous changes that would eventually lead to the establishment of the world's first Communist regime. As the Bolsheviks transformed Russia into the Soviet Union, their new government nationalized private property, seized assets, ignored demands from foreign governments for repayment of debt, and forged new international alliances. The political, social, economic, and foreign policy profile of one of the world's great powers changed quickly and dramatically. Could the risk of upheaval been mitigated—or at least recognized in advance?

Nearly a century later, historians still argue over how and why the Bolshevik Revolution took place. Some emphasize the economic crisis generated by Russian participation in World War I. Others place greater emphasis on the mobilization of peasants and workers already active before the war began. Other experts stress the cruelty and incompetence of the ruling Romanovs. Still others point to economic problems, like runaway inflation. Still others emphasize the emergence of a coherent and ambitious Bolshevik leadership.

A risk event has complex and interrelated causes, and there is simply not enough available historical data to definitively determine the probability that the rarest of them will come to pass. Bolshevik Revolutions don't come along very often. Yet, if we had monitored political developments in Russia in January 1917, we *would* have recognized that the situation was unstable—and getting structurally worse. That assessment would have helped policy makers and investors better prepare themselves for the upheaval soon to be unleashed by an unstable Russia. How that can be done is the subject of this book.

## Interdependencies with Other Risks

For our purposes, it is useful to separate political risk from economic, financial, and other types of risk. But in reality, one form of risk can easily generate another. Gamal Abdel Nasser's rise to power in Egypt in 1952 (a political event) led to the expropriation of the Suez Canal in 1956 (a political and economic event), which had a direct financial impact on those who owned shares in it. The politically motivated seizure of farmland by the Mugabe government in Zimbabwe (2000–05) has led to, among other things, hyperinflation (an economic risk) and famine (a threat to social stability).

This problem is not a new one. We can look back to the surprisingly momentous consequences of a decision made in 1575 by King Philip II to default on Spain's debt.[9] A series of economic and political risks produced a politically motivated credit default, the independence of the Netherlands, and the decline of Spanish imperial power.

Philip II inherited one of the world's superpowers, giving him effective political control of Spain, southern Italy, the Netherlands, Flanders (part of today's Belgium), and parts of France. Added to these possessions was Spain's extensive colonial empire in the Americas. Philip's army and navy were probably the best in the world. Soon, he would send the Spanish Armada to invade England (and almost succeed).

So much power must have seemed a good thing, but the burdens that come with it had driven his father into a monastery. In 1575, Philip found himself fighting a series of seemingly intractable wars. His navy had been battling the Ottoman Empire in the Mediterranean for more than a decade and his army had struggled with Dutch separatist rebels for four years.

These wars were expensive, and Philip was running out of money. Most of his income came from the revenues collected from those widespread territorial possessions. Unfortunately, taxes had to be approved by local parliaments (or estates). Almost all the provinces had one, making it more complicated to simply raise taxes. After many years of war, these parliaments were increasingly upset by new requests for cash. Philip II had to borrow the money. Spain happened to be closely allied with the city-state of Genoa, the Wall Street (or the City) of the time. The Genoese gladly lent Philip money, as long as he paid the interest. But after years of borrowing, it became harder and harder to make those payments. Philip faced the difficult choice of asking his estates for new taxes or renegotiating the loans with the Genoese.

For Philip II, both options proved problematic. He first tried to increase taxes, but the Spanish estates said no. His Genoese creditors then refused to renegotiate the interest rates on his loans. With no better option, Philip decided to default in September 1575.[10]

The impact of this political act was swift and drastic. Genoese bankers refused to extend further credit to the Spanish crown. Without funds, Spain could no longer pay the large mercenary army fighting the rebel Dutch provinces on its behalf. By July 1576, the Spanish army in the Netherlands, which had not been paid in months, mutinied and began to attack Spanish-held towns. This unrest eventually provoked the sack of Antwerp (one of the great industrial centers of Europe) and the massacre of as many as 18,000 citizens. The Spanish reputation in the Netherlands and Europe collapsed almost overnight, as did any chance that Spain might quell the Dutch rebellion.[11]

Philip's quandary reveals how one type of risk produces and fuels another. Spain's political risks from wars with the Dutch and the Turks, combined with economic imbalances, significantly increased the risk of a sovereign credit default. The default then generated a new series of political and economic risks and imbalances.

## Political Risk and the Past

What do the Bolshevik Revolution and a 16th-century Spanish debt default have to do with the political risks facing today's policy maker and investor? Though political risks have become increasingly complex, the forces driving a politically motivated 16th-century credit default or a 20th-century revolution are not fundamentally different than those that create similar risks today. An especially important constant: political interests often trump economic ones in the performance of markets. In many cases, as in Russia in 1998, economists have argued that a certain event, like a default, will not happen because it would so badly damage that state's economy. Yet, the politicians who will decide whether to default may very well make their decision with political, rather than economic, goals in mind.

Consider the problem of expropriation, the classic political risk faced by companies directly investing abroad. Mexico's 1938 decision to nationalize its hydrocarbons sector provides a landmark example of how political motives can shape economic actions. It has also served as a kind of "best practice" model for the nationalization of natural resources in Venezuela, Bolivia, Russia, Kazakhstan, and Algeria. Iraq may well be next.

In March 1938, Mexican president Lázaro Cárdenas signed an order expropriating Mexico's petroleum industry, which until then had been dominated by foreign companies such as Standard Oil of New Jersey, Gulf Oil, and Royal Dutch Shell. The decision yielded estimated losses of $200 million for U.S. companies and similar losses for the Anglo-Dutch investors.[12] It also illustrates several factors that have traditionally led governments to seize private property and foreign direct investments: ideology, nationalism, domestic interest groups, national economic development, and geopolitics.

The nationalization of the oil industry formed one important element of a wider series of reforms under the slogan "Mexico for Mexicans." Cárdenas sought to consolidate his power among core supporters from the labor movement and the political Left. The nationalization fit with a developing anticapitalist and nationalist agenda, and rewarded key domestic political constituents. The biggest winner was the petroleum workers union, which gained access to a steady stream of revenues and side benefits. The statist-minded Cárdenas also saw the foreign oil companies as an obstacle to Mexico's economic development. As with future oil industry nationalizers in other countries, Cárdenas believed that his administration, not foreign companies, could best manage Mexico's economy and natural resources.

A final, and perhaps defining, factor was the geopolitical environment of the time. In the 1930s, the United States had begun to shift its approach to Latin America from "gunboat diplomacy" toward a "good neighbor" policy. With a political crisis looming in Europe (which led to World War II), the likelihood of an American or European backlash against Mexico had significantly diminished.

The nationalization was a resounding political success, and Cárdenas is revered in Mexico to this day. It also helped the ruling Institutional Revolutionary Party (PRI) maintain its grip on power by providing bases for patronage and by burnishing its nationalist credentials. But in economic terms, the expropriations and the creation of a national oil company (PEMEX) were a disaster. They provoked the flight of foreign know-how and capital; by 1940, foreign investment in Mexico had plummeted to a quarter of the level that the country had attracted two decades earlier.[13] The loss of foreign expertise made oil exploration much more difficult. Revenues declined, and national debt increased.[14]

Mexico's 1938 oil expropriation continues to impact the political risk landscape in Latin America, where President Hugo Chávez's agenda in Venezuela borrows heavily from the logic of Cárdenas's decision. Seven decades later, Mexico has a pressing need to reform the energy sector and to upgrade declining fields with the help of outside investors. Venezuela will face precisely the same problems in coming years, as foreign oil firms are driven from the country and as oil profits diverted for politically inspired spending projects push state-owned energy company PDVSA's production into sharper decline.

### Understanding Political Risk

What is the best way to analyze political risk? Given the complexity of its causes, its many potential impacts, and the diversity of forms it takes, there is no easy answer. Any political event that can (directly or indirectly) alter the value of an economic asset can be considered a political risk. A declaration of war, an act of terror, a law that expropriates private property, and a change in the rules governing foreign investment are all examples of political risk. Governments, rebel groups, nongovernmental organizations, individuals, and anyone else who engages in a political action can create political risk.[15] The impact of a particular

**TABLE 1.1** Types of political risk

| Main types of risk events shocks | Examples |
| --- | --- |
| Geopolitical | International wars |
| | Great power shifts |
| | Economic sanctions and embargoes |
| Global energy | Politically decided supply and demand issues |
| Terrorism | Destruction of property |
| | Kindapping/hijackings |
| Internal political strife | Revolutions |
| | Civil wars |
| | Coup d'etat |
| | Nationalism |
| | Social unrest (strikes, demonstrations) |
| Expropriations | Confiscations of property |
| | "Creeping" expropriations |
| Breaches of contract | Government frustration or reneging of contracts |
| | Wrongful calling of letters of credit |
| Capital market risks, currency, and repatriations of profits | Currency controls |
| | Politically motivated credit defaults and market shifts |
| | Repatriation of profits |
| Subtle discrimination and favoritism | Discriminatory taxation |
| | Corruption |
| Unknowns/uncertainty | Effects of global warming |
| | Effects of demographic changes |
| | Political events that cannot be foreseen |

risk depends on who must absorb its worst effects. Corporations can lose people, money, or infrastructure as a result of political events. Governments can lose all of those things, as well as their independence.

There are a wealth of tools, methods, and ideas that can help corporations and policy makers better understand and forecast political risk. Effective management of political risk requires three skill sets: an understanding of which tools and methods are best suited to a particular political environment, awareness of how a particular analyst's style and temperament may produce a particular kind of bias, and an ability to transcend preexisting assumptions about what is possible to successfully communicate a forecast.[16]

## Style and Temperament

The disposition of those who assess risk helps determine how accurate or biased the analysis and understanding of political risks will be. Philip Tetlock argues that analysts can be divided into two types: "hedgehogs" and "foxes."[17] The hedgehog knows one big thing—and may display a near-fanatical adherence to it—while refusing to consider alternatives. The fox knows many things—and can draw on a wide array of data and analytical frameworks in making forecasts. Tetlock argues that foxes, who tend to be more tolerant of counterarguments and see the bigger picture, make better risk analysts. But risk analysis is contextual. In some cases, the simplicity of hedgehog analysis yields better results; in others, the complexity of fox analysis produces a more accurate forecast. When it comes to communicating the analysis, the hedgehog approach is sometimes better suited for reaching decision makers and cutting through existing cultural and organizational biases.

Foxes tend to be less successful than hedgehogs with scenario analysis. They can imagine many competing scenarios and too often exaggerate the probability of each of them. Hedgehogs believe in simple explanations, often consistent with a broader set of ideological beliefs, and can be overly confident forecasters. Equally important, they can remain unwilling to reconsider the merits of rival hypotheses after they have made a forecasting error.

The best forecasters whom Tetlock studied have two characteristics. They are eclectic thinkers who are tolerant of counterarguments. They also avoid the common mistake of overestimating the probability of change. The approach to political risk we will set forward in this book reflects this basic spirit. We are eclectic in our methodology rather than wedded to a single model of political risk or political change. And we are cautious about exaggerating the probability of fundamental change, whether for better or for worse.[18]

## Making Risks Known

Another key component of understanding political risk is its successful communication. If a risk is not properly communicated, timely identification and accurate analysis are useless. Al Qaeda's attacks on New York and Washington, DC, on September 11, 2001, killed nearly 3,000 people, the largest death toll produced by warfare or terrorism on American soil since the end of the Civil War. In hindsight, all the data needed to predict the attacks was there. So was much of the analysis. Al Qaeda–associated Islamic terrorists had in the 10 years prior to September 11 tried to crash planes into tall buildings (in Paris, for one) and had attacked the World Trade Center in 1993. The U.S. government's domestic security agencies had at least in passing considered an airplane suicide plan scenario.[19]

Yet, miscommunication between security agencies, failure of imagination, and the constraints on risk managers who must process large amounts of often competing bits of information on many different sources of risk prevented any warning of imminent danger from being successfully transmitted to those in a position to thwart the attacks. Some things get lost in the information flow. Others are blocked by social and organizational biases.

One common type of bias is bureaucratic. Organizations develop idiosyncratic cultures and processes that produce specific worldviews. During the Cuban missile crisis, the Kennedy administration worked hard to avoid a "tunnel vision" scenario in which institutional assumptions about Soviet intentions and behavior might have ignited direct and unnecessary confrontation with Moscow.

Idées fixes and wishful thinking constitute another type of bias. When German forces invaded the Soviet Union in June 1941, Stalin's initial reaction was to discount the reports. The invasion did not fit his expectation, and he rejected it. Could reporting of the risk have been successful, given Stalin's personality and his reputation for punishing the bearers of bad news? Difficult personalities and biases of decision makers pose a challenge to effective risk management.

These are only two of the many biases that can block accurate and timely reporting of risk. Ultimately, our understanding of political risk is inherently tied to our cultural and ethical values.[20] The potential events we consider most frightening are those that threaten the things we most want to protect, like our independence and the value of our assets and investments. Thus, perception of risk is as important as the risk itself. We don't necessarily face more risks than our ancestors did. In many respects we are more secure.[21] The plagues, famines, and political unrest faced by those who came before us (think Mongol invasions) now offer little more than entertainment (think "Conan the Barbarian").

Generations past often blamed gods or fate for unforeseen and unhappy events. Modern societies understand risk differently.[22] Our risks may have not increased, but economic globalization and the sophistication of our technology have expanded both the complexity and the interdependence of the challenges we face, including nuclear proliferation, terrorism, state failure, and the more rapid pace of political and social change. As the stakes for global stability have risen, the need to better understand and more successfully manage political risk has become more urgent.

## Book Overview/Roadmap

In this book we discuss a broad range of political risk types, ranging from global risks, which play out in the international system, to country risks, which manifest themselves in a specific society or government, to micro-level risks, which occur at the substate and industry level.

But we will start by acknowledging how much we *cannot* know. To understand political risks, it is essential to accept that much is beyond our ability to forecast. Many have argued that the interaction between the enormous variety of actors making policy decisions—individuals, groups, and states—and human psychology, history, and economics, as well as the natural environment, has created a world that is largely driven by unexpected, undeterminable, and frequently catastrophic events.[23] It is worth exploring first the things that are unpredictable and uncertain—and there are many. The next chapter will focus on this theme.

However, much *can* be predicted, and there is a significant amount that corporations and governments can do to understand and mitigate the negative potential of political risk. The following six chapters will focus on broad types of political risk, the geopolitical (those resulting from international wars or great power politics), expropriation, regulatory changes, or social unrest (a broad category that can include anything from civil wars and revolutions to mass demonstrations). Each chapter will detail how each risk is identified, weighed, and mitigated and explain how companies and governments did and didn't assess the risk effectively.

Understanding risks is only half the game. They must also be effectively communicated. In chapters nine and ten, we consider the challenges of ensuring that risks are understood by the right people at the right time. The final step in the process—mitigation. Even if you correctly identify a risk it is not always obvious what a firm or government should do about it.

We are not at the mercy of fat tails. Now we turn to why that is.

# Dealing with Uncertainty | T W O

If we begin with certainties, we shall end in doubts;
but if we begin with doubts, and we are patient in them,
we shall end in certainties.

—Sir Francis Bacon

Today, the palm-fringed beaches of Yucatán and Cozumel are known mainly as a holiday getaway spot for raucous college students. But in 1519, the Yucatán coast saw the beginning of what perhaps comes closest in human history to an alien invasion. Hernán Cortés and 600 Spaniards sailing from Cuba landed there and set in motion a remarkable chain of events that would culminate in the Spanish conquest of the Americas.[1]

Cortés, like many adventurers of the time, came in search of great riches and new lands for himself and his king. Once ashore, he eventually made contact with the Aztecs, who then controlled a powerful empire of city-states extending across much of today's Mexico. As the Aztecs and their emperor, Montezuma, struggled to understand the sudden appearance of fair-skinned, bearded, armed, and armored men on horseback, Cortés forged alliances with rival city-states and prepared his battalion-sized warband to conquer a civilization of as many as 30 million people.[2] Within two years, Cortés had crushed the Aztec Empire, killed a succession of its emperors, and laid the foundation for 300 years of Spanish colonial rule in Mexico.

Spain boasted one of the most feared armies in Europe, and its frontal assault tactics were devastating for a foe unfamiliar with European norms of warfare. The impact of Spanish cavalry and firearms has been overstated (the former were too few, the latter unreliable), but Spanish armor and steel-edged weapons offered a material technological advantage when used against warriors from a civilization that lacked ironworking.[3]

Yet the Aztecs were not defeated by superior tactics and technology alone. Cortés drew strength from three additional factors. First, he cultivated allies among the Aztecs' most bitter local rivals, who provided the conquistadors with both manpower and strategically useful information.

Second, there was disease. In H. G. Wells's classic story of a Martian invasion, *War of the Worlds,* aliens conquer the Earth's native population, but are ultimately felled by the common cold, to which they have no immunity. In fact, Wells drew inspiration for his story directly from reports of the numerous encounters that took place between European explorers and indigenous people from 1492 onward. During the Spanish conquest of Mexico, the natives, not the invaders, fell victim. Various estimates have placed Aztec deaths from European diseases like smallpox at 10% to 50% of the population between 1520–21,[4] making it an early (though inadvertent) use of a biological weapon of war.

Third, and most interesting for our purposes, the shock of the new and unexpected paralyzed the Aztecs. When people do not know how to respond to a catastrophic event, they often ascribe it to the supernatural. The common story of Cortés's conquest credits the initial Aztec inaction to their association of Cortés with the myth of Quetzalcoatl, an important god in the Aztec pantheon. In Aztec mythology, Quetzalcoatl was portrayed as a light-skinned, bearded figure with light eyes who would one day return. Spanish chronicles of that time assert that Montezuma II, the Aztec emperor, believed that Cortés's appearance represented Quetzalcoatl's return. Modern scholars have cast doubt on that view. But there is little question that the Aztecs were fascinated with the newcomers, their manners, style of dress, beliefs, and technology. Whatever the precise circumstances, Montezuma and his subjects were catastrophically slow to respond to the Spanish threat.

Nothing in the Aztecs' experience prepared them for the horses, muskets, steel, and infantry shock tactics that suddenly threatened their survival.[5] Yet, when it comes to political risks, the unimaginable happens more often than you might think.

Unlike risk (which is probability times impact), uncertainty implies an inability to determine the probability or the impact (or both) of a certain future event. The main task and challenge of risk management is to transform uncertainty into probabilistic, measurable assessments, or risks. That is not always possible. Risk analysts and managers must accept that they will always have to contend with some level of uncertainty.[6]

The United States military didn't find weapons of mass destruction following its 2003 invasion of Iraq, but the search did produce an important insight in the form of a much-derided comment from then-Defense Secretary Donald Rumsfeld.

> Reports that say that something hasn't happened are always interesting to me, because as we know, there are known knowns; there are things we know we know. We also know there are known unknowns; that is to say we know there are some things we do not know. But there are also unknown unknowns—the ones we don't know we don't know. And if one looks throughout the history of our country and other free countries, it is the latter category that tend to be the difficult ones.[7]

## Grappling with Unknowns: Understanding "Fat Tails"

How does an organization deal with "known unknowns" and "unknown unknowns"? No one accurately predicted the end of the Cold War, the Bolshevik Revolution, or the 9/11 attacks. Or, to take a more recent corporate example, there is the story of Arla Foods.

In its September 30, 2005, issue, the Danish newspaper *Jyllands-Posten* published a series of 12 cartoons depicting the prophet Muhammad. This attempt to provoke public debate in Denmark triggered an explosion of anger across the Muslim world. Outrage over what was seen as an insult to Islam was subsequently directed not only at *Jyllands-Posten,* but at Denmark and its business interests.

Many in Denmark fully expected angry reactions to the cartoons, but the magnitude, intensity, and persistence of the crisis and its damage to both private and diplomatic interests were completely unforeseen. The sophistication and organization of the reaction in many countries was particularly surprising as e-mail and mobile phone text messaging dramatically boosted efforts to coordinate collective action against Danish products.

Saudi religious leaders targeted Arla Foods, one of Scandinavia's largest dairy producers, and called for boycotts of its products during Friday prayers. Images of Arla butter and cheese were shown on Saudi television as part of the coverage of the cartoon controversy.[8] Denunciations echoed across Islamic Web sites and via e-mail and mobile SMS messages, and the protests reportedly cost the company $1.5 million per day.[9] As the boycotts had everything to do with Arla's country of origin and nothing to do with its products, the firm was powerless to respond.[10]

No one advising Arla before the cartoons were published could have foreseen this low probability, high impact risk. Even after they were published, it would have required extraordinary foresight to do so: they did not provoke an uproar in the Middle East until ten months after they first appeared. The cartoons became an issue only when a small group of religious activists decided to make them one.

Perhaps the most difficult aspect of all risk management is in providing accurate probabilities for events that are both rare and potentially devastating. Nassim Nicholas Taleb's provocative book *The Black Swan: The Impact of the Highly Improbable* argues precisely that the most important events in the world tend to be those that are rare, extreme in their impact, and not predictable statistically (or otherwise) with any consistency. Such events are rare enough that they cannot be accurately described by a bell-shaped (standard normal) statistical distribution that relies on historical data series.

Taleb's insight is that modern society has been conditioned to think about risks and probabilities in terms of "normal distributions," or bell curves, and that this is a deep analytical flaw. Normal distributions indicate that catastrophic events are extremely unlikely to happen. Historically, when these models have been applied to calculate the likelihood of catastrophic events, like mortgage meltdowns, financial crashes, sovereign credit defaults, and terrorist attacks, they have failed badly.

In the standard statistical assumption about how the world works[11] (see figure 2.1), you notice that the ends of the curve are "thin." This signifies that events in those ranges are very unlikely to occur. "100-year" floods happen far more often than once a century. The same goes for financial crises.

This approach works for polling samples, for example, because these surveys assume that the distribution of political views present in a large enough group of people will be approximately equal to the views of the entire country. It is often assumed that other political and social behavior can be predicted with a similar set of tools. This assumption is misleading, because many of the risks we face today do not follow a normal distribution, but one that is highly skewed. Really unexpected things happen far more often than our usual statistical models would indicate. Taleb calls these events "black swans." They are more commonly (and less poetically) known as "fat tails" (see figure 2.2).[12]

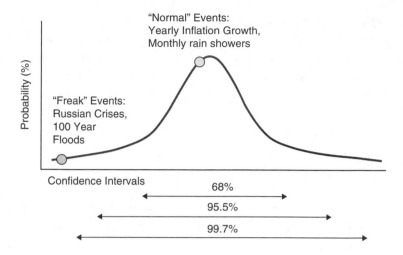

FIGURE 2.1 Standard bell-curve distribution and assumptions

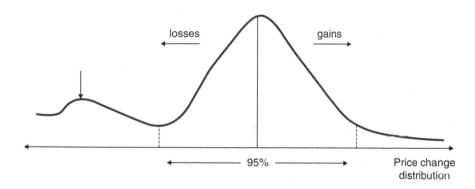

FIGURE 2.2 "Fat tail" or "long tail" for downside risk

For Taleb, this shows that people have very limited predictive ability when it comes to rare events. Before European explorers first landed in Australia, they assumed that all swans were white. Every swan they had ever seen had been white. Yet, in Australia, they found a previously unknown species of black swan, forcing scientists to refine their definition of what a swan was. The understanding that swans were white was a theory built on inference. The theory had been affirmed many times—until a single black swan proved the theory wrong.[13] Taleb's black swan represents an event that is extremely rare, yet also has an extreme impact, disproportionate to its probability. Taleb then argues that these events cannot be predicted or perceived in advance, because human beings are especially bad at predicting irregular events, even if they are relatively good at assigning probabilities to more likely ones.[14] And to Taleb, critical events in the world, from the spread of Christianity and Islam to World War I and 9/11, are fat tails. Accordingly:

> History and societies do not crawl. They make jumps. They go from fracture to fracture, with a few vibrations in between. Yet we...like to believe in the predictable, small incremental progression.[15]

This is a disturbing proposition. As we discussed earlier, predicting the Russian Revolution or Arla Food's troubles would have been impossible; even now, with the benefit of hindsight, it is difficult to agree on what caused them. Even if the causes are well known, it is impossible to say how an event will occur. If you drop a glass, you know it will break. But you cannot predict with any confidence where each piece will come to rest.

In the case of 9/11, even if we had known that terrorists wanted to attack U.S. interests and that their plan would involve airplanes, it would still have been extremely difficult to figure out the number, place, timing, and tactics that were used.[16] In fact, Taleb argues that accurate forecasting of catastrophic events is simply impossible.[17] These are "black swan" events.[18]

Taleb's approach has fundamental limitations. First, most organizations are more likely to face the impact of frequent minor disturbances (strikes, corruption, etc.), rather than catastrophies like revolutions, wars, and state failure.[19] The collective impact of many smaller events can surpass that of a fat tail event.

Consider the cumulative effect of corruption. As part of the cost of doing business in Nigeria, work permits, access to utilities, and so forth sometimes require bribes for local officials. Foreign corporations accept risks to their reputations, and even legal action, at home by playing this game. By itself, petty corruption ranks relatively low as a political risk, more an annoyance than a disaster.[20] Yet the impact of petty corruption over several years can be catastrophic for a country's stability—even its survival—and for a company's bottom line. In several African countries, the cumulative effects of petty corruption have undermined the ability of governments to deliver basic services and security—sometimes even within the capital city.[21] During the 1990s, corruption contributed to risks of state failure in countries like Congo, Liberia, and Sierra Leone.

But these risks can be predicted, and their gradual effects can be measured. It's like the risk of smoking. The risk over time from smoking cigarettes is death, which is a pretty well-established (and catastrophic) fact. Yet there is no unpredictable "black swan" death from smoking: all the facts are known. Arguing that all catastrophic events and disasters are only obvious in retrospect ignores the fact that people regularly engage in risky behavior they know will have serious and predictable consequences.

An organization facing political risks does not have the luxury of worrying only about black swans, but must assess all risks in a comprehensive way. Low-impact risks like smoking and petty corruption *do* cumulatively result in catastrophe over time. There is significant value in predicting the things we can. But the question of how to deal with those earthshaking events that we cannot envision, much less predict, remains important.

Those who would apply Taleb's theory to political risk face another important problem. Unlike financial, economic, or environmental risks, political risks are usually generated by individuals, people with particular and identifiable sets of motivations and limitations. This makes them predictable—and not black swans. If we can map these incentives and constraints, it is considerably easier to forecast downside risks (and the limitations on upside outcomes).

Let's look at Business Bank, a small and successful private bank in Uzbekistan. In 2005, the Uzbek Central bank closed Business Bank and liquidated its assets.[22] Press coverage noted that the closure came without warning. Western diplomats pointed out that Business Bank had been praised during a meeting of the central bank just days before.[23] If you were Business Bank's owner or one of its business partners, this closure and liquidation would seem a catastrophic "black swan" event.

Banks are not shut down for no reason. The Uzbek Central bank cited unspecified (and probably bogus) violations of the state's banking and finance laws as the basis for its decision. But in the months before the seizure, Business Bank's parent corporation, Naitov Group, had partnered with the U.S. firm SkyTel to enter the Uzbek mobile telephone market, bringing it into conflict with mobile telephone investments held by Gulnara Karimova, the eldest daughter of Uzbekistan's president.[24] The presence of politically influential people in the mobile phone sector should have raised all sorts of red flags.

Further, press coverage suggested that a pending investment in Business Bank by the European Bank for Reconstruction and Development (EBRD) was also a primary trigger for Business Bank's liquidation.[25] The EBRD has had a long and contentious relationship with the Uzbek government, especially on issues of human rights and transparency, and the involvement of the EBRD in an already politically troublesome business may have driven the Uzbek government to act.

This is why politically motivated events like the seizure of Business Bank *are* predictable. Most political risks hinge on the actions and policies of people and organizations. That implies, in most cases, planning and deliberation. So, with perfect intelligence, it would be entirely possible to predict a large number of high-impact and low-probability political events. If the United States and Soviet Union had had better spies and better risk-reporting mechanisms, both Pearl Harbor and the 1941 German invasion of Russia could have been predicted. The same goes for 9/11 or for most terrorist attacks. One analyst of strategic studies, Richard Betts, notes that in politics, "pure bolts from the blue hardly ever occur."[26] Perfect intelligence and warning could predict all threats that originate from human actions.

Of course there is no such thing as perfect intelligence. For one, there is the issue of complexity, especially when it comes to revolutions, civil wars, and other forms of large-scale conflict. In 1917, following the tsar's abdication, Lenin, then in exile in Switzerland, saw an opportunity to create a Communist revolution. Between Switzerland and Russia lies Germany, with which Russia was at war. To take the shortest route to Russia, Lenin needed the support of the German government. He was able to win official German help to cross the front lines and return to Petrograd, then Russia's capital.

The Germans provided this service to Lenin in hopes of fueling instability within Russia. Did they believe he could topple the Russian government? Would they have provided him with safe passage had they foreseen the sort of government he would create? The answer to both questions is probably no. Lenin succeeded more than anyone, probably including Lenin himself, thought possible. Many factors, including luck, played a role in his ultimate triumph.

So, in many respects, the Bolshevik Revolution of 1917 was both unpredictable and unexpected. But it was not a black swan. Both the British Foreign Office and their Russian allies knew the Germans were providing transportation and funding for Lenin to cause trouble at home. They knew this before Lenin got off the train at Petrograd's Finland Station.[27] The Russian Provisional Government, which took power following the tsar's abdication, knew Lenin would prove a threat, and yet it did nothing to stop him. Had Lenin remained in Switzerland, the history of the 20th century could have taken an entirely different turn. But his return was not a "bolt from the blue," despite the large number of events that might have changed the course of history and the complexity they added to any forecast of Russia's future.

### Risk Mapping and Data Collection

To better understand how political risk works, let us start with things that are known and can, to some extent, be understood and forecast. We must first distinguish between ordinary and catastrophic risks. Figure 2.3 plots risk frequency (how often it is likely to occur) versus magnitude of impact (how big an effect it would have if it did occur). Financial institutions use tools like this to plot the operational risks they face. They are also useful in understanding how political risks are distributed. This right-sloping curve shows that most organizations face many low-impact risks that happen with regular frequency (say, changes in taxation rates or minor strikes) and a few high-impact/catastrophic risks that happen relatively rarely (like World War II or the 9/11 attacks). The noncatastrophic events (ordinary risks) can be plotted using standard statistical techniques, such as normal distributions, given that they happen relatively often—and therefore provide risk analysts with plenty of data. Unfortunately, that doesn't apply to the high-impact, low-probability events—the fat tails.

Creation of a risk map can help an organization develop a common risk language and identify the kinds of risks it faces. For operational risk, financial institutions routinely collect data from their losses on previous events. With this information, they can create a large database that allows them to determine the probability of similar losses in the future. For catastrophic events, standard statistical data does not have much predictive power (although statistical models do offer ways of modeling the impact of fat tails[28]).

Political risk maps abound and can be useful. Yet political risk is not as quantifiable or "mappable" as operational or other financial risks. In part, that is because losses from political risk events are harder to quantify than losses from financial risks. The cumulative losses from 9/11, for example, are still being debated.

A problem with risk maps: things get left out. They too often look like maps of the medieval era. Early modern maps always contained some degree of uncertainty, of half-drawn contours, as much of the world remained undiscovered country. At the edges of these maps, artists sketched terrifying sea snakes,

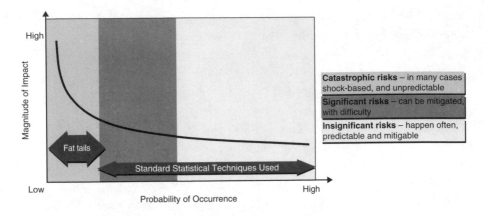

**FIGURE 2.3** Distribution of "catastrophic" and "ordinary" risks

human-headed sharks, and dragons, all ready to devour the explorer as he crossed into the unknown. Catastrophic events can inspire much the same confusion and terror.

Much of what we call political risk is in fact uncertainty. This applies to all types of political risks, from civil strife to expropriations to regulatory changes. Political risk, unlike credit or market or operational risk, can be unsystematic and therefore more difficult to address in classic statistical terms.[29] What is the probability that terrorists will attack the United States again? Unlike earthquakes or hurricanes, political actors constantly adapt to overcome the barriers created by risk managers.[30] When corporations structure foreign investments to mitigate risks of expropriations, through international guarantees or legal contracts, host governments seek out new forms of obstruction, such as creeping expropriation or regulatory discrimination, that are very hard and legally costly to prove.[31] Just as with Heisenberg's principle:[32] observation of a risk changes the risk itself. There are ways to mitigate fat tail–type events. But analysis of these risks can be as much art as science.

**The Value of Contrarian Thinking**

It is wise to accept, as Rumsfeld did, that there are sharp limits on what we can know. Too much certainty can generate some very big mistakes. Remember when Director of Intelligence George Tenet told President George W. Bush that finding weapons of mass destruction in Iraq would be a "slam dunk?" Or when analysts and journalists forecast, as many did in 1990, that Yugoslavia would prove the best (most stable) place in Eastern Europe to invest? Too much confidence stops policy makers from thinking about the unthinkable.

The subprime mortgage crisis in the United States illustrates a similar problem: elaborate risk analysis systems can breed false confidence. Most of the financial institutions involved used sophisticated risk management approaches. But they were lulled to sleep by their own perceived analytical sophistication and took on too much high-risk debt.

Their models did not consider the possibility of a devaluation in the housing market and a simultaneous credit contraction. As the crisis began to unfold, *The Economist* noted, "The lifeguards had been scanning the horizon for an oil-price shock, a bankrupt buy-out or a terrorist attack. But when the big wave struck last week it surprised them by coming from inside the financial system."[33] Simply put, organizations too rarely challenge their own most basic assumptions. The U.S. intelligence community and the U.S. military use a "red team" approach to avoid precisely this problem. Red teams are groups of selected analysts charged with playing devil's advocate and directly challenging conventional wisdom and existing plans. They use "what if" types of questions to find the flaw in a decision, forecast, or piece of intelligence. It is time-consuming work, and like auditors at corporations, they are not always viewed kindly by those they second-guess. It also frequently helps to expose dangerous false assumptions.

But the process only works if those who evaluate its findings do so with an open mind. In the run-up to the war in Iraq, the U.S. administration led a massive war-gaming exercise called Millennium Challenge 2002.[34] The game was predicated on the U.S. invasion of a country that clearly stood for Iraq. The gaming exercise involved all four branches of the U.S. armed forces, and reportedly cost about a quarter billion dollars.[35] The planning for the invasion by Blue Force (standing for the United States) was based on using the blue team's enormous technological superiority to overwhelm the enemy Red Force, which was to simulate possible Iraqi responses. The red team, led by retired General Paul van Riper quickly unraveled the blue team's invasion plans.

> Van Riper used motorcycle messengers to transmit orders to Red troops, rendering useless the Blue team's super-sophisticated eavesdropping technology. He kept the

Red forces in constant motion. When the Blue team's fleet entered the Persian Gulf, he used suicide-bombers in speed boats to sink several of its ships. Managers then stopped the game, "refloated" the Blue fleet, and resumed play. Robert Oakley, a retired U.S. ambassador who played the Red civilian leader, told the *Army Times* that Van Riper was "out-thinking" Blue Force from the first day of the exercise.

Despite his success, Van Riper complained that the game's managers had restricted some of his moves and blocked others altogether. According to the *Army Times* summary, "Exercise officials denied him the opportunity to use his own tactics and ideas against Blue, and on several occasions directed [Red Force] not to use certain weapons systems against Blue. It even ordered him to reveal the location of Red units.[36]

Van Riper quit in protest, charging that the event had been unfairly scripted to confirm the Pentagon's preconceptions about the efficiency of high-tech, networked warfare. Van Riper's red team accurately predicted the kinds of low-tech but effective tactics that Saddam Hussein's army—and, later, Iraqi insurgents—would use against U.S. and allied forces.

## Scenarios

Scenario analysis is a particularly useful means of understanding uncertainty and fat tails. Where data are lacking and standard statistical analysis will not work, scenario analysis proves useful in understanding how the future might develop. It does not produce probabilities and predictions; it is a collaborative and iterative process that helps to prepare an organization for a number of plausible paths. The main objective is to inspire creative problem solving and to spur managers to think about unthinkable outcomes.

Consider the example of Royal Dutch Shell, which successfully used scenarios in the 1970s to prepare for the possibility of an oil crisis. The company's success in weathering the price shock triggered by the 1973 Yom Kippur War cemented scenario planning as a viable tool for the firm.[37] Pierre Wack, who led the first scenario planning group at Shell Française, successfully argued that the firm's existing planning system was flawed, because it drew too heavily from projections of past trends in oil production and consumption to inform major decisions on infrastructure and capital investments.[38] Wack's argument was essentially that Shell was not preparing for fat tail events: linear forecasts could not foresee major breaks with historic trends.[39]

Starting in 1971, Wack's scenarios focused primarily on energy markets, but went well beyond assessments of commodity price fluctuations or the possibilities for new crude oil discoveries. His team's approach divided the operating environment into known "predetermined elements" and uncertain ones, what Shell knew and what it didn't know. He then developed alternate futures based on assessments not only of Shell's core knowledge areas, such as how oil is most efficiently drawn from the ground and moved to market, but also of geopolitical trends related to the oil industry and the different incentives faced by oil-producing and consuming states.[40] Wack's team treated the governments of oil-producing countries as rational, self-interested actors seeking to increase the state's wealth and its security. In the process, Shell's scenarios uncovered a possible future gap between the amount of oil that consuming states needed to meet their projected demand and the amount of oil that producing states were likely to pump, given political and economic constraints.[41] One of the six scenarios that Wack developed in 1972 demonstrated that only a 10-year period of low economic growth could maintain oil demand at existing levels in relation to available supplies.[42]

At first, Shell's managers treated Wack's scenarios with skepticism. Following the onset of the oil shocks of the 1970s, his work won wider acceptance. It revealed that a shock was far more likely than most believed, but it also forced management to contend with the problem of uncertainty and to allow for the possibility of fat tail effects.[43] As a direct result, Shell was better prepared than its competitors to withstand the worst effects of an oil shock.[44]

Wack noted that scenarios serve two purposes: they help us anticipate and understand risk, but they also uncover strategic options and opportunities that we might never have imagined.[45] Nearly 40 years after his group introduced scenario planning to the firm, Shell has expanded its planning exercises to focus on multiple levels of analysis and to generate potential scenarios at the project (not just the global) level. Internally, managers assessing specific investments or capital projects must demonstrate that they can withstand both local and global alternate scenarios.[46] Shell's successes owe a great deal to the development of analytically rigorous "signposts," indicators that allow managers to see how current trends indicate which scenario may be developing.[47]

## Assessing Country Stability

Financial institutions use the Value at Risk (VaR) method to assess many different kinds of risk. VaR, a mathematically sophisticated way of analyzing the probability that a portfolio will decline in value over a particular time period, offers a precise way of estimating a given portfolio's ability to weather market volatility.

For political risk, analysis of a country's stability accomplishes much the same thing. Some catastrophic events may be literally unpredictable. It is much easier then to measure a country's ability to survive various forms of catastrophe. In other words, instead of predicting when an earthquake will hit, predict what would happen to a particular city if and when it does.

To capture the broader definition of stability (which can include government changes that are not adverse), think of it as a state of political equilibrium.[48] The stability of a state lies in its ability to maintain its political equilibrium in the face of different shocks. A shock can be almost anything—an earthquake, a flood, a drought, or an epidemic. Hurricane Katrina along the U.S. Gulf Coast (2005) or the tsunami that devastated parts of Southeast Asia (2004) provide two obvious examples. Other shocks are man-made—terrorist attacks, assassinations, or revolutionary and secessionist movements can impact the political stability of a country. Shocks can originate outside a country, as when Iraq invaded Kuwait in 1990. Or they can originate from within, as when demonstrations and unrest brought down the Bolivian government in 2005.

A shock is far less likely to undermine the stability of a strong, resilient state. The fiercely contested and controversial 2000 presidential election results did not destabilize the United States or its government because the ultimate legitimacy of the country's governing institutions were never seriously called into question. But an equally contested election in an unstable state can ignite dangerous political upheaval, as the "Rose Revolution" toppled Georgia's government in 2003. Measurements of stability allow political risk analysts to gauge which states—and at a more micro level, which economic sectors, social groups, institutions, and projects—will likely be most dramatically impacted by sudden and unforseen events. The resilience of the U.S. government and the American economy following the September 11 terrorist attacks was entirely predictable—though few foresaw the attacks themselves. New York was never in danger of civil unrest. The U.S. economy and specific companies took significant hits, but the financial system (the terrorists' target) proved resilient. The Federal Reserve

Bank was able to pump some $100 billion in liquidity into the market for each of the next three days, averting a financial crisis. Ultimately, it was the Taliban government in Afghanistan that could not survive the 9/11 attacks, as the United States invaded the country just 26 days later.

A terrorist attack in a less stable society could elevate social tensions and trigger communal violence. That's precisely what happened with the 2005 assassination of former Lebanese prime minister Rafik Hariri, a public murder that fueled a sharp rise in tensions between the country's pro-democracy and pro-Syrian factions. It is too early to tell how this crisis will end, but the killing has thrown Lebanon into a period of profound political unrest, one in which risks of instability have sharply intensified. These risks have shifted both regional politics and international perceptions of Lebanon as a sound investment bet.

In a weak state, a shock can come from something far less dramatic than a terrorist attack, such as an increase in the price of basic commodities. In 1998, in the wake of the East Asian financial crisis of the previous year and the collapse of its currency, Indonesia's government felt compelled to impose austerity measures that fueled, among other things, higher unemployment and a rise in the price of rice. The riots that followed toppled the authoritarian Suharto regime, which had held power since 1967.

Stability can be measured and calculated. But, though stability metrics are useful, they come with two important caveats. First, the stability of a political regime is not necessarily a good indicator of the stability of its policy, because some regimes, however resilient, have a way of generating their own shocks. As the Hugo Chávez government in Venezuela has consolidated power, it has launched radical nationalization plans for several industries. His government remains fairly stable, but the country's policy environment is anything but. At the same time, the fall of some governments can dramatically improve a country's business climate, as a new more business-friendly government embarks on a steadier and more predictable path. Beyond Suharto, consider the collapse of Communist governments in Poland, Hungary, and Czechoslovakia in 1989 and 1990.

Second, assessments of political stability, however accurate, cannot by themselves predict how markets will perform. Some governments, companies and even individuals thrive in a climate of political instability, finding ways to succeed in difficult and complex environments. As Harry Lime (Orson Wells) tells his friend Holly Martins (Joseph Cotton) amid the rubble of postwar Vienna in Carol Reed's classic film *The Third Man:*

> In Italy, for thirty years under the Borgias, they had warfare, terror, murder, bloodshed—they produced Michelangelo, Leonardo da Vinci and the Renaissance. In Switzerland, they had brotherly love, five hundred years of democracy and peace, and what did that produce? The cuckoo clock.[49]

## Dealing with the Unknown

Andrew Grove, the former CEO of Intel Corporation, titled his autobiography *Only the Paranoid Survive*. Grove's book details how corporations should handle what he calls a "strategic inflection point," a radical technological, marketplace, or regulatory change. Grove argues that abrupt (sometimes radical) shifts in the trajectory of a trend, create both risks and opportunities for every organization.

A company's success in adapting to these game-changing events depends on its ability to spot them as early as possible and on the flexibility and competence with which its organization adapts to the new circumstances it creates. One such political/regulatory inflection point,[50] the Telecommunications Act of 1996, allowed increased competition in the U.S. telecom sector, especially among long-distance and short-distance carriers, and in the cable television industry. The event was not unpredictable. Congress debated the idea long before the legislation was approved. But the act's implications were far harder to forecast. It produced a number of corporate mergers valued at more than $150 billion. Some of them were successful, like the acquisition by SBC Communications of AT&T in 2005. Others were disastrous: the 1997 MCI/WorldCom merger, worth $37 billion at the time, became a symbol for corporate scandal as the company spiraled into bankruptcy.

## How to Prepare

Beyond adaptability there are a few general rules that make a significant difference. Experts on corporate and government management of uncertainty, like Paul Bracken, highlight several core themes and approaches.

## Isolating

We can manage future risks by isolating and separating critical assets, either to lower their overall vulnerability or simply to ensure that not all our critical assets are open to the same set of threats at the same time.[51] This is the principle behind portfolio diversification and the distribution of "deterrent" nuclear weapons across submarines at sea, land-based missiles in hardened silos, and aircraft at widely distributed bases.[52] In short, don't put all your eggs (or assets or weapons) in one basket.

## Smoothing

Uncertainty can also be managed by distributing risks over time and across various theaters, business subsidiaries, and entities. Firms confronting Wall Street pressures for consistent corporate earnings may choose to take on some expenses sooner than planned and to confront selected risks later. That way, they spread uncertainty and risk into manageable quantities.[53] "Isolating" means spreading risks, costs, and vulnerabilities across space. "Smoothing" means spreading them across time.

## Warning

Warning systems and political forecasting can also be used to better prepare for specific contingencies. Warning systems incorporate specific reporting requirements, internal structures, and "triggers" based on preselected criteria to inform decision makers of impending threats.[54] It is a trip wire designed to warn in advance that trouble is on the way.

## Agility

Reducing the time and costs of response to crises can substantially lower the risks associated with them. Flexibility in strategy, the use of plant and equipment that can be moved quickly and efficiently, and the reduction of unnecessary bureaucratic oversight in operations can help a firm respond more nimbly when unforeseen trends or events emerge.[55]

## *Alliances*

Alliances among firms and private corporations, nongovernmental organizations (NGOs), international institutions, and private stakeholders can help mitigate the risks inherent in uncertainty by spreading risk among them. The response to recent disasters such as Hurricane Katrina reveals the importance of coordination between levels of government and private organizations.[56] Similarly, when it comes to foreign direct investment, many corporations work with local stakeholders, NGOs and community groups to win public approval for projects and to diminish the risk of being branded a "bad neighbor." After the mid-1990s, Shell actively engaged local communities while developing new gas fields in Peru to avoid the kinds of problems it encountered in Nigeria's Niger Delta.[57]

## *Environment Shaping*

Organizations can mitigate risk by influencing the environment where they operate.[58] They can lobby legislative bodies for more favorable regulation. They can also speak directly with local stakeholders and ordinary citizens in areas impacted by their operations. The international mining company Anglo American has spent large sums of money in several countries to help shape public perceptions of its work. In 2006, $50.3 million went not only for training and infrastructure that directly benefited the firm's business but for support for community activities, the arts, and education.[59] This investment helps maintain friendly relations with local social and political leaders and an environment in which disputes can be more easily resolved. The point may seem obvious, but some companies shape their environments more successfully than others.

## Wal-Mart and Katrina

Consider Wal-Mart's preparations for and response to Hurricane Katrina. The federal and local governments failed to respond effectively to the storm's impact, but Wal-Mart was ready to provide significant relief. Before the storm hit, the company's business continuity office increased its usual complement of between 6 and 10 employees to more than 50, who drew from existing contingency plans based on previous hurricane experiences to develop a firmwide response. Wal-Mart used its own hurricane tracking software and weather forecasts, providing high-quality information on the projected effects of the storm.[60] The ability of managers in the field to make decisions regarding business operations and the presence of senior managers equipped with satellite phones allowed Wal-Mart's strategy to be executed efficiently and in coordination with local authorities.[61]

Wal-Mart's Brookhaven, Mississippi, distribution center had 45 trucks full of relief supplies loaded, and had secured a dedicated fueling line at a local gas station in anticipation of Katrina's landfall.[62] Ultimately, Wal-Mart was able to deliver donations totaling $20 million in cash and over 100 truckloads of necessities to the affected areas, as well as continued employment for workers displaced by the disaster and food for 100,000 meals—within days of Katrina's impact.[63] By many accounts, Wal-Mart was better prepared for the hurricane than either the local or the federal government. The success of its response was a function of its thorough business continuity planning process and of a highly efficient distribution system. The government response, on the other hand, was plagued with silo-style management flaws, as various groups and agencies failed to communicate and coordinate effectively.[64]

### The Risk Society

The advance of globalization has created an interconnected world, one in which the boundaries that once separated domestic from international problems have eroded. Governments are no longer the only players in the political arena; plenty of sub-state groups and individuals have joined the game. It is not simply the belligerent, heavily armed countries that now stir up trouble. It is also weak states that become safe havens for those who would rather disrupt the global marketplace than shop there. Most of us use new technologies like the Internet for information, communication, and entertainment. A few use it to recruit militants, disseminate hatred, or to attack the infrastructure of the Internet itself.

Threats are no longer bound by traditional political borders, social structures, and geographic boundaries. Some have argued that we now live in a risk-dominated world—a "risk society"—one in which a fast-growing number of threats have made risk calculation virtually impossible.[65] Faced with this increasingly complex landscape, governments and businesses now focus simply on minimizing the risk of worst-case scenarios.

During the Cold War, there was a clear and dominant threat that shaped the security conception of the Western world—the Soviet Union. Dangers were calculated in numbers of Soviet bombs, troops, tanks, ships, and other measurable factors controlled by a dominant and centralized Soviet leadership. Organizations and governments could deal with such large, slow-moving threats through preemption, diplomacy, and, if need be, direct action.

Risks like global warming, nuclear terrorism, and revolutions, on the other hand, can only be mitigated—not eliminated. The current era has no Soviet-scale dominant threat, but rather an array of dangers with different levels of consequence (e.g., pandemics, refugee crises, and the cross-border diffusion of dangerous technologies). Coupled with the new security environment is the advance of globalization. The rapid expansion in the movement of people, information, ideas, money, goods, and services across international borders has created unprecedented challenges for risk managers.

Local ethnic conflicts or state failures in distant countries can now quickly produce ripple effects across the globe. This transformation has empowered substate actors and individuals to play a greater role in international politics.

These risks often cascade from one into another.[66] The most frightening of them may compel governments or corporate decision makers to take action against the danger before it develops into a full-blown crisis. This is the so-called precautionary principle. To a large extent, this was the thinking behind the preemptive U.S. invasion of Iraq in 2003. [67]

NATO's military involvement in Yugoslavia in 1999 is widely considered a case of post-Cold War risk-society planning. The leaders of NATO governments understood the turmoil in the Balkans in terms of risk probabilities—and they feared that inaction might generate catastrophic consequences.[68] Tony Blair, then British prime minister, best captured this idea:

> [T]wenty years ago we would not have been fighting in Kosovo. We have to establish a new framework...the world has changed in a more fundamental way...globalization is not just economic. It is also a political and security phenomenon...we cannot turn our backs on conflicts and the violation of human rights in other countries if we want to be secure.[69]

In short, many leaders feared that inaction might have consequences in other parts of the world—a type of domino theory. They feared that what appeared to be genocide against Albanians within the tiny province of Kosovo would generate instability in Albania, Macedonia, Turkey, and then Greece. Rather than face this potential catastrophe, NATO governments decided to hit the already bankrupt Yugoslavian government with a 10-week precision bombing campaign to force it into submission.

To view the world through the prism of the "risk society" is to believe that states and corporations are more vulnerable to instability and dangers than ever before. Governments and corporations therefore must be more vigilant in monitoring problems (and potential problems) across the globe. They must develop protective measures to avoid, or at least to safely absorb, the fallout from many different kinds of threats. Defensive measures can no longer be reactive, but must be actively constructed to deal with emerging threats before they fully form. Leaders may need to take preemptive measures to meet security challenges. According to the theory, the new complexity of global threats will require governments and businesses to live with greater uncertainty than ever before.

Ironically, efforts to aggressively anticipate emerging dangers and to take preventive measures to avoid them can themselves create confusion and a potentially volatile political situation—especially among actors who are already paranoid. One government can interpret a neighbor's defensive move as a belligerent military act. "Is he arming because he is afraid of me? Or because he wants my land?" Companies must take a harder line in negotiations with one government to protect their interests with others.

## Adapting Successfully

Fat tails and uncertainty affect different governments and companies in different ways, and the ability to adapt to these risks can be critically important. In 1543, not long after the Spanish obliterated the Aztecs, another set of European explorers, the Portuguese, made contact with the Japanese Empire. Nearly five centuries later, Japan still has its emperor. The Aztec and Portuguese empires have long since collapsed.

Following this first Portuguese contact, Dutch, British, and Spanish merchants and missionaries arrived in Japan, with Western tools, technologies, sciences and religious doctrines—as well as ambitions to dominate the country. The Japan they encountered was weakened and divided by civil wars. The Europeans had better weapons and superior navies. European missionaries drew Japanese converts to Christianity (half a million by 1615). European influence spread steadily across the country. Japan might have suffered a fate similar, if not to the Aztecs, then to Vietnam, the Philippines, or China, which, to varying degrees, were all brought within European spheres of influence between the 1500s and 1800s.

Yet the Japanese adapted. They had two advantages over the Aztecs: They were immune to diseases such as smallpox, and they possessed a highly literate culture with a tradition of craftsmanship and ironwork. These traits allowed the Japanese to quickly absorb Western technology. When the Europeans introduced military technology like rifles and cannons to Japan, the Japanese copied them. Local warlords put them in mass production and incorporated them into military strategy.

By the end of the 16th century, guns were at least as common in Japan as they were in Europe. Japanese engineers also adopted Western ship designs (galleons) and European castle architecture. Using these innovations, the Tokugawa Shogunate ended the civil wars between the Japanese warlords and centralized government authority. Concentration of power and the adaptation of European military technology transformed the Tokugawa into a political and military force formidable enough to resist Western pressure and influence and to halt the spread of Christianity. In 1637, the Tokugawa government mobilized more than 100,000 samurai to crush 30,000 Christian samurai and peasants who rose up against the leadership in the Shimabara Rebellion.

The Japanese could not have anticipated the arrival of the Portuguese nor the tactics they would use to try to dominate them. Yet, unlike the Aztecs, they responded to these threats very effectively. First, Japan was able to "shut out" all foreigners. When complete isolation became impossible in the 19th century, Japan embarked on a uniquely successful program of modernization. By the early 20th century, roughly 50 years after Japan had decided to rapidly industrialize, its modernized army and navy were able to decisively defeat imperial Russia, one of the great European powers. With that victory and its annexation of Korea, Japan emerged as an important world political player and entered the field of "geopolitics," to which we now turn.

# Geopolitics | THREE

Who rules East Europe commands the Heartland:
Who rules the Heartland commands the World-Island:
Who rules the World-Island controls the World.
—Halford Mackinder[1]

The above quote may sound like the musings of a Bond villain bent on world domination. But it comes from one of the founding fathers of geopolitics, Halford John Mackinder (1861–1947). A British academic and sometimes politician, Mackinder developed the influential strategic theory that control of Central and Eastern Europe could provide control of the entire Eurasian landmass—"the World-Island"—and therefore of the world.

Most politicians treat academic theories lightly, perhaps with good reason. But Mackinder's geopolitical formula, as further developed during the 1920s and 1930s by German strategists like Karl Haushofer and Erich Obst, inspired Nazi planners as they formulated the invasion of Russia, where much of the Eurasian "Heartland" lies.[2]

There are many reasons why that plan ended in catastrophe.[3]

Geopolitics, despite its problematic intellectual beginnings,[4] remains crucial for any understanding of global politics (or, at the very least, how policy makers understand global politics[5]). At its most basic, geopolitics is the study of how geography, politics, strategy, and history combine to generate the rise and fall of great powers and wars among states.[6]

What do we mean, then, by geopolitical risk? Two things, in particular: the risks posed to economic actors and governments by the relative rise and decline of great powers and the impact of conventional wars on states and corporations.

Geopolitical risk, more than any other kind of political risk, can pose an existential threat, such as mutually assured destruction during the Cold War, the impact of a large-scale conventional war on markets, or nuclear proliferation. In a fundamental sense, geopolitical events, particularly international warfare, can make or break financial markets. The London Stock Exchange achieved preeminence because of war (or rather, a series of wars, military blockades, and economic sanctions—all tools of geopolitical statecraft). It lost its preeminence to the New York Stock Exchange because of another war (World War I).

### Geopolitical Events and Capital Markets

London owed its rise as the preeminent global financial center to a shift in geopolitical circumstances. Amsterdam, a great trading and industrial power from the late 16th century, had become the main center for international finance by the latter half of the 18th century. The Amsterdam Stock Exchange was probably the first stock exchange in the modern sense of the word.[7] But a series of wars with Britain and France in the late 17th and 18th centuries weakened the Netherlands and forced many of Amsterdam's traders to seek safe haven in London. The invasion of the Netherlands by revolutionary France in 1794 provided the final blow. The decline of the Amsterdam Bourse and the rise of the London Stock Exchange were in a way quirks of geopolitics, as the Netherlands were far easier to invade than the islands of Great Britain.

London's fortunes fell more suddenly, the result of an international crisis in July 1914 and the onset of World War I, which soon followed. Until that time, Britain dominated international finance at least as much as it dominated global politics. London was vital to the system of credit and currency exchange that supported international trade, including that of its future adversary, Germany.

The signs that a general European war could end London's position as a financial center emerged during the last week of July 1914, when Austria's ultimatum to Serbia sparked a global stock market crash and a liquidity crisis, with devastating effects on global trade. Despite warnings from British bankers that war would inflict tremendous damage on both Britain's financial system and its reputation as guarantor of international trade, Britain joined the fight in August 1914.

The war burdened London with increasingly large levels of debt, allowing New York to pick up the slack in the international system and to become a vital lender to a number of countries, including Britain.[8] The U.S. government, which undertook reforms to its nascent Federal Reserve System, survived the 1914 crisis and emerged from the war in a much stronger position than when it began.[9] The changes enacted during wartime helped to ensure New York's rise to dominance of the international financial system. London recovered, and remains a global financial power in its own right, but World War I, a geopolitical crisis, ended its paramount importance to the financial world.

If politics and war served as catalysts for New York's ascendancy in financial markets, it sometimes takes a Cold War to create an entirely new class of financial products. The 1950s, a time of growing tensions between the United States and its allies and the Soviet bloc, were also a time of geopolitically driven financial innovation. Eurodollars—U.S. dollars held by foreign banks outside the United States—proved a major contributor to changes in the international financial system in the 1960s and 1970s. Their impact extended far beyond the Cold War–era decision that spawned it.

In fact, choices made by the political leadership of the Soviet Union, one of the world's least liberal states, gave birth to Eurodollar deposits, which eventually made capital more mobile and loosened the control that sovereign states held over the global financial system. The Soviet decision to move some of its dollars from U.S. banks to U.K.-registered banks in the 1950s was a pragmatic one motivated by geopolitics: The Soviet Union acquired U.S. dollars thanks to its exports, largely for crude oil, and held this currency in U.S. banks to pay its various foreign obligations. But given the Cold War tensions at the time, Soviet leaders worried that economic sanctions might freeze or otherwise restrict its U.S. dollar accounts. Months prior to its initial Eurodollar deposit in 1957, the Soviet Union had invaded Hungary, a move that worsened an already tense international environment. By holding the dollar deposits in a British-registered bank, the dollars were far less likely to come under threat from U.S. authorities.[10]

Eurodollars proved useful not just for the Soviets, however. Eurodollar deposits continue to be a major part of the international capital market and are still used by governments and corporations for a variety of purposes. In the 1960s, the volume of Eurodollar deposits rose rapidly, as governments loosened banking regulations and controls on foreign currency. Eurodollars, which were typically used by banks to issue loans and whose deposits faced significantly fewer regulations than regular U.S. dollar deposits, became increasingly attractive as a source of capital. As these deposits grew and had a greater impact on international financial markets, the United States and other governments found it increasingly difficult to manage the international financial system.[11]

## The Vexing Nature of Geopolitical Risks

There are at least three factors that make analysis and identification of geopolitical risk more difficult than for other forms of political risk. They are duration, bias, and complexity. These issues pose challenges for all risk analysis, but they are especially complex when it comes to geopolitics.

First, let's take duration. Geopolitics can take a long time to play out. The most obvious instance is identifying and analyzing the relative rise and fall of great powers. This is something of a parlor game—after all, the careers of most political analysts last about 40 years, while great powers sometimes take much longer than that to rise and fall. It is impossible to tell how long it took the Byzantine Empire to decline,[12] yet for about five hundred years its fortunes ebbed and flowed with a number of dramatic defeats and victories. Even with hindsight it is hard to tell when exactly this particular state was on a terminal path, and 500 years is the type of hindsight that only future historians can afford.

Another more recent example is that of the United States, which has been judged to be in decline relative to other powers a number of times in recent decades. Supposed inflection points have included the stagflation of the late 1970s following the Vietnam War and the late 1980s, when Japan was seen as the emerging great power (Michael Crichton's novel *Rising Sun* and the eponymous movie based on it are interesting cultural artifacts of that fear). But the end of the Cold War in 1991 left the United States as the only superpower left, and Japan went into an economic tailspin from which it has yet to fully recover. Might the United States have finally entered a period of relative decline? Yes. In fact, we will make that very case toward the end of this chapter. But as one analyst wrote in 2003:

> Between 1990 and 1998, the United States' gross national product grew 27 percent, Europe's 16 percent, and Japan's 7 percent. Today, the American economy is equal to

the economies of Japan, the United Kingdom, and Germany combined. The United States' military capacity is even more in a league of its own. It spends as much on defense as the next 14 countries taken together.[13]

A second factor that adds complexity to geopolitical risk analysis is risk identification and analytical bias. There is no shortage of experts ready to sound the alarm on all sorts of geopolitical threats—from enemy states, to the causes of the decline of this or that great power (the power of budget deficits to permanently stunt America's growth provides a perennial favorite), to new types of threats on the horizon, such as terrorism, global warming, and disease.[14]

Samuel Huntington's influential, if controversial, "clash of civilizations" theory offers a case in point.[15] Huntington maps a world of future geopolitical conflict driven by wars among great civilizational or cultural blocs. Yet, U.S. government officials, Russian generals, and al Qaeda supporters have each used it to bolster arguments in favor of this or that worldview. Yet, like earlier ideas set forth by Mackinder and Haushofer,[16] Huntington's theory raises an important question common to all geopolitical theories: Does it truly allow us a glimpse of the future? Or is it simply a self-fulfilling prophecy used by different groups and individuals to further their particular agendas? Figuring out geopolitical risks is no straightforward matter: identification of risks drives political interests, which by definition are biased.[17]

Complexity poses a third set of problems. Geopolitical risks tend to reinforce one another and to develop feedback loops, as one type of risk generates another, reinforcing the first. Arms races provide an example. Country A, fearing invasion by Country B, begins to arm. Country B sees its neighbors' new weapons and arms in self-defense. The fear takes on a life of its own, fueling an arms race. As the stakes rise, one of the two countries decides that only a preemptive attack can protect its security. World War I erupted, at least in part, because several of the great powers of the day (France, Russia, Germany, Austria-Hungary) had established precise mobilization schedules in advance that were activated when a rival began to mobilize. As soon as Austria-Hungary and Germany began to mobilize, France and Russia felt compelled to do the same. Yet, the decision to go to war was not automatic. There were painful debates in the various capitals between army and politicians as to whether to mobilize or not. While the politicians went along with the mobilization decision and set in motion the set of events that resulted in a war, this was not a foreordained outcome. Geopolitical analysis has a hard time identifying such complex relations.[18]

### Early Warning and Geopolitical Risks

Attempts to identify and to analyze emerging geopolitical dynamics in today's world—whether the potential for international wars, the rise of China, the new-found assertiveness, of Russia, or the potential impact of Iran's nuclear program on energy markets and regional security dynamics—is essential for both corporations and governments. Identifying geopolitical threats before other governments or market competitors do can be essential for profitability and even survival.[19]

Having access to news before anyone else is, needless to say, a useful thing. A cursory look at the growth of the news media, whether CNN, CNBC, BBC, and Fox News or wire services such as Dow Jones, Reuters, and Bloomberg, highlights the growing international demand for accurate, real-time information. Governments, whether through embassies or intelligence agencies, often try to gather additional information about both friends and foes. Early warning will not determine whether a great power is in decline and is likely to act belligerently to slow the erosion of its power; that is the realm of long-term analysis. But early warning helps determine whether a short-term economic or security crisis looms.

An important caveat: the right information is useless unless it is correctly processed. In 1941, Soviet intelligence services warned the Kremlin of an impending German attack. Alarm bells rang in the United States before both Pearl Harbor and the 9/11 attacks. In all three cases, policy makers failed to process the information and to act on it.[20]

### The Benefits of Early Warning: Napoleon and the House of Rothschild

If early warnings are successfully received and understood, they can make an enormous difference. But a glimpse of the future is not always enough. In 1815, Napoleon had just escaped from captivity on the island of Elba and had begun to reform his army to march on the rest of Europe.[21] Markets, unsure whether

Napoleon would succeed (and undermine government bonds in Britain) or fail (and send British bonds soaring), remained on edge. Was it possible to know with certainty the outcome of the conflict before it reached the British markets? Nathan Rothschild is rumored to have achieved just that—effectively receiving tomorrow's newspaper today.

The head of the Rothschild banking family, Nathan Rothschild had financed significant elements of the anti-French forces—providing subsidies to British allies in continental Europe and supplying British forces with gold bullion in the field. Among his competitive advantages was his bank's maintenance of an effective network of informants and couriers who provided information and news, often ahead of governments or the markets. With the telegraph still decades away, the Rothschilds had the next best thing.[22] As the legend goes, Rothschild received news of the Battle of Waterloo before the British government or the London exchanges. Some have claimed that Rothschild made £25 million to £135 million at the London exchange by trading on the news days before it reached London. As with all good stories, there is a kernel of truth in it, but the reality is much more complicated—and reveals important lessons about political risk.

It is true that on the night of July 19, the Rothschild couriers delivered their boss in London a copy of a Brussels newspaper printed the night before. Thus, Nathan Rothschild learned of Napoleon's defeat nearly 48 hours before the official British dispatch reached the Cabinet. News of the battle's outcome was also confirmed by another Rothschild courier from Ghent. But the Rothschilds made no large sums of money on this news. In fact, Napoleon's defeat nearly ruined them. Months before, on hearing news of Napoleon's escape from Elba, Nathan Rothschild had begun buying up large amounts of gold bullion, forecasting a long military campaign against a resurgent France. When Napoleon was defeated quickly and decisively at Waterloo, the Rothschilds were left holding bullion that was depreciating as market fears eased. Rothschild probably made money from early news of Waterloo's outcome, but analysis of shifts in government bond prices indicates that the amount probably did not exceed £7,000—far less than he would have made in commissions on supplying bullion during a protracted campaign.

This case illustrates the undeniable value of immediate and accurate information—but it also demonstrates that identifying risks is not enough. They must also be correctly analyzed. His information network usually allowed Rothschild to adapt to changing circumstances, but, in this case, his forecast of a long military campaign inflicted serious financial losses.

### Frameworks and Theories

Analysis of geopolitical risks depends greatly on approach and on different schools of thought that we will now briefly describe. One problem is that many experts tend to shoehorn all the evidence to fit their favored theory. For political risk analysis (whether geopolitical or not), it is best to think of different types of analysis as complementary tools. Some work better in explaining and forecasting some situations than others.

#### Historical Analogies

More than any other type of political risk management, geopolitical risk depends on knowledge of history. A person who earned a penny every time the literature on geopolitics mentioned the Peloponnesian War, World War I, or the 1814–15 Congress of Vienna (which settled the Napoleonic Wars) would have enough money to have financed all three events. But not all historical analogies are equally useful, and many are overused.

History can also be used selectively. During the 2003 debate in the United States on whether to invade Iraq and depose Saddam Hussein, historical analogies seemed to be everywhere. Those in favor of the invasion invoked the post–World War II experience in Germany and Japan, where the United States and its allies successfully facilitated the development of a range of stable governmental and civic institutions. Invasion critics cited France's traumatic occupation of Algeria. Some pointed to the Marshall Plan, others to the Battle of Algiers.

That said, the (rather hackneyed) adage that those who do not know their history are destined to repeat it holds rather well in geopolitical risk. Hitler's ill-considered invasion of the Soviet Union provides an example for the ages.

Sweden's king Charles XII (in 1707) and Napoleon (in 1812) invaded Russia. Charles's invasion ended Sweden's reign as a great European power. Russian Cossacks followed what remained of Napoleon's divisions all the way back to Paris. Hitler and his army planners closely studied Napoleon's invasion plans and determined that his strategy had taken too long to develop. Hitler settled on a three-pronged attack strategy (one army striking in the north, one in the middle, and one in the south) that was specifically designed to quickly overwhelm Soviet troops. But the Nazi command, overconfident of a speedy victory, planned for neither the muddy Russian autumn nor the harsh Russian winter. A failure to supply troops with adequate winter clothing and supplies played a crucial role in Germany's inability to hold Soviet territory. Nor did the Germans plan for the dogged Soviet resistance they encountered once the Soviet command and Stalin recovered from the initial shock of invasion. Remorseless cold, the burdens of long and vulnerable resupply lines, and a determined Soviet counterattack eventually crippled the Nazi war machine.

But it was not a lack of speed that defeated Sweden's king or France's emperor. It was the same defensive prowess, relentless scorched-earth tactics, and the harshness of its winter that ultimately decimated the Wehrmacht. The Nazi command learned nothing from history.

### Theories for Geopolitical Risk Analysis

Yet, well-informed knowledge of history is not enough. Other, theory-driven approaches can also prove useful. In general, analyzing different kinds of risk is done through a number of different analytical lenses. Debates over which tools work best dominate the study of international relations. We think it best to steer clear of these debates. Instead, we'll treat them as a set of lenses for a single camera, each of them potentially useful, depending on the desired angle and distance.

We began the chapter by citing Mackinder's theory that domination of Eastern Europe provides the foundation for global dominance. Since then, many other theories of how geopolitics operates have been used to identify and analyze geopolitical risks. Generally, most geopolitical theories try to explain the world as it exists today as well as its future state.

Geopolitical theories tend to be highly speculative, much like scenario analysis. The value of a good geopolitical theory similarly lies in providing a glimpse of a possible future. Many recent geopolitical theories do not focus on the state system, because they are premised on the view that future threats to the great powers will originate not from other states, but from challenges that states do not or cannot control. True or not, this idea provides a glimpse into the anxieties of the current world, where terrorism, global warming, and demographic change have replaced mutually assured destruction or the advance of foreign tanks in the collective imagination.

GLOBALIZATION   The theory that the spectacular growth in international trade, industrial production, travel, and communication of recent decades has become increasingly independent of the state system has emerged as the dominant geopolitical idea of our time. The mobility of goods, people, and services can undermine as well as strengthen a state. Likewise, the question of what makes a state successful in a globalized world is a tricky one. Can states insulate parts of their culture, economy, and society from the impact of globalization (new McDonald's restaurants or new immigrants)? What will globalization mean for the traditional idea of a world system made of states? Will globalization create zones that cannot be governed—on the Internet, in derivatives markets, or in the deserts of Somalia? A globalizing world creates new geopolitical risks and opportunities for states and corporations alike.

ENVIRONMENTAL DEGRADATION   Consider the geopolitical implications of large-scale environmental degradation, poverty, and demographic growth.[23] Will environmental damage (like desertification) combined with growing demographic pressures fuel ethnic and social pressures in weak states, as well as tensions between states in areas facing shortages of key resources?

The description of this world can look like something out of a Mad Max movie,[24] with global chaos and ungovernability as the dire end state. Many of these theories have not panned out, and they have frequently been criticized for having a neo-Malthusian bent—that is, claiming that states and peoples will eventually fight over increasingly scarce natural resources.[25] Yet, theories that explore the relationship between environmental change and social conflict deserve our attention.

Take global warming. Government officials in Russia, Canada, Norway, and other countries have recently begun to think seriously about how the melting of the polar ice caps will impact the discovery of new hydrocarbon resources and the opening of new shipping lanes.[26] This frees up not only new commercial avenues but also the possibility of tensions created by competing national claims over what had previously been frozen wastelands.

THE CLASH OF CIVILIZATIONS   A theory mentioned earlier that has had significant impact is that of a world increasingly dominated by cultural blocs based on the world's great religions. Huntington's theory posits that the borders that separate concentrations of people of different religious traditions (which pass through places like Bosnia, Nigeria, and Kashmir) will become the fault lines for future warfare and conflict.

## Theories of International Relations

International relations is the study of how states interact with one another. A brief review of this field highlights how international relations theories underpin much of the analysis of geopolitical risks. Unlike specific geopolitical theories, international relations theories do not predict which great power will rise or decline or where the next international conflict will take place. Instead, they provide systematic (often contradictory) ways of thinking about how the international system operates.

To illustrate the best known international relations theories, we'll detail how adherents to each of these schools of thoughts might formulate a policy solution to a real-world problem and consider possible U.S. responses to Iran's nascent nuclear program.

REALISM   Perhaps the oldest theory of international relations, realism dates, by some accounts, to Thucydides and the Peloponnesian Wars.[27] (Add a penny to your collection.) Its foundation is premised on the conviction that states exist in an anarchic world, one with no international force or institution capable of arbitrating disputes between and among them. As a result, states exist in perpetual fear of being attacked, overtaken, or conquered by rival states (the "security dilemma"). The theory also assumes that states are rational actors (which, admittedly, will not explain exceptions, such as why Caligula declared war on the sea, or why Idi Amin proclaimed himself the Last King of Scotland) and will act to maximize their economic and military power.

Realists understand international politics as a zero-sum game: all state power is relative to that of other states, and one state's gain is, by definition, another state's loss. Thus the security dilemma: one state can only become stronger at the expense of other states. So when a great power rises or when a state becomes militarily or economically stronger, it inspires insecurity and fear in other powers. This creates conflict. In the realist worldview, the best way to alleviate conflict is through alliances that create stable balances of power, forcing states to behave peacefully.

Realism and its intellectual offshoots[28] represent a tragic view of the world,[29] in which warfare and geopolitics can never be eliminated as long as there are sovereign (and selfishly rational) states with independent military capabilities. International institutions (such as the United Nations) matter, but only at the margins. They are merely reflections of existing balances of power and cannot sustain great influence.

In the case of Iran, two realists might offer very different prescriptions. One might argue that it is irresponsible to allow Iran to acquire nuclear weapons and insist that it must be prevented at all costs and by any means necessary. Another might argue that Iran's neighbors should develop nuclear arsenals of their own to restore the regional balance of power—and, therefore, the region's stability. No realist would argue that the United Nations or International Atomic Energy Agency could have any impact on Iran's nuclear plans.

LIBERAL INSTITUTIONALISM  The traditional critique of realism comes from neoliberal thinkers, especially institutionalists. Liberal institutionalists share the realist belief in an anarchic world, but they believe that international institutions (such as treaties and organizations) can and do provide a framework that can mitigate the security dilemma. They also argue that realists ignore the internal workings of the state and obsessively focus only on security issues.

Neoliberal institutionalists argue that institutions can overcome fears of cheating and unequal gains and allow cooperation to emerge between states.[30] They hold that states, especially in a multipolar world, by participating in treaties and international organizations, can mitigate the security dilemma and focus on winning relative gains. Further, by participating in multilateral institutions and trade, states can become increasingly interdependent, which further reduces friction and the risk of war. Given its focus, much of the literature on institutionalism deals with how to create international institutions that work and ensure that their members neither cheat the institutional rules nor act as free riders (actors who benefit from a collective action without paying their fair share of the costs).[31]

In the case of a nuclear Iran, a neoliberal institutionalist[32] could provide varied policy recommendations, though these would emphasize a multilateral approach to the issue, preferably one involving diplomatic consensus reached within existing international organizations like the U.N. Security Council. This might include a gradual tightening of economic sanctions on Iran. He would not renounce the use of force as an option of last resort, but would try to build a multilateral consensus in favor of military action before taking this step.

CONSTRUCTIVISM    Constructivism is a radical departure from both the realist and neoliberal institutionalist traditions of international relations. An outgrowth of literary deconstruction and postmodernism,[33] it focuses on how ideas, social identities, and theoretical concepts are created and employed in strategic politics. For instance, in explaining the end of the Cold War, Alexander Wendt analyzes how the breakdown of the Soviet Union's Leninist thinking opened the door for Gorbachev's glasnost and perestroika.[34] The main idea is that nothing is foreordained in international politics and that strategy and geopolitics are heavily dependent on how they are conceptualized.

Our hypothetical constructivist analyst could address the question of what the United States or the international community should do in the case of Iran's nuclear arsenal in a number of ways—from recommending direct U.S. diplomatic engagement with Iran, to regime change in that country. Overall constructivism is more a critique than a school of thought and does not lend itself to policy prescription.[35]

FOREIGN POLICY ANALYSIS    Foreign policy analysis is not so much a theory as a field of study that looks at how states make foreign policy decisions. In general, foreign policy analysis concerns itself with the sources of decision making. It differs from international relations theory in that it strongly considers the locus of foreign policy decision making to be based in domestic politics. Most international relations theories (especially realism), like traditional geopolitics, only look at how states interact with one another, but foreign policy analysis "unpacks" the foreign policy decision-making process.

There are a number of things an analyst employing foreign policy analysis could look at, including a state's institutions, regime, elites, ideology, and interest groups. There are many variations and schools of thoughts about foreign policy analysis (with different ideas about, for instance, whether bureaucracies are more important than elites in decision making, and when). Foreign policy analysis applied to the question of the Iran nuclear issue would try to break down what motivates the various parties in the Iran nuclear crisis, and ask a number of pertinent questions. What are Iran's motives? What is motivating the respective positions of the United States, Israel, and the European Union? What drives their foreign policy? What institutions, interest groups, or interpretations of history motivate them?

The foreign policy analysis method is complex, messy, and contentious. But at its best, it yields some of the finest geopolitical analysis. This was the case with a July 1947 article by George F. Kennan, a high-ranking diplomat in the U.S. embassy in Moscow, that provided the basis for the United States' Cold War containment policy.

The article, titled "The Sources of Soviet Conduct" and published in *Foreign Affairs,* exemplified geopolitical analysis at its best. As its name implied, it detailed the sources of Soviet behavior as extensions of its Communist ideology and of Russian history. The article described how Russia's geopolitical condition—as a flat, open landmass lacking natural barriers to invasion—left it perpetually insecure in the face of potential marauders like the Mongols, Swedes, Napoleon, and Hitler. As a consequence, Kennan argued, Russia had always sought expansion, both to create buffers and to fulfill a sense of "manifest destiny."[36] The article further described how Soviet ideology and current policy making, married with Russian expansionist experience, would lead the Soviets to try to extend the reach of communism throughout the world—and into Western Europe in particular.

Kennan's analysis identified the Soviet expansionist threat and suggested a number of ways to counter it. The essay appeared in 1947, a year when Greece, Turkey, Italy, and even France seemed on the brink of seeing domestic power passed to Communist parties with ties to Moscow. Kennan's proposal, which dealt mostly with countering Soviet propaganda and influence, advocated a number of "soft power" measures, such as better education and support for democratic governments and a commitment to lead by example across the world. These ideas contributed to the development of the Truman Doctrine (which provided significant economic and military aid to Turkey and Greece) and of the U.S. containment policy, which was meant to stop the spread of Soviet power across the globe.[37]

Kennan's historical analysis proved astute and stood as the basis for mitigating the risk of Western governments turning Communist. There is, however, a problematic side here as well: the analysis could be misapplied. Consider the impact of America's containment policy on Vietnam.

Kennan intended that containment be conducted on a peaceful basis wherever possible, by attracting people and their governments to side with the United States through education and military and economic aid. By the time of Vietnam, however, the containment policy had morphed into the "domino theory," which posited that the fall of one country to communism might well trigger the fall of others.

Proponents of the domino theory argued that the U.S. government had to intervene militarily to prevent this from happening. But the domino theory ignored the local historical and political context in favor of an abstract idea. U.S. policy makers did not recognize that Vietnam's Communists were also nationalists, a failure of analysis that contributed significantly to the U.S. defeat in that conflict. Adherents to the domino theory also failed to recognize that nationalism in the states around Vietnam would limit the spread of communism beyond Vietnam's borders. Ultimately, Kennan's article and the ways in which it has been misused reveal the advantages of foreign policy analysis and the problems that rigid adherence to a single abstract theory can create.[38]

## Mitigating Geopolitical Risks

By definition, governments have always been geopolitical risk-mitigation enterprises because they are charged with protecting their territories and peoples. Most states, when faced with a threat from a rival power, have a number of traditional means at their disposal. These range from diplomatic moves, to economic sanctions and foreign aid, to military action, to combinations of these means. The choice of tools depends on factors ranging from domestic politics, to regime type, to economic, international, or sociocultural constraints.

In the previous section we detailed how governments have traditionally dealt with geopolitical risks. The literature on international relations, with its focus on alliances, strategy, and the construction of threats explains just that.

The United States, like other governments, is increasingly interested in applying corporate risk management techniques to strategic problems, and sees inspiration in creating scenarios that are methodologically similar to those employed by Royal Dutch Shell.

Risk management as a philosophy is becoming ever more popular. In the past governments focused on dealing with threats, which are specific and can be eliminated or contained.[39] Risk, on the other hand, is a probabilistic concept. Risks never go away and must constantly be mitigated. Instead of aiming for specific solutions, risk management is about coping with known and unknown possibilities.[40] Risk management is also a tricky issue, because it generates other risks,[41] possibly creating feedback loops.

An interesting result of the use of risk management techniques to deal with national security and geopolitics: preemptive warfare. Launching a war to defeat your rival before he can attack you is not a new phenomenon, but having a military doctrine based around this idea, such as the Bush Doctrine,[42] is a novel concept, and one that is tied to the idea of risk. Recent United States–led interventions, whether the NATO bombing of Kosovo (1998) to preempt ethnic cleansing by Milosevic's regime or the war in Iraq (2003), were implemented with the hope of "*averting* speculative scenarios rather than *attaining* specific outcomes."[43]

Do preemptive wars successfully mitigate geopolitical threats? That is a matter of considerable debate. Preemptive wars have produced strategically mixed results for those who prosecute them. NATO's Kosovo bombing was successful in preventing the Milosevic regime from ethnically cleansing the province's ethnic Albanians, but it also provoked a more antagonistic relationship between the United States and Russia.

### The Benefits and Drawbacks of Preemption

Consider two more examples of the intended and unintended effects of preemptive war: Israel's 1967 attack on Syria, Jordan, and Egypt in what became known as the Six Day War and the United States' 2003 invasion of Iraq. When measuring the success of preemptive strikes on a perceived threat, it is important to consider a strike's short- and long-term implications as well as whether the strike achieved tactical and strategic objectives.

Israel's 1967 preemptive attacks on Jordanian, Egyptian, and Syrian forces produced a quick military victory. Just 19 years after the founding of the state of Israel, the political leadership in Tel Aviv became convinced that the country's neighbors were determined to attack and destroy the young country. Israel has already fought border skirmishes with Egypt and Syria. Egypt had remilitarized and blockaded the strategically vital Straits of Tiran. The threat to Israel was clear, and belligerent speeches from Egyptian leader Gamal Abdel Nasser made the threat appear immediate.

Israel then launched simultaneous attacks on Syria, Jordan, and Egypt, surprised their militaries, and expanded its territory by acquiring the Gaza Strip, the West Bank, and the Sinai Peninsula. We can't know what would have happened had Israel not attacked first. Some analysts argue that miscommunication veiled the likelihood that the conflict between Israel, Syria, Jordan, and Egypt was on the verge of a diplomatic solution. Others warn that had there been no preemptive attack, the combined Syrian, Jordanian, and Egyptian forces would have easily overwhelmed the smaller Israeli forces and destroyed the country. In this sense, Israel's preemptive strike was a success.

The United States' 2003 invasion of Iraq provides an example of a less successful use of preemption. Following the September 11, 2001, attacks, President George W. Bush's administration determined that Iraqi dictator Saddam Hussein was developing weapons of mass destruction and that he might use them against the United States—a compelling case for a preemptive strike. The fall of his regime would also allow the United States to cultivate a democratic government in Baghdad, triggering democratic momentum across the Middle East.

The preemptive attack achieved its tactical objectives: It toppled Saddam Hussein's government and prevented it from obtaining and deploying weapons of mass destruction (although it later became clear that he did not in fact have such weapons at the time of the invasion). But it failed to achieve its strategic objective of creating a wave of democracy across the region. The U.S. strategic position in the Middle East in 2008 was arguably weaker than it was before the strike on Iraq, and Washington's ability to militarily defend its interests elsewhere in the world was diminished by the ongoing troop commitment in Iraq.

In traditional geopolitics, the key actors are typically states rather than companies. After all, corporations cannot do much to prevent geopolitical shifts from happening. As we described earlier in the chapter, most British and German bankers bitterly opposed movement toward World War I, which they rightly perceived as disastrous, but they could do nothing to prevent it. Typically, when corporations face risks of embargoes or war, they make contingency plans—by planning for alternate work sites and, in some cases, acquiring insurance against war damage.

That explains the divergent fates of two German aircraft manufacturers, Fokker and Pfalz. Both companies created military aircraft for the German army during the war. But once the war ended, Pfalz was shuttered while Fokker produced commercial aircraft in Holland and the United States. What accounted for the difference? The main factors were intellectual proprietorship, geographical mobility, and some element of neutrality.

When the Treaty of Versailles restricted German aircraft production, Fokker and Pfalz at first appeared to have equally poor prospects. In fact, the Fokker D.VII fighter was the only weapon that the treaty explicitly prohibited. But the Allies' demand to destroy the Fokker factories in Germany did not push the company out of business. The founder and owner, Anthony Fokker, fled to his native Netherlands, where he reestablished the company. Fokker corporation could be relocated and relaunched because the founder was able to preserve the know-how of production (planes and engines were smuggled out of Germany to the Netherlands, and Fokker himself was involved in the design and testing of planes), as well as his business acumen and leadership. Fokker successfully redirected production to the civilian aircraft sector in both Holland and the United States. Thus, his ability and willingness to relocate saved the company, despite the hostile geopolitical environment.

The Pfalz corporation, on the other hand, went bankrupt following the Treaty of Versailles, when French troops occupied Germany's western territories and confiscated the company's equipment. The factories were later reused by various companies. A company under the name of Pfalz Flugzeugwerke (PFW) was reformed in 1997. But the corporation ceased to exist under its original ownership not long after the end of World War I. Pfalz could not simply relocate its production or start civilian plane manufacturing as Fokker had done because its wartime success relied less on intellectual property, technical innovation, and managerial talent than on simply taking advantage of wartime opportunities. Before the war, Pfalz engaged in licensed production of aircraft models of various companies. During the war, it launched a number of original models, but Fokker's models performed better.

Companies cannot prevent wars between states, but they can prepare for different geopolitical scenarios and develop contingency plans and insurance policies for projects that have geopolitical exposure. Most companies (with a few exceptions) do a pretty poor job at this, for a number of perfectly rational reasons.

First, most companies do not have the luxury of planning 20 years ahead, particularly when management is often judged by its annual (and even quarterly) performance. Second, most corporate management is simply not structured to consider how geopolitical shifts could affect corporations. Third, and most importantly, most corporations still consider risks to be normally distributed (they take the shape of a "bell curve" in terms of probability and impact), whereas political risks are often much more likely than normally distributed risk events would suggest.

How could companies better plan for geopolitical risks? For a large corporation, or one dealing in the international economy, it is important to consider the following:

- Keep an open mind on long-term risks. While most companies' short-term bias is understandable, not having planning for the big events that can be either grave threats or great opportunities can pose a significant risk. Over the past 50 years, major geopolitical changes have occured at least once a decade. Think of the decolonizations of the 1950s and '60s, the U.S.-Soviet entente of the 1970s, the end of the Cold War, or the post-9/11 world. Large geopolitical changes happen regularly. It pays to pay attention.
- Structure yourself organizationally to be nimble and know your strengths in case of a major shock. In Fokker's case, the company's ability to move production to a neutral country and to maintain control of its intellectual property was a quick and creative solution to a crushing event.
- To address geopolitical fat tail risks, plan for radically different worlds. That is what Royal Dutch Shell does with its energy scenarios, which contain a number of geopolitical variables. These scenarios are then used to develop internal strategies that can be quickly applied if the world changes. Except in specific industries, such as oil and gas exploration, such planning remains exceedingly rare.
- Consider buying political risk insurance. It is possible for corporations to buy insurance for specific projects with geopolitical risks, such as wars between states and business disruptions associated with war-related embargoes and border closings. Insurance has significant limitations, as we shall discuss, but in particular circumstances, it can prove invaluable.

INSURANCE AND GEOPOLITICS    Some political risk insurance policies cover losses from wars, civil wars, politically motivated internal violence, and terrorism (though since 9/11, terrorism insurance has become a separate field).

But for geopolitical risk, insurance is a bit tricky. First, wars between and among countries are not all that common. Most of the world's organized conflicts since the end of World War II have been civil wars within developing countries.[44] Buying insurance to offset the risk of World War III doesn't make much sense, especially given the small and illiquid nature of the political risk insurance market. In the case of a major conflict, such obligations would in any case be difficult to fulfill, and a corporation would have bigger issues to deal with than collecting on an insurance policy.

But political risk insurance can also cover the symptoms of great power tensions, like embargoes and trade disruptions. Given that most political insurance is negotiated directly with insurers, it is often possible to write policies that cover the effects of country or economic sanctions. One interesting recent case involving the former Soviet Union highlights some of the benefits and problems of political risk insurance.

Despite U.S. trade embargoes, U.S. corporations engaged in significant business with the Soviet Union, including investments in strategic industries. In the early 1970s, U.S. investment in the Soviet KamAZ (Kama River) truck plant (in Tatarstan, Russia) is estimated to have reached $500 million.[45] The French-based Renault corporation built the plant, but several U.S. firms supplied the equipment,[46] and U.S. insurance corporations and the U.S. Export-Import (Ex-Im) Bank provided insurance and loan guarantees.[47]

When the Soviets invaded Afghanistan in 1979, KamAZ trucks were used to transport troops across the border in violation of U.S. export agreements. The Afghanistan invasion generated U.S. economic sanctions and trade restrictions (and thus financial losses) for the U.S. firms involved in the investment.

One of the main companies affected, Ingersoll Rand,[48] was prevented from providing engine assembly lines to KamAZ. Some of Ingersoll Rand's losses (and those of other U.S. companies) were recoverable thanks to the existing political insurance policies that covered the possibility of embargoes.

Investment in a militarily sensitive Soviet industry was recognized as risky from the outset, which is why many of the U.S. firms involved in it bought private and government insurance policies. The main U.S. investments were made in 1971–72, only a few years after the Soviet invasion of Czechoslovakia in 1968. Given previous Russian military actions (and the sales of military hardware to other Communist states involved in different conflicts) and the common use of trucks to transport military personnel, U.S. companies bought insurance to mitigate the potential risks posed by investing in a controversial Soviet project.

But insurance policies did not cover (and could not have covered) the reputational—or public relations—risks these companies accepted. The use of American-built trucks by Soviet troops for the invasion of Afghanistan created plenty of bad publicity for the U.S. companies involved with KamAZ. It also triggered congressional investigations and more restrictions on U.S. investments in the Eastern Bloc.

Political risk insurance has other limitations. Most insurers, especially those run by governments, require corporations claiming insurance protection to turn over their investments to the insurer. Most insurance only covers about 90% of the value of the investments.[49] Finally, most insurance requires a legally enforceable event, such as an embargo or act of war, to produce a payout. In other words, it is practically impossible to insure against certain occurrences: the economic and financial consequences of, say, great power decline or the relative rise in strength of a competing nation and its companies.

## Capital Markets and Geopolitical Analysis

The era of great power wars, colonial adventures and a steady stream of revolutions may have passed, but correctly analyzing geopolitical risk is no less important for business leaders today.[50] This is not necessarily easy or straightforward (losses are also common), and it depends on a thorough understanding of both the historical background and of the theories we have just discussed.

### Making Money and Chinese Saber Rattling

Take, for instance, China's determination to use any means necessary to prevent Taiwan from declaring independence. The Chinese Communist Party claims Beijing's sovereignty over Taiwan and believes that any move by Taiwan's government to formally declare the island nation's independence would pose a fundamental challenge to the party's legitimacy. A Chinese invasion of Taiwan is often discussed as a real possibility.

This widely perceived risk has fueled Taiwanese market volatility whenever election cycles or official remarks raise the specter of Taiwanese independence and, therefore, of a violent reaction from Beijing. When Taiwanese president Lee Teng-hui advocated Taiwanese independence in a speech in 1995, China staged a missile exercise in the Taiwan straits. The following day, the Taiwanese stock exchange (TAIEX index) fell 4.2%.[51] Lee delivered another explicitly pro-independence speech in 1999, triggering a market slide that pushed the index lower by 20% over the course of a month. In March 2000, the index fell 2.6% on the day that Chen Shui-bian was elected as the first Taiwanese president from the Democratic Progressive Party, a party founded on the principle of Taiwan's independence.[52]

Yet, fears that China will invade Taiwan are misplaced. China's strategy for tamping down Taiwanese public demand for independence has been far too nuanced and far too successful for the risk of invasion to raise too many concerns. For China's leaders, losing Taiwan would prove a disaster. Losing a war against U.S. and Taiwanese forces would be worse. That is one reason why an all-out Chinese military invasion is highly unlikely. More relevantly, China is also shrewdly co-opting Taiwanese businesses that are unhappy with restrictions on direct investment in the mainland and giving them a powerful financial incentive to exert their influence within Taiwan in favor of policies that preserve a peaceful status quo. Beijing hopes that Taiwan's deepening reliance on the mainland economy will strengthen the island's mainland-friendly constituencies. Given these constraints, and China's "mixed" Taiwan strategy (belligerent posturing plus nurturing of economic interdependence), most investors consistently overestimate Beijing's threat. The knowledge that the TAIEX dips whenever China and Taiwan rattle their sabers is useful information for savvy market participants.

### Geopolitical Tensions in Iran and Oil Markets

Understanding the timing and "volatility zones" of a specific issue can be just as important as the ultimate outcome for market participants. Even if it is impossible to predict the endgame of a particular political or policy dispute with a high degree of confidence, mapping out a time line that details when tensions are likely to build or recede, and drive market and investor sentiment, can be critical for certain types of investors. If you know when things will appear to worsen (or improve)—regardless of the ultimate outcome—you can better understand the market volatility that these developments produce. The story of the round of U.S.-Iran tensions that began in 2004 provides a good recent example.

It became clear in 2003 to many observers in the United States, key European Union states, the United Nations, and the International Atomic Energy Agency

(IAEA) that Iran was working to acquire the technology needed to enrich uranium from start to finish entirely within its borders. Many analysts argued that, if they succeeded, the Iranians could develop nuclear weapons in the intermediate term. If so, Iran's success would directly undermine the nuclear nonproliferation efforts of the world's nuclear powers, as other Middle Eastern states—like Saudi Arabia, Turkey, Egypt, and even Iraq might one day feel compelled to respond by developing nuclear arsenals of their own. Some worried that Iran might share nuclear material with allied militant groups like Hezbollah. Some feared that Iran might launch a nuclear attack on Israel, despite Israel's ability to retaliate with its own nuclear weapons.

As tensions grew, a preemptive U.S. or Israeli strike on Iran's nuclear facilities began to appear increasingly plausible—even likely. Imagine the impact on global markets, particularly energy markets, of such an attack. Energy investors monitored the situation closely, and markets reacted each time the risk of conflict appeared to rise. Many experts began to talk of an "Iran premium" in the price of oil.[53]

In early 2005, tensions appeared to recede. The IAEA adopted a less confrontational stance and sent encouraging signals that Iran was edging toward some form of acceptable compliance. At the United Nations, Iran's talks with Russia, France, and Germany appeared to yield progress. Oil traders began to ask two questions: "Have we turned the corner in this conflict?" and "Can we expect the Iran premium to come out of the oil price in the coming months?" Regardless of the end game of "attack or no attack," there was a key timing issue with respect to tensions and markets. If you believed the corner had been turned, all else being equal, oil prices could be expected to soften. If you believed that tensions would soon return, oil would likely move in the other direction.

Thoughtful analysis of the incentives, agendas, and bargaining positions of the relevant countries—particularly of the domestic political incentives that Iran's leaders had for pushing ahead with nuclear development—suggested that this was a temporary cooling of tensions. By summer, some believed, the political temperature would rise again. Oil market investors who took that bet in early 2005 did very well. The IAEA, United Nations, European powers (including Russia), and the United States became increasingly frustrated and impatient with Iran's diplomatic stall tactics. Tensions spiked, an attack on Iran again appeared plausible, and the "Iran premium" returned to oil prices.

### *From Global Politics to Global Capital Markets*

While geopolitical trends and developments impact global capital markets, much of the dynamism and risk associated with liquid global markets is in fact local and regional. National-level political decisions that do not even register in the realm of geopolitics, such as the resignation of a finance minister or tensions between a central bank head and a prime minister, can move currency, bond, and equities markets.

The impact of geopolitics on markets can be trumped by other, local drivers. In recent years, as geopolitical tensions have risen between Russia and the West, Russia's local markets have actually improved dramatically. From a U.S. perspective, Russia has been a bad story for Washington but a very good story for Wall Street.[54] These local and regional drivers of political risk provide the theme for the next chapter.

# Political Risk and Capital Markets

## FOUR

Newspapers and politicians pay little heed to what they
are told by professors of politics. But they take very
seriously—sometimes far too seriously—what
they are told by the economists.
—Susan Strange[1]

In late 1994, Jaime Serra Puche, a rising star in Mexico's Institutional Revolutionary Party (PRI) and the country's newly appointed finance minister, was expected
to manage a currency devaluation without stirring up a lot of political or economic trouble. The celebrated negotiator, famous for delivering on the North
American Free Trade Agreement (NAFTA) failed on both counts. Mexico experienced a massive, rapid devaluation of its currency (the peso). The currency's
downward spiral helped strip the PRI of its dominant hold on Mexico's political
landscape. Saddled with expectations that he remain faithful to his party's political agenda, despite the demands of modern capital markets, Serra was probably
doomed to fail. But the real story is about the PRI and its approach to maintaining single-party power, a decades-long dominance dependent on the power iof
graft and patronage.[2] The PRI, run as a kind of massive-scale Tammany Hall
organization, bolstered its power by dispensing economic spoils to the leaders
of trade unions, state and agricultural employees, and regional political parties.[3]
The operation was, as Peruvian novelist Mario Vargas Llosa aptly called it, "the
perfect dictatorship."[4]

Yet the manipulation of economic policy for political gain would ultimately
break the PRI's grip on power. Its inability to retire its patronage machine contributed

substantially to the 1994 peso crisis and the party's first ever political defeat two years later. This crisis illustrates perfectly how political factors can trigger a financial crisis.

In the years preceding the 1994 currency collapse, the Carlos Salinas administration (1988–94) carried out ambitious market-oriented economic reforms that brought a significant reduction in inflation—and the North American Free Trade Agreement. Before the peso crisis, Mexico's economy was in reasonable shape, though a growing account deficit would probably have made an eventual currency devaluation necessary.[5]

Economic factors alone cannot explain the peso crisis. A devaluation could have been managed to ensure a soft landing. Instead, the Mexican currency crisis was driven by poor political decisions: "The state of illiquidity at the end of 1994 was due to unexpected shocks that occurred throughout the year, and the inadequate policy responses to those shocks, according to economist Jeffrey Sachs."[6] Mexico was running a current account deficit, at least in part, because the ruling party had increased government spending to curry favor with voters in an election year—a formula that had served the PRI well for the previous 70 years.

The Salinas government launched its spending spree, enabled cheap credit, and avoided engineering a much-needed correction in the exchange rate. It was no secret in early 1994 that Mexico would have to devalue its currency. Markets expected it, and waves of investors headed for the exits to beat the rush. But the PRI decided that a preelection devaluation or a rise in interest rates amounted to a pill it was not prepared to swallow. Not in 1994. Not six years after Carlos Salinas had won only by the narrowest of margins, quite possibly as a result of electoral fraud.[7]

Other political surprises followed. The left-wing Zapatista guerrilla uprising in the state of Chiapas frightened foreign investors. Three months later, the PRI's presidential candidate, Luis Donaldo Colosio, was murdered during a campaign stop in Tijuana, Mexico's first high-profile political assassination in decades. Ernesto Zedillo, an uncharismatic technocrat, took his place. A series of kidnappings of prominent businessmen added to investor anxiety. The government's decision that sound corrections to fiscal, monetary, and exchange rate policies were too politically risky in this environment made matters worse.

The political strategy paid political dividends as Zedillo was elected president of Mexico in December 1994. But in the process, the PRI had activated an economic time bomb with a very short fuse. Less than a month after Zedillo's victory, the PRI decided the moment had arrived to devalue the peso by 15%—to

4 pesos per dollar. It was too little too late. Market players panicked as the peso quickly fell from 4 pesos to more than 5.5 pesos per dollar, and then to 7.45 in March 1995, triggering Mexico's worst economic crisis in half a century. Fears that Mexico would default on its sovereign debt prompted the International Monetary Fund and the U.S. government to stabilize the peso with a $50 billion bailout.

The "December mistake," as the crisis came to be known, crippled Zedillo's political standing. The PRI's rivals demanded political and economic concessions in exchange for support for his stabilization plan. Zedillo's rivals within the PRI called on him to resist. By 1996, he had little choice but to defy hardliners within his party and to implement an electoral reform package that proved a significant step toward political liberalization. A year later, the PRI lost its absolute majority in the lower house of congress for the first time since it was created in 1929. In 2000, Vicente Fox became Mexico's first non-PRI president in 71 years.

The moral of the story: What at first appears an irrational choice might not be. Those who assume that presidents, prime ministers, and members of parliament care more about sound economic policy than about their political fortunes are doomed to the occasional surprise, because political leaders sometimes make market-moving (even market-crashing) economic decisions to satisfy their political needs. Economists knew that the peso was overvalued; some called for devaluation well before the crisis began.[8] Players in capital markets recognized the Mexican budgetary and currency imbalances; foreign capital had already begun flowing out of the country. Yet, very few market analysts understood that the PRI would decide it *could not* devalue the peso, for political reasons.[9]

### How Politics Impact Capital Markets

Currency controls and devaluations, financial regulatory changes, declarations of war, strikes, sovereign credit defaults, the confiscations of banks' assets, corruption, outright theft, and fraudulent bookkeeping are just a few of the many political factors that influence money flows and change the value of an investment, whether a stock, a currency, a bond, or a commodity.

A growing number of investors and business decision makers now understand that political choices and events move capital markets and alter the value of

TABLE 4.1 Some ways in which politics can impact capital markets

|  | Government actions | Nongovernmental political events |
|---|---|---|
| Direct impact | Currency devaluations | Boycotts |
|  | Sovereign credit defaults | Terrorism |
|  | Currency controls | Strikes |
|  | Regulatory changes | Civil wars |
|  | Confiscations of bank assets |  |
| Indirect impact (market panics) | Declarations of war |  |
|  | Changes in government makeup |  |
|  | Public statements |  |
|  | Elections |  |

portfolio investments. But as they develop their economic models and indexes, the ones they use to calculate a country's sovereign creditworthiness, they consider economic factors (like levels of inflation, growth, and deficits) with no systematic way of including political risk in the equation. The architects of these economic models too often push political risk into the miscellaneous uncertainties category, what statisticians call the "error term."[10]

A government announces that it will change the value of its country's currency or limit the ability of individuals and investors to hold or trade it. That is a common form of political risk, one that impacts just about everyone with an interest in the value of that particular currency: holders of the country's debt, foreign companies operating there, exporters to that country, and those who live there. The United States' Overseas Private Investment Corporation (OPIC), whose mission includes the insuring of U.S. investments abroad against political risks, estimated that between 1966 and 1999, about one-fifth of its claims arose when corporations found themselves unable to convert profits earned abroad into other currencies.[11]

Politically driven currency risks come in three basic forms. First, a government can simply devalue its currency. In the case of the peso crisis, the Mexican government revalued the peso's value relative to the U.S. dollar. Second, political events that generate investor concerns about a currency's value can force a devaluation. Any number of events—the collapse of a ruling coalition, a cabinet reshuffle, a political scandal—can trigger that level of anxiety.[12] Third, governments can impose regulations that make it difficult for others to convert or transfer the local currency into another—by limiting the amount that a company or individual can hold, regulating the timing of exchanges, increasing taxes and fees on conversions, or imposing an outright prohibition.

Consider Malaysia's experience during the 1997–98 East Asian financial crisis, which reveals how heavy-handed government intervention in capital markets can stabilize an economy, though at significant cost to investors. The Asian financial meltdown triggered enormous capital flight from the region, including from Malaysia. Asian exchange rates collapsed, prompting a vicious cycle of capital outflows and asset price deflation. Thailand, Indonesia, Korea, and the Philippines turned to the International Monetary Fund (IMF) for emergency financial assistance. Malaysia, on the other hand, managed the crisis alone. Initially, Malaysian finance minister Anwar Ibrahim responded with orthodox market policies, raising interest rates and cutting public spending to improve fiscal and trade balances. But these austerity measures threatened major Malaysian businesses, including many that supported then Prime Minister Mahathir bin Mohamad and his ruling party, United Malays National Organisation.

On September 1, 1998, Mahathir introduced strict capital controls and famously blamed "speculators" (notably George Soros) for instigating Malaysia's economic troubles. He also sacked Anwar Ibrahim. Mahathir restricted capital outflows by requiring nonresidents to wait one year before converting their ringgit proceeds from Malaysian securities sales. Later, this restriction was replaced with a stiff exit tax on capital gains. Mahathir eliminated the offshore market for ringgits by repatriating all of Malaysia's currency, prohibited lending by Malaysians to foreigners, and recalibrated the Malaysian exchange rate. After taking control of the capital market, Mahathir reduced interbank interest rates and passed a fiscal stimulus package to rejuvenate the economy.[13]

The prime minister imposed these currency controls to manage the economic recovery without jeopardizing the government's ability to distribute wealth across the country to reinforce its political popularity. The unfettered workings of free markets might have threatened the delicate balance among the country's various ethnic communities and its constituent federal states. In addition, Asia's financial crisis had put an end to Suharto's 30-year rule in Indonesia, and UMNO's leaders had no desire to share his fate. Finally, Anwar had won praise from financial market players for effective stewardship of the finance ministry and was positioning himself for a run at the presidency. By sacking him, Mahathir removed a political rival. To prevent another round of capital flight following Anwar's ouster, Mahathir announced the capital control one day before removing Anwar from office.

Mahathir's risky policy choice paid off politically and, over time, economically. Though Malaysia's GDP declined by 7.4% in 1998, it rebounded with 6.1% growth in 1999 and another 8.2% in 2000. Mahathir remained in power until his retirement in 2003.

Investors must contend with changes in currency values as well as trading rules and regulations, but their impact depends on the degree and type of exposure. For a local producer, a currency devaluation makes products cheaper to sell abroad. But for those holding a local currency, the effects are largely negative. Investors are often dependent on the free flow of money across borders. When this process is interrupted, they may not be able to transfer profits out of the country or even to pay their employees. Exporting firms are not paid, bond dividend payments are not made, and everyone faces a surge in paperwork as they learn the new rules.[14]

This is why Malaysia's actions had significant costs for portfolio investors who were holding its currency or assets denominated in it. The Singapore Stock Exchange ran a very liquid over-the-counter trade in Malaysian equities. When the Malaysian government imposed currency controls, it also banned the trade of Malaysian shares on the Singaporean exchange, leaving investors there with $4 billion worth of shares in more than 100 Malaysian companies that were suddenly "frozen," and therefore temporarily worthless.[15]

Not all currency devaluations or restrictions are politically motivated. Governments can impose currency controls or engage in devaluations for what they see as sound economic reasons; such motives certainly played a part in Mahathir's decision. It is not always easy to separate a government's political considerations from its economic motives in analyzing currency policy-related risks. But for most market players, attention to political motivations is a vitally important part of any sound risk management strategy.[16]

**Emerging Markets—Where Political Analysis**
**Meets Economic/Financial Analysis**

In 2003, Goldman Sachs released an important piece of research on emerging markets. *Dreaming with BRICs: The Path to 2050.*[17] In it, the authors argued that by 2050 Brazil, Russia, India, and China would have larger economies than any country in the world except the United States and Japan. The report has helped fuel intense interest in the inevitable shift in the balance of global political and economic power over the next half century. It has provided intriguing glimpses of a world no longer dominated by U.S., European, and Japanese interests.[18] Some analysts have argued that it makes little sense to throw Brazil, Russia, India, and China together into a single emerging market category. These four economies have four very different sets of advantages and vulnerabilities. Others question the economics behind the prediction. Still, the report has generated compelling debate, and the term "BRIC" has become universally known in political, financial, and economic circles.

But the BRIC story has one fundamental flaw. To combine so many complex variables into such a long-range forecast, the report's authors had to make a series of questionable political assumptions. The largest is that the governments of these four countries would exist in pretty much the same form for the following 47 years. Given how much political systems and attitudes toward state intervention in economies can change, that's quite an assumption. What sort of political leaderships governed Brazil, Russia, India, and China in 1956, 47 years before the Goldman report appeared? Russia formed a single republic within the Soviet Union. Only two of the four countries, India and China, had (roughly) the same form of government they have today; India was already a democracy; China was—and still is—a one-party authoritarian state. Brazil was a democracy in 1956—though the country later endured a period of military dictatorship between 1964 and 1985.

More importantly, in 1956, *none* of the BRICs pursued the economic course that they do today. Had you predicted in 1956 that by 1992 the Soviet Union would yield 15 capitalist successor states and that China would become a capitalist powerhouse, you would have faced more than your fair share of ridicule. The fundamental problem with 50-year political predictions is that virtually *no one* gets them right. We simply cannot know how leaders in Brazil, Russia,

India, and China will define their political and economic interests half a century from now.

Thoughtful analysis of the impact of politics on capital markets depends on the ability and willingness to accept the limits of what can be known. An understanding of politics will not necessarily tell you whether a stock price will rise or fall tomorrow, but it can tell you where and how political events may limit or alter an investment's value. At the very least, it can tell you whether the underlying political assumptions of an economic forecast are plausible.

In no area is political risk more relevant than in analysis of globalization and the rapid growth of emerging markets. Globalization—the processes by which ideas, information, people, money, goods, and services cross borders at unprecedented speed—has been the driving force in international politics for the last two decades. Globalization has meant, among other things, explosive economic growth and investment abroad. The core developed states (the United States, Japan, several Western European countries, and others) have aging populations and more mature economies, offering relatively low risks and, therefore, relatively low returns. But over the past several years, nothing has fueled the optimism of pundits and the ambitions of investors more than the words "emerging market." In that magic phrase, there is hope for a more stable and less violent future. Investors see growth and underpriced assets. Yes, there are risks. But emerging markets will surely emerge, and there's plenty of money to be made in the meantime.

But ask a random sampling of global investors to name some emerging-market countries, and you will get a long list of states that do not belong in the same political or economic category. Some of those markets will emerge. Others will not, at least not in their present forms. Each faces challenges unique to its social and political circumstances.

In general, political risk analysis has more to offer in emerging markets. An emerging market country is one in which politics will matter at least as much as basic economic fundamentals for the performance of markets.[19] Developed industrial countries are often defined as states in which economics and culture are independent of politics. In Germany, you probably won't need political connections to operate a grocery store. In many developing states, however, it can be expensive or even dangerous to run a small business without them. Capital and business acumen will help you turn a profit, but only if you also know how to navigate a politicized economic and regulatory environment.

A defining distinction among emerging market states: How different are their responses to the demands of globalization? When India ran dangerously low on foreign exchange reserves in 1991, the Reserve Bank of India was forced to airlift some 47 tons of gold to London as security against a $400 million emergency loan. Facing bankruptcy, the ruling Congress Party made a political decision to begin to dismantle decades of state control of the economy and to open India as never before to foreign investment. Reform debates and plans had begun to form years earlier, but the crisis atmosphere created by the threat of collapse in 1991 provided a tipping point. The country's political infighting still ensures that liberalization moves forward by fits and starts. Plenty of political and cultural obstacles remain. But India is emerging because its political leaders have tightened their embrace of globalization.

Nor is there any way to separate China's aggressive growth strategy from the country's authoritarian politics. Former leader Deng Xiaoping determined in the late 1970s that the Communist Party's future legitimacy would depend on its ability to attract foreign capital and know-how to the still isolated country and to deliver the Chinese people from poverty to prosperity. China is emerging because its leadership finds political benefit in a commitment to economic liberalization.

In Russia, on the other hand, the political leadership's commitment to globalization is more limited. Russia, unlike China and India, is blessed with an abundance of crude oil and natural gas deposits that the state can manage for both economic and geopolitical advantage. The Kremlin has opened the Russian economy to foreign investment in a range of retail and other sectors, but the five-fold rise in global oil prices between 2002 and 2008 ensures that much of Russia's wealth can be pumped from the ground. A full embrace of globalization is not necessary when it is not politically useful.

## Ways of Analyzing Political Risk in Markets

Political risk can be directly relevant for changes in the values of bonds, stocks, currencies, and commodities. The how, when, and where depend on a number of highly specific circumstances.

One study of a very specific subject—the liberalization of financial markets in a group of middle-income emerging market countries—finds that the openness of capital markets in countries like Chile, South Korea, Mexico, and Turkey varies a great deal—a result of the varying ways in which political leaders in these countries define and pursue their political and economic interests.[20]

There can be no grand unified theory that explains how political risk impacts all capital markets. There is only a broad range of tools and methods that can help us apply ideas to the particular cases for which they are best suited.

Some of these tools take the form of answers to a specific set of questions:

- Regime type: Do different types of regimes behave differently when it comes to markets?
- Ideology: What are a government's stated policies and ideas?
- Constraints: What kinds of voting, constitutional, organizational, and political interest groups limit the ability of a government to act?
- Policy changes: What policy changes can impact markets?
- Elections and government makeup: How do elections impact markets?
- Exogenous factors: What role do wars, panics, etc., play in the performance of markets?

### Regime Types

Dividing emerging market countries into broad categories can help us understand how they interact with markets. Call these groups the best bets, potential backsliders, resource nationalists, and authoritarian globalizers.

First, the best bets, the true emerging markets. Countries like Brazil, India, Mexico, South Korea, and many of the former Communist states that have recently joined the European Union have embraced openness to globalization as their route to prosperity. Politically, these countries are governed not by the whims of individual leaders and small elites but by the legitimacy of strong (and fairly independent) political institutions and the rule of law. To protect their stability, governments of the best-bet countries have committed themselves to disciplined fiscal and monetary policies. They believe that foreign investment in their economies and the reputations their governments have earned for honoring their international commitments are among their most prized assets.

The potential backsliders include states that continue to emerge, but in which special political and social circumstances threaten to generate a slide toward various forms of isolation. Turkey,[21] Lebanon, and Israel figure among this group. These states risk more than the label of laggard. If their considerable political and security challenges are not well managed, the gains these countries have enjoyed over the last generation could be lost.

States like Russia, Iran, and Venezuela fall squarely into the third group: the resource nationalists. The governments of these countries have leveraged their countries' energy wealth to consolidate power at home and to flex their muscles abroad. All three have changed the rules for foreign investment in what they consider to be "strategic sectors" of their economies—especially natural resources. With revenue pouring in from high energy prices, the governments of these states believe they can afford to declare independence from the need to observe some international rules of the road and norms of behavior.

Resource nationalists often have elected governments, but they also fall short of the key elements of genuine rules-based democracy. The whims of leaders still matter much more than in more politically mature states. To varying degrees, ruling elites in these countries use the law as a tool to consolidate political control. Domestic institutions such as courts, legislatures, and civil society organizations struggle to preserve their independence.

Finally, there are the authoritarian globalizers. The elites that govern states like Saudi Arabia and China have decided to gamble on opening their economies to the energies of globalization. Although the nature of their embrace of globalization varies considerably, both governments have accepted the need for foreign presence (and therefore foreign influence) in their economies (and therefore their societies). These are the countries in which the stakes for global political and economic stability are unparalleled, as their regimes could eventually face tough challenges that are a direct by-product of their increased openness to people, ideas, and information from abroad.

To varying degrees, the increasingly free movement of ideas, information, people, money, goods, and services bolsters the stability of the best bets, potential backsliders, and resource nationalists. The authoritarian globalizers are another story. In these states, small elites hold a virtual monopoly on political power. Foreign influences that encourage their citizens to challenge that monopoly pose a serious long-term threat to their positions. The Chinese Communist

Party leadership and the most powerful members of the Saudi royal family have decided that they must learn to live with this threat, because they calculate that a higher standard of living for their peoples and the growth of a middle class give them a better shot at long-term survival.

But authoritarian states are potentially brittle and face several unique challenges. First, unlike established democracies where intense political competition is the norm, political rivalries among elite factions within an authoritarian state can threaten the survival of the regime. Second, authoritarian globalizers typically base their legitimacy on their ability to provide for their people, leaving them particularly vulnerable to changes in the international environment. China's economic stability, increasingly important for the health of the global economy, continues to depend on political decisions made within the Communist Party elite—in particular, a Politburo Standing Committee composed of fewer than a dozen men. Imagine the political pressures these men might face if a global recession dramatically reduced the country's economic growth. How would the Saudi government cope with a sustained and substantial long-term reduction in the price of oil?

### Ideology, Constraints, Policy Changes

We can also divide governments by ideology. Revolutionary governments (especially of the left-wing variety) play a more direct role in local markets than other governments do. Following World War I, the Bolshevik government in Russia chose to default on its outstanding sovereign bonds, debts which had been accumulated by its tsarist predecessor. The decision instantly transformed France, which held about 75% of Russia's sovereign debt in 1917, into an international debtor.[22] In fact, France lost more that $4 billion, about one-fourth of its reported 1913 assets,[23] or in today's terms upwards of $80 billion—an object lesson in the importance of asset diversification.

Markets can also misinterpret the nature of a government's ideological commitments. The political ideology that helps lift a party to power does not always signal how it will govern. This is especially true of countries in which there are strong institutional constraints on a ruling party's ability to exercise power freely. Consider Luiz Inácio Lula da Silva's 2002 election as president of Brazil. Lula, head of the leftist Workers' Party (PT), defeated the incumbent administration's centrist candidate José Serra of the Brazilian Social Democratic

Party (PSDB). It's not difficult to understand why so many analysts and investors believed Lula would lose. He had come up short three times before—in 1989, 1994, and 1998—as doubts grew among middle-class voters that he could (or would) keep inflation under control. Observers had little apparent reason to doubt that Lula's perceived "radicalism" would sink his candidacy one more time.

Investors underestimated not only the probability that Lula would win, but the likelihood that his government would honor campaign pledges to pursue sound macroeconomic policies. In particular, investors feared a Lula victory would bring a default on Brazil's external debt, generating a sharp devaluation of the Brazilian currency and a surge in inflation as it became apparent that Lula would win.[24]

But the new Lula administration neither defaulted on Brazil's sovereign debt nor engaged in the kind of fiscally expansionary policies that markets feared. Investor concerns weren't entirely groundless. Lula's presidential predecessor, Fernando Henrique Cardoso, had been elected in 1994 thanks largely to his ability to rein in inflation while serving as Brazil's finance minister. Much of the effort of his two administrations was focused on winning approval for structural reforms that were needed to consolidate the government's macroeconomic adjustments. Lula had opposed government-sponsored plans to privatize state-owned enterprises and reduce pension expenditures, and his party repeatedly accused Cardoso of worrying too much about Brazil's debt obligations and neglecting the need for greater government spending on social welfare. No wonder that so many investors feared the newly elected Lula would allow his government to default on the country's external debt.

But a few experts[25] were able to accurately forecast both Lula's victory and the political incentives he would inherit to stick to restrictive fiscal and monetary policy. This is how political risk analysts can anticipate market trends. Looking at a candidate's electoral track record and his party's political platform makes sense—as a starting point. But the political drivers that would determine both the outcome of Brazil's 2002 election and its market implications were critically important. Preelection opinion polls suggested that an economic slowdown was feeding a desire for political change, and that Serra would struggle to expand his share of the electorate beyond about 30%. In addition, Lula's previous defeats had persuaded the candidate and his party to moderate their electoral message.

Voter perceptions in 1994 and 1998 that the PT might threaten the gains associated with low inflation not only led Lula to call for "responsible change" in 2002, but also generated strong incentives to chart a moderate economic course once he was elected. Voters did not directly associate market volatility with Lula, but he recognized that unless his administration could tackle inflation, he would quickly lose public support. Careful study of the political incentives facing Lula, his party, and Brazilian voters allowed political risk analysts to look beyond the conventional wisdom and to build an accurate forecast that was useful for investors.

There are also constitutional, organizational, and bureaucratic constraints on a government's room for maneuver. The Mexican constitution requires state ownership of the oil industry. If a pro-market, liberal government wants to privatize some part of the industry, it will need enough votes in parliament to amend the constitution.

In 1996, a nominally reformist, pro-market coalition government won power in Romania for the first time since the fall of communism in 1989. Its ideology and political platform called for the sweeping judicial, political, and pro-market reforms needed to meet the requirements for membership in NATO and the European Union. For four years, the new government struggled with little success to implement its plans; it is now remembered as a well-intentioned but deeply incompetent administration. Why did it fail? It inherited a national bureaucracy that was both corrupt and heavily staffed with supporters of the previous Social Democratic Party government. The bureaucracy, ill disposed to the new government and mired in the old statist ways, stalled some plans and simply refused to implement others. As reformist president Emil Constantinescu later admitted, "We had won the elections but not the power."[26]

Interest groups can also limit a government's freedom. To some extent, all governments look to lobbyists, industry groups, nongovernmental organizations, and other interest groups for various forms of support, creating a dependency that can work in both directions.

There's another lesson here from the 1998 Russian financial crisis. On August 15, 1998, the chief Europe economist of a large Western bank briefed its executive committee on Russia's sovereign debt. Like most other Western financial institutions, this bank had purchased substantial amounts of short-term GKO Russian bonds. It had also loaned money to others who held the bonds. So soon after the turmoil of the previous year's Asian financial crisis, committee members were hungry for persuasive reassurance that the Russian government could continue to meet its debt obligations. The Russian economy was hardly booming, but it was performing far better than at any time since the collapse of the Soviet Union. In 1997, for the first time since 1991, Russia had seen positive GDP growth (albeit less than 1%), its inflation rate had dropped to about 15% (down from about 1,500% in 1992), and it enjoyed a positive trade balance.[27] The GKO bonds offered very attractive returns. By late 1997, some analysts had begun to talk of Russia's economy as the next "star" emerging market, and "the world's financial markets swung from viewing Russia as a complete loser to deciding that it was very interesting."[28]

But some economic indicators—a high budget deficit, falling commodity prices (about 80% of Russia's exports), and the government's commitment to a strong ruble—made fears of a default seem reasonable. The Russian government, faced with a budget deficit and restricted in its ability to collect taxes and revenues or to borrow from the Russian central bank, repeatedly resorted to short-term borrowing via short-term government bills (the GKOs) to finance its deficits.[29] To complicate matters further, the costs of security in Chechnya and strikes by Russian miners weighed heavily on the government's time and money.

The chief economist in question did what good economists do: he performed sovereign credit analysis to determine whether Russia could pay its debts. He considered the country's GDP growth, per capita income, inflation, fiscal balances, external debt, default history, and other economic factors. Weighing them, the economist issued his verdict: the risk of a Russian sovereign debt default was not significant.[30]

Two days later, the Russian government imposed a moratorium on some of its debt, effectively amounting to default. It allowed the currency to float in relation to the U.S. dollar. Within a month, the ruble that had bought between 17 and 20 U.S. cents was worth a nickel. Inflation surged over the course of the year to more than 80%.

Why did economists miss the crisis? They recognized that Russia *could* pay its debts, but they did not address the essential political question: *would* Russia pay its debts? The ruble devaluation and credit default were, in part, a government response to domestic interest groups.

Some analysts did warn that Russia might default, in part because they recognized that important political interest groups within Russia favored a sharp devaluation. Between December 1997 and April 1998, Yeltsin sacked a number of reformist government officials, including a prime minister and a finance minister, provoking doubts about the ability of individual members of the government to negotiate emergency loans and stoking tensions within the parliament.

This executive and legislative tension made it difficult to implement tax and land reform or cut spending, which in turn delayed passage of a budget for months.[31] During the same period, the private sector operating environment became less stable, as unpaid workers in the energy, agriculture, medical, education, and mining sectors went on strike and began to call for Boris Yeltsin's resignation.

The strong ruble was becoming a political liability in the government's relations with key groups of workers and trade unions. By devaluing the ruble, Yeltsin's government could more easily meet wage demands. Russian industry groups favored devaluation, because they saw a strong ruble as a drag on their ability to export, especially at a time when world commodity prices were already low. Both the left-wing opposition in the Duma and factions within Yeltsin's cabinet were unwilling to keep the ruble strong at the expense of political stability. Then came a collapse in global oil prices, which squeezed the government's finances even further. By devaluing Russia's currency, the Yeltsin government could no longer service its short-term sovereign debt. Yet, forced to choose between shocking foreign investors and antagonizing powerful domestic interest groups, the Yeltsin government decided to improve its standing at home.

### Government Makeup and Election Results

The composition of a host government can generate risk for capital market investors as well, given that government officials make decisions on regulation, default, and a number of other policy questions. A change of finance minister may implicitly or explicitly signal a change in the government's *willingness* to pay its debts. A change of economics minister may alter expectations about a country's growth potential, impacting its *ability* to service its debt.[32] Changes in the leadership of a central bank, other government resignations, and, of course, the outcomes of elections can generate uncertainty and risk, as well.

When looking at how politics impact markets, elections play a special role. (This is true only, of course, in countries that hold genuinely competitive elections. Contests in places like North Korea, Zimbabwe, or Saddam Hussein's

Iraq, or even Russia or Vietnam don't count.) For starters, there appears to be a relationship between electoral contests and financial changes.[33] In Latin America between 1970 and 2000 about 76% of changes to currency regimes intended to make a currency more stable occurred just before elections.[34] As in the case of the prelude to Mexico's peso crisis, governments tend to defend the value of a currency before an election and to let its value slide afterward.[35] For those with risk exposure to currency valuations, this is especially useful information.

In fact, quantitative political analysis has much to offer when mapping the relationships and correlations between political movements and markets. There are many discrete ones that when used in conjunction with qualitative judgments can provide useful forecasts.

For instance, you wouldn't typically expect the landslide reelection of a party known for its Islamist roots to make foreign investors feel that their capital is secure. Yet in Turkey in 2007, financial markets cheered the triumph of the Justice and Development Party (AKP) in the July 22 general election. A day after the election, the Istanbul stock market's benchmark IMKB-100 index rose 5% while the Turkish lira gained 2.3% against the dollar.

Why would financial markets celebrate the reelection of a party suspected of trying to undermine Turkey's secular constitution and to impose some version of an Islamic form of government? The AKP was, after all, the reincarnation of a political group that the Turkish state (rightly or wrongly) banned for challenging Turkey's political order.[36]

The AKP won the elections, in part, because the party had proven an astute manager and capable steward of Turkey's economy following its first election victory in 2002. During its first five-year term, the AKP's commitment to fiscal discipline and economic modernization paved the way for an unprecedented period of macroeconomic stability. Turkey's annual growth rate averaged around 7.3% in the period 2002–06, while inflation declined from 29.7% in 2002 to 7.7% in October 2007. Foreign investment surged from $1 billion in 2002 to more than $20 billion in 2006.

To win reelection in 2007, the AKP ran on its economic accomplishments. The Turkish and international media, missing the point, focused their attention on the party's social policy, branding the balloting a "battle for Turkey's soul."[37] Voters, much more concerned with pocketbook issues than with disputes over secularism, provided the AKP with nearly 47% of the vote—a massive figure by Turkish standards. The AKP became the first government to win reelection in 20 years, and the first since 1954 to increase its vote (up from 34% in 2002). Following its landslide victory, the party built on its already strong majority in parliament.

Another reason that foreign and domestic investors welcomed the result had little to do with the AKP's policy platform—or even with Turkey. Market players were biased in favor of single party government. Too many parties within a coalition government mean too many internal rivalries to manage and too many political demands to satisfy—a problem that creates uncertainty, unpredictability, and incoherent policy. Having earned the trust of the investment class over the previous five years, the AKP's landslide ensured it need not share decision-making power.

Electoral systems with single-seat districts (the United States, U.K., India, Canada, Australia) empower fewer parties. As a result, political competitors must appeal to broader, more diverse collections of voters. This allows politicians to rely (relatively) less on rewarding organized special interests with expensive policy favors and (relatively) more on representing voters as consumers or taxpayers. When debt payments compromise support from vital political constituencies, as they did in Russia in 1998, governments are sometimes less willing to pay. The more necessary or unpredictable that domestic special interest support, the greater the risk of debt default—especially to foreign creditors. But in electoral systems that produce high party system fragmentation (lots of political parties, as in Turkey or Italy), parties must find consistent sources of voter support in exchange for championing policy favoritism for their core constituents.

The classic financial measure of sovereign country risk, the likelihood that a country will default on its debt, is the bond yield spread. In simple terms, a yield spread is a measure of how much riskier one country's bonds are than another's, because it reflects how much return one particular bond must offer an investor to prevent him from buying a safer one. If a U.S. Treasury bond (considered safe, since the U.S. government is thought highly unlikely to default) returns 5%, then the bonds that Argentina or Russia (which have both defaulted on their debt within the last 10 years) issue might return, say, 8%. In this hypothetical case, the spread is 3%.[38]

As in the case of Turkey, elections offer a useful time line for assessing likely changes in the strength of government and market expectations of sovereign risk. Governments that are expected to fragment as parties proliferate or coalitions splinter into warring factions should appear much riskier than governments in which power is being consolidated. Political analysis offers early warning of these kinds of risk.

But bond yields and other useful statistics do not provide a complete picture of a country's stability. There were also factors unique to Turkey that help explain why the AKP's victory reduced political risk. The country's most determined secularists wanted voters to believe that an AKP triumph would prove as damaging for Turkey as the Hamas 2007 victory in the Palestinian Territories has proven for many Palestinians or the Islamic Liberation Front's (FIS) 1991 victory in Algeria proved for stability in that country. A strong plurality of Turkish voters saw it differently. Many appear to have considered the AKP more like a conservative Christian Democratic party in Western Europe than like Hamas or the FIS.

Ultimately, in analyzing the impact of political risk on a country's economy and markets, both qualitative and quantitative measures are needed. Indices and statistics alone do not explain the outcome in Turkey, but simple country-based qualitative analysis misses important and revealing risk and risk-mitigation factors—like the historical (and market-moving) perception that fewer parties within a governing coalition create less risky governments in market terms.

### Policy Changes

Regulatory changes can have an enormous impact on a country's investment climate, but monitoring these changes is difficult work. They can be subtle enough that even an attentive analyst can miss their significance. Their most important effects are not always immediately obvious.

The decision makers who lead multinational companies want hard data, and they rely on macroeconomic indicators to help them make investment decisions. Inflation figures, fiscal balances, and other revealing statistics are crucial elements of most country risk indices. Investment houses tend to form their own estimations of these indicators, but much of their information comes from the central governments of the countries in question. These governments sometimes have political motives for manipulating the information they provide, creating a new risk for investors, particularly those that trade in sovereign debt.[39]

This is a bigger problem than you might imagine. Since early 2007, Argentina's government has been suspected of manipulating inflation statistics via the Consumer Price Index (CPI). This has taken a variety of forms, including the replacement of multiple heads of Argentina's National Institute of Statistics and Census (INDEC), the direct manipulation of components of the CPI, and the proposed introduction of a new CPI calculation method.

In October 2006, the government requested that INDEC turn over the names of stores and sources for its CPI methodology. INDEC refused to do so in order to maintain statistical integrity. The head of INDEC was then replaced by a government economist, reportedly for refusing to directly manipulate inflation statistics. Under the new administration (also replaced at the end of 2007) the CPI was calculated using data that would underestimate inflation.[40]

Why would the Argentine government do this? Understanding the politics behind a government's manipulation of statistical data is essential for anyone with economic assets at stake. The answer provides another example of how political factors can generate economic outcomes that have little to do with economic rationality.

In 2005–06, Néstor Kirchner's government, for reasons both historical and ideological, found itself unable to manage inflation. The problem was not new; Argentina suffered hyperinflation throughout most of the 1980s. In the early 1990s, the government brought inflation under control by pegging the Argentine peso to the dollar and through a program of privatization and financial austerity. But these decisions contributed to Argentina's 1999–2002 economic crisis, a meltdown that helped elect Kirchner's populist government. Inflation returned, and by 2005, the Kirchner government had neither the fiscal discipline needed to tame it nor the political motive to simply accept (and try to manage) its worst effects. Financial austerity measures would have undermined the purchasing power of workers represented by trade unions that actively supported the government. Higher inflation would upset investors and the business community. Neither choice appealed to much of Argentina's population.

In addition, the Argentine government chose to manipulate the CPI numbers because inflation has a direct effect on public debt and is used to adjust around 40% of total government debt. By holding the inflation statistic down, the government pays less on current outstanding debt.

Did the CPI manipulation work? Yes and no. On the one hand, investors were no more fooled by this than foreign governments were by the Soviet Union's fake records of food harvests. Capital markets compensated for the manipulation by increasing Argentine bond spreads, which more than doubled during this time frame. On the other hand, Kirchner's party managed to win another round of elections. In 2007, his wife Cristina became president.

## Conclusion

Investors are vulnerable to domestic constituencies and interest groups, whose actions directly impact capital markets and can provide politicians with good reasons to act in ways that seem "irrational" in market terms. In extreme cases, these competing domestic interests can create situations that are far more dramatic than a currency devaluation or a debt default. But there are times when the stakes are even higher. When revolution, insurrection, and regime change are in play, foreign exchange rules may look like an afterthought compared with other, more pressing risks. To those risks we now turn.[41]

# Domestic Instability—Revolution, Civil War, State Failure

## FIVE

Sweeping emotions feel vulgar or untrue to those sophisticated
to the point of detachment from real life. Yet, without this
factor, any understanding of revolutions falls flat.
That is why clerks, bankers, generals, and social
scientists so often fail to see revolutionary
upswing even when looking at it directly.
—Teodor Shanin[1]

In January 1978, Tehran experienced a "revolutionary upswing." Protesters flooded the streets day after day in mass demonstrations against Shah Mohammad Reza Pahlavi, the Iranian monarch, hated by many of his subjects for the repressiveness of his regime and for his close alliance with the West. A year after the protests began, the political fallout for the West—and the economic cost to Western companies—would be immense. Trade between Iran and the United States, valued at $5.7 billion in 1977, would be effectively wiped out. A new government would expropriate vast amounts of U.S. and other foreign-owned property.[2] These companies would recoup some of the losses years later in an international claims tribunal, but a combination of Iranian hostility toward America and U.S. embargoes would guarantee a loss of potential revenue for these firms for decades to come. The shah would be gone; Iran would be ruled by a theocracy hostile to the West. The Islamic revolution and the regional political realignment it provoked are still very much with us. After the Japanese attack on Pearl Harbor and the September 11 terrorist attacks, the shah's overthrow in 1979 may well represent modern America's greatest intelligence failure.

Revolutions offer just one example of the kind of sudden and violent challenge or change of regime that can quickly undermine both corporate and geopolitical interests. Of all the categories of political risk faced by corporations and states alike, domestic (intrastate) violence and strife is both the broadest and most widespread. Today, when we speak of the risk of civil strife, we include any kind of severe regime or government instability and crises such as state failure, civil war, revolutions, coup d'états, and riots.

Growing exposure to risk from civil strife can be partly explained by structural changes in the post–Cold War state system, changes that have increased the likelihood of state collapse—the creation of new, potentially unstable states across the former Soviet Union and the cutoff of superpower subsidies to traditional allies. But it is also a logical by-product of an increasingly globalized marketplace, as an ever larger number of companies have begun to invest—and to expose themselves to risk—in an unprecedented range of emerging market countries. Today, as the "flattening" effect of globalization exposes more and more businesses to overseas competition, many business decision makers have cut costs by shifting or expanding their operations overseas. As a result, it's not just the big oil and mining companies that must manage risks created by threats of revolution, civil war, state collapse, or coup d'état.

### Identifying Civil Strife before It Happens

Exposure to risks of domestic instability have broadened and deepened, but the capacity to manage them has not. The Iran example provides a good introduction to many of the indicators and warning signs of civil strife. Before the mass demonstrations and nationwide strikes began, Western diplomatic and intelligence agencies and the approximately 30,000 American expatriates then living in Iran and working in its oil sector saw little cause for concern. The shah, an ally of the United States, controlled (at least in theory) one of the strongest, most modern militaries in the developing world. His army boasted the latest and most advanced British-made tanks—vehicles so expensive that not even the British military could yet afford them. Why should a man with 50,000 special security police (SAVAK) at his disposal worry over internal dissent?

Many factors ignited the revolution, including the return from exile of a charismatic opposition leader, Ayatollah Khomeini. President Jimmy Carter's political pressure on the shah to liberalize in the face of popular resistance played a role, effectively transforming the shah's rule into a halfhearted dictatorship, illustrating the danger of civil strife associated with slow, incremental steps toward political liberalization. More than any other factor, it was the failure of the shah, and of outsiders, to recognize the true depth and intensity of popular Iranian anger toward his government that blinded almost everyone to the latent potential—under the right circumstances—for revolution.

Revolutions and civil wars are notoriously difficult to predict. Yet, there are ways to determine how prone a particular country or region might be to dangerous levels of instability.

For a first indicator of potential political turmoil, watch the young. Few of the elderly in any society enjoy manning barricades or throwing Molotov cocktails at police. Young people are another matter. Two-thirds of Iran's population is under the age of 30.[3] Any state with an exceptionally high number of people between the ages of 15 and 25[4] has more revolutionary potential—all else being equal—than a country with an average age of 40. Any country with a relatively male-heavy youth population is more likely to generate violence (both internal and external). In some respects, places like China and India, where tradition and family planning combine to create a strong preference for male babies, may in time portend more violent trouble.[5] Other commomly tracked indicators include infant mortality, lack of access to housing and potable water, and other measures of human misery. This is not to say that poor or youthful places are always more violent than a more prosperous and older neighbor, but these factors, in combination with others, can create a volatile mix.

Thus, one approach to analyzing domestic political instability is to use a series of indicators that are strongly associated with political unrest. The strength of each indicator is monitored as it fluctuates over a given period of time, and a composite level of risk is then created. Usually, this method involves both qualitative and quantitative aspects. Some indicators (like inflation or infant mortality rates) are easily measured in quantitative terms. Other indicators, like the level of a state's democratic development or its corruption, require a more qualitative approach. Though one-off events like revolutions or civil wars can be virtually impossible to predict, measurements of a country's stability can reveal which countries are unusually vulnerable to these sorts of risks.

Another way to analyze domestic instability is to look at cities. Historically, cities have provided the center stage for a variety of internal political upheavals. Capital cities are symbolic centers of a country's political life. They are also home to a country's most important government buildings—and therefore the staging ground for coups d'état, rebellions, revolutions, mass strikes, and other popular demonstrations. Paris offers a paradigmatic example: it was the center of the French Revolution of 1789; of Napoleon's seizure of power; of rebellions in 1830, 1848, and 1871; of mass popular demonstrations throughout the twentieth century, including the student uprising in 1968; and, more recently, of a series of antiglobalization protests in 2003 and violent ethnic riots in 2005. St. Petersburg and Moscow have played a similar role in Russia, as have Mexico City in Mexico, Managua in Nicaragua, Cairo in Egypt, Algiers in Algeria, Istanbul in Turkey, Tehran in Iran, and so on.

A city's demography, infrastructure, and political significance can be gauged to see if they suggest a likelihood of instability and violence, and can also measure the degree to which individual cities and city crises impact states and thus can serve as vehicles for the transmission of urban crises to states, as well as the extent to which rural crises can overwhelm cities. Experts can then better determine just what types of cities with which combinations of transmission factors are most likely to affect state stability.[6]

Consider Manila, capital of the Philippines. Since its rebuilding by Spanish conquistadors in 1574, Manila has been the country's political and economic center. An urban concentration with more than 16 million people,[7] Manila is a typical developing-world capital. It contains all of the main government branches and a disproportionate percentage of Philippine industry and economic activity. It also suffers from the typical issues that affect many megacities of the developing world, such as income disparities and a constant inflow of rural migrants.

The politics of urban Manila have long had a significant impact on the politics of the Philippines. This was evident during the protests against Ferdinand Marcos's authoritarian regime, which began in the late 1960s and peaked in the early 1970s when protesters attempted several assaults on the presidential palace. The antigovernment movement had acquired a specific metropolitan character by 1983, when almost a million of Manila's residents (then about a fifth of the city's population) attended the 1983 wake of slain opposition leader Benigno Aquino Jr. In 1986, approximately the same number gathered on the city's main avenue, Epifanio de los Santos (popularly known as EDSA), and successfully rallied for Marcos's ouster.

In what would prove a double-edged dynamic, Metro Manila was seen both domestically and internationally as a proxy for the country's political senti-ment. Local conventional wisdom then evolved that forcing a government from power required support from the military—and a sufficient number of people in Manila's streets. As a result, the Philippine political elite (Manila-based, of course) has sought to exploit critical municipal constituencies on several occa-sions since 1986. The first effort, in January 2001, was successful, when a largely middle-class movement forced President Joseph Estrada out of office. Then, in May 2001 and July 2003, pro-Estrada politicians unsuccessfully attempted to motivate poor constituencies against his successor, Gloria Arroyo. All of these factors helped to ensure that, during times of political crisis, developments in Metro Manila will determine the course of events in the rest of the country. If prominent social organizations and groups like the Catholic Church, business community, students, middle class, and urban poor do not actively participate in an incipient political conflict, it is much less likely to destabilize the country.

## Types of Civil Strife

One of the very few confident predictions social scientists have made since the statistical modeling revolution of the 1960s has been the connection between democracy and war. Perhaps the only thing approaching a *law* of politics is that democracies do not go to war with one another.[8] While democracy has not offered the same level of immunity to domestic political violence, in general, the more democratic a state, the less likely that it will suffer potentially destabilizing levels of civil strife.

In the past, this observation had led some to believe—falsely—that the political stability of nondemocratic states will increase in steady and predict-able increments as they move toward democracy. Today, it is clear that partial democracies—states with an autocratic government that makes halfhearted and limited moves toward democracy—are much less stable than either strictly auto-cratic states or full democracies. Why is this so? Autocratic, repressive regimes clamp down on all forms of political dissent (think Tiananmen Square), making political tensions between the populace and government both less likely to sur-face and, when they do, less likely to spread.

Standard indicators cannot tell what form instability will take when it erupts. Iran's young population is potentially as likely to spell trouble for the ruling theocratic regime as it is for the West. Similarly, in Manila, an urban riot can topple a government that is business-friendly as easily as one that is not. What is needed, then, is a way to interpret that data, and what different types of civil strife mean.

One categorization of political risk sees all forms of civil strife—from riots to revolutions—as "internal/societal" political risks. According to this framework, risks as diverse as riots, civil war, and coups d'état are classified as *internal* because both their causes and their effects occur within the territorial boundaries of the state. They are logically opposed to *external* risks, such as interstate war or international terrorism, which cross political boundaries between states.

Civil strife is a *societal* risk. Phenomena such as riots, popular revolutions, endemic violence, and civil war originate within a country's broader society and are not caused directly by the government. These risks are logically opposed to *governmental* risks, political risks that originate from the government itself, such as property nationalization or tax and regulatory discrimination. Below, we consider five distinct types of civil strife: revolutions, civil wars, state failures, coups d'état, and riots.

### Revolutions

How do we know a revolution when we see one? Political scientist Samuel Huntington offered an early and influential definition: Revolution is "a rapid, fundamental, and violent domestic change in the dominant values and myths of a society, in its political institutions, social structure, leadership, and governmental activity and policies."[9] By combining a rapid change in the political control of the state—and the creation of a new state elite—with the simultaneous, mass-participatory social transformation of society as a whole, revolutions are unequaled in their ability to produce rapid and truly transformative long-term political risks for both firms and governments.

Revolutionary change that sweeps away the old political order in a country can also sweep away the old economic order, with dramatic consequences for domestic and foreign businesses alike. Businesses can sometimes become entangled in the rivalries that revolutions create. Far-left revolutions that espouse radical political and economic programs of wealth redistribution and collective (i.e., state) ownership of property, such as the Communist revolutions of Russia and Cuba, are particularly problematic for corporations.

Following the Russian Revolution of October 1917, the Bolshevik government expropriated all private land, agricultural holdings, banks, and industrial enterprises, including assets held by foreign investors. As supporters of the tsarist order, these foreign investors were not welcomed by the new Communist regime. Following the economic devastation of the Civil War, Lenin's New Economic Policy of the 1920s allowed a degree of foreign investment back into the country. But the Soviet government refused to compensate companies that lost property in 1917, despite repeated attempts on the part of foreign governments to reach an agreement.

U.S. companies lost everything in Cuba following the January 1959 revolution that brought Fidel Castro to power. The new Communist regime's revolutionary goals were in direct opposition to capitalism, and the new state expropriated private property of both domestic and foreign actors. As Cuba moved more toward the Soviet orbit and relations with the United States worsened, the situation for U.S. companies declined dramatically. Refineries held by U.S. oil producers that refused to refine crude oil imported from the Soviet Union—the U.S. government encouraged them not to—were nationalized in 1960. These expropriations, valued at roughly $1 billion,[10] formed part of the larger ideological conflict between the United States and Cuba that led to the severing of diplomatic relations and the subsequent U.S. embargo.

Not all revolutions result in property confiscations, gulags, cults of personalities, and secret police-like surveillance. If Communist-inspired revolutions send shivers down the spines of investors, revolutions inspired by the desire to overthrow communism can have the opposite effect. On November 17, 1989, Czechoslovakia's "Velvet Revolution"—one of the anti-Communist revolutions sweeping across Eastern Europe at the time—ousted that country's Soviet-dominated Communist government and ushered in the first democratic elections in 40 years. The sheer speed of this transformation brought a great deal of political uncertainty and inexperienced leadership, but the new government's focus on the rehabilitation of free-market principles—like private ownership and liberal business law—created extraordinary commercial opportunities. Revolutions inspired by a liberal ideology frequently create markets with new openings for entrepreneurial investors.

Russia, China, Nigeria, and Iran have all experienced substantial social turmoil, upheaval, and revolutionary change. Their histories illustrate a larger truth: a revolutionary past does not imply a revolutionary future. In fact, you could as easily argue that these are cases of "nonrevolutions" waiting to happen. History tells us that a revolution or a violent or noninstitutionalized overthrow of a central government requires a combination of factors to succeed, including strong political opposition with charismatic leadership within the country; external support for political change, possibly from a stronger and influential neighbor; broad support for an unofficial revolutionary movement from a politically engaged population; and a weak government, often combined with ineffective political institutions.

Not all these factors are necessary for a revolution to occur. As we have seen, the Iranian revolution of 1979 can be largely attributed to a strong opposition with a charismatic leader, acting against a background of common socioeconomic grievance that mobilized an angry population. More recently, Ukraine's "Orange Revolution" in 2004 grew from a strong and popular political opposition movement that mobilized a politically engaged population, winning invaluable external support from the European Union.

Even when all these factors are in play, there is no guarantee that revolutionary upheaval looms just beyond the horizon. Forecasting "nonrevolutions" is just as important as explaining when they are increasingly likely. Without the right combination of factors in place, a revolution can be difficult to achieve, despite pressures on an incumbent government. Iran, China, Russia, and Nigeria provide examples of states where revolution remains unlikely, despite the presence of many troubling factors associated with regime instability.

In several of these states, the leadership is simply too genuinely popular to be vulnerable to a violent, noninstitutionalized overthrow. As of this writing, former Russian president (now prime minister) Vladimir Putin enjoys overwhelming popular support within his country's borders, and is credited—by his own people (as well as by *Time* magazine, which made him Person of the Year for 2007)—with bringing political stability and strong economic growth to Russia after he took office in 2000. As long as Putin retains his central position on Russia's political stage, his considerable stockpile of political capital and public goodwill will ensure that "flashing indicators" such as corruption, foreign policy entanglements, and violent domestic separatist movements will have little impact on Russia's state stability. In China, the central government continues to enjoy popular support, drawing on both popular nationalism and new social initiatives that address many of the social grievances that might provoke unrest. China's environmental disasters, rural violence, mass migration to cities, and rapid economic change do not necessarily move the country toward dangerous instability. In Iran, despite the unpopularity of the regime among many young people, there remains broad public agreement that some form of Islamic republic—combined with a strong elected presidency—has legitimacy. As a result, there is limited support for a radical change in the Iranian political system. Further, in each of these states, governments can be expected to use violence (with loyal militaries and police forces) to quell dangerous levels of unrest, creating a further deterrent to destabilizing antigovernment activity.

Weakness or fragmentation of internal opposition is also an important factor in making revolutions unlikely in these countries. Russia and China have effectively quashed political opposition movements and hampered the development of civil society. This prevents the opposition from drawing enough public support to credibly threaten mass mobilization and a sustained campaign against the government. In Nigeria, activist groups are fragmented and often have conflicting goals and agendas. A complex web of religious, economic, and ethnic fault lines complicates the political scene. While these divisions persist, the central government, along with the opposition, is seen as the overall arbiter of political stability, and the emergence of a united and powerful revolutionary movement is unlikely. That said, the same ethnic and regional divisions that diminish the risk of a revolution in Nigeria can lead to other forms of instability, such as ethnic riots and even civil war.

But a severe economic crisis could fatally undermine the popularity of an incumbent government and help to engage and mobilize the public over a common cause. This risk is particularly acute in states where current political and economic stability is based on resource-driven economic growth, such as Russia, Iran, or Nigeria. Government failure to deal with a major environmental crisis, in China for example, could also generate risks. But in all these cases, other destabilizing scenarios, such as riots, ethnic clashes, coups d'etat, and civil warfare are more likely than a revolution to topple the government.

### Civil Wars

A civil war can be defined as a violent conflict within a country fought by organized groups that aim to either take over central or regional power or force a change in government policy. The U.S. Civil War was launched by Southern secessionists hoping to establish control of their region (the South); the Spanish

Civil War was fought for control of the entire country. There is disagreement over how to differentiate civil war from other forms of domestic political violence. A common threshold is a death toll of at least 1,000 killed over the duration of the conflict. By this definition, there have been about 125 civil wars since World War II. About 20 civil wars were ongoing as of April 2007.[11]

Civil wars have occurred in rich and developed states, but most occur in countries that are poor, regionally divided, and weakly autocratic. Separatist movements driven by the suppressed or manipulated nationalism of an ethnic or religious minority are a major cause of such wars, exemplified in both the Nigerian Civil War (the 1967–70 conflict driven by the attempted secession of several provinces to form the Republic of Biafra) and more recently in the violent disintegration of the former Yugoslavia in the 1990s. As a result of the heightened risk posed by nationalist-inspired movements, models used for generating predictions of civil war rely heavily on mapping religious and ethnic/linguistic differences within a state's boundaries.

CORPORATE MANAGEMENT STRATEGIES FOR CIVIL WAR    The eruption of civil war need not force a company's immediate withdrawal from the country in question. "You can't move 15 million tea bushes. That's where they are, so that's where we are."[12]

For Joseph Wertheim,[13] of the Connecticut-based firm Tea Importers, Inc., this explains in a nutshell why his firm stayed in Rwanda, despite the brutal violence of the Rwandan Civil War of the early 1990s. Operating in the region since 1975, Tea Importers, Inc.—in tandem with its Rwandan partner firm SORWATHE—was for a long time the only U.S. investor in Rwanda, one of the poorest countries in the world. Today, it remains the sole American privately controlled producer of tea in the country, with more than 650 acres in cultivation.

During the 1990–94 civil war, this small U.S. firm suffered a series of losses common during such conflicts. The company's tea processing factory was shelled by rebel forces, its vehicles were stolen, and its office furniture and computers were looted, with nearly $250,000 in total damages.[14] The company's employees were also placed at risk, with some management personnel being forced to flee the country via roads that had become unsafe to travel. As for the company's operations, they were forced to shut down for the duration of the armed conflict, and to wait it out and see what, if anything, would be left of its plantation.

This example clearly illustrates the most obvious risks associated with violent civil war: damage to property, physical threats to employees, and the dangers and problems associated with degraded or unsafe public infrastructure. It also shows the risks of wasted time, and all the associated costs of failure to comply with time-sensitive delivery contracts.

Though Tea Importers, Inc. faced the kinds of risks that few small companies can survive, its leadership decided to continue with its long-term business in Rwanda after the war ended. Crucially, the firm's foresight in purchasing the necessary political risk insurance coverage bolstered its ability to absorb the financial losses incurred during the war—and the company managed to expand its operation in 1997.[15]

Another example is Skanska,[16] a Swedish multinational construction company that managed to run multiple, simultaneous projects in places that were at war or highly unstable, like Somalia, Colombia, Kosovo, and Kashmir. Skanska focuses primarily on *project-level* risks. It operates in conflict-torn countries so long as they are not under United Nations sanctions and the political risks are judged to be tolerable at the project level. Had the firm relied only on country-level political risk reports, they probably would not have profited from investment opportunities in these places.[17]

At the same time, operating in the middle of a civil war, while potentially profitable at a project-level, can bring significant reputational risks for a multinational corporation. Perhaps the best example of this phenomenon is the experience that De Beers had with African "conflict diamonds."[18] With nearly $8 billion in annual revenues and 40% market share in the global diamond industry, De Beers has long been at the forefront of diamond-rich conflict zones during civil wars, including those in Angola, Sierra Leone, and Liberia.

Yet, since 1990, De Beers has reduced its exposure to war-torn nations as a result of negative publicity over "conflict diamonds." Criticism in the West was driven by nongovernmental organizations and resulting pressure from shareholders. In some cases, De Beers suspended or terminated its mining operations; in others, such as Liberia and Sierra Leone, it ended its purchase arrangements as well. De Beers pulled out of Angola in 1999 despite a long-standing and profitable alliance with the UNITA rebels during the country's civil war. Its strategy in Angola had been to purchase UNITA diamonds in-country through its Central Selling Organization, but at an arm's-length distance from the rebels in the interest of "plausible deniability."[19] At the same time, De Beers had purchasing

agreements in place with the state-owned corporation Endiama, effectively playing both sides of the conflict to insulate itself from risk should one side gain
a decisive advantage. The company even hired private South African forces to
protect Endiama diamond assets from UNITA, while continuing to do business
with the rebels.

By the late 1990s, the company shifted its focus to more stable African
nations that posed fewer security and reputational risks. De Beers embarked
on a two-pronged strategy, reducing its exposure to war-torn regions (though
it has maintained purchase operations in many cases) while aggressively backing the Kimberley Process, which certifies that diamonds are conflict-free. The
company now claims that 100% of its diamonds are conflict-free, although the
United Nations and others dispute that claim. As competition from Russia
and elsewhere has eroded its long-standing monopoly, De Beers has tried
to reposition itself, from a marketing perspective, as the industry leader for
clean diamonds. Looking to the future, De Beers is poised to reenter many of
the troubled nations it left in the 1980s and 1990s, as peace is consolidated in
Liberia, Sierra Leone, Angola, and the Democratic Republic of Congo. This
provides a major new opportunity for the world's largest diamond company, though one fraught with potential risks given the fragility of peace in
regions like the eastern Congo and De Beers' zero-tolerance policy on conflict
diamonds.

These cases illustrate two important points. First, it is possible for corporations to find ways to successfully operate during a civil war. But second, as
De Beers learned firsthand, an increasingly politically informed public may punish corporations it believes are acting unethically or in an exploitative fashion
during periods of violent conflict. Oil companies doing business in countries
with unpopular and discredited regimes (such as those of Sudan and Burma)
have also been targeted by public boycott campaigns, and this reputational risk
remains for any company that decides to do business with an unsavory government or rebel group in times of violent conflict.

### State Failure

State failure typically refers to the complete or partial collapse of state authority,
such as in Somalia and Bosnia. Failed states have little or no political authority
that can enforce the rule of law within the state's borders, and they are usually

associated with widespread crime, violent conflict, and humanitarian crises.[20] Failed states, like civil wars, often involve sustained military conflicts between governments and insurgents, as well as genocide, mass murder, and the displacement of citizens by government or insurgent forces. According to one study, 127 state failures occurred between 1955 and 1998.[21] Today, from Afghanistan to Zimbabwe, state failure remains a persistent risk for governments and corporations alike.

In the early 1980s, Zimbabwe was regarded as a market-friendly environment, with an independent judiciary, stable political institutions, and one of the best education systems in Africa. It also had an impressive cadre of talented politicians and ministers, led by the Western-educated Robert Mugabe. Circumstances there have changed.

Since 2000, when the Zimbabwean government started its accelerated land reform program, the economy has shrunk by one-third and inflation has exceeded levels at which normal commerce can be conducted. Government policy has become increasingly uncertain. Skilled workers have fled. Infrastructure, suffering from a lack of investment, has decayed. Power, fuel, and food shortages are now common. The black market has thrived, as has government corruption, and the judiciary can no longer maintain even a semblance of independence.

Despite all this, a number of foreign companies remain in the country, deflecting criticism that they are operating under a repressive regime by insisting that they have a responsibility to their employees. Some foreign investors have sought out opportunities to pick up cheap Zimbabwean assets, but many firms, and mining companies in particular, are believed to be clinging to investments in the hope that their intrinsic value will be realized once the political climate improves. One platinum miner, Zimplats, is even considering a $340 million expansion program.

How do companies operate in a country that verges on state failure? Hyperinflation forces many firms to adjust wages on a quarterly (or even monthly) basis to offset the erosion of employees' buying power. Shortages compel them to supply their workers with food to maintain their productivity. Companies must also accept responsibility for investing in and maintaining roads and bridges—and for generating their own power. Zimplats has agreed to fund the construction of a power substation. In other words, these firms must provide a wide range of goods and services and invest in basic infrastructure—functions that are normally considered the responsibility of governments.

Companies must also cope with constant and significant risks of political and social instability. Increasing crime levels, political protests, and the risk of wider conflict can force firms to undertake threat and vulnerability assessments, implement risk management programs, and plan for worst-case scenarios, including full evacuation. Many companies will opt to downscale operations, with only essential staff remaining behind. This allows them to maintain operations with lower levels of risk, while positioning themselves to quickly ramp up operations once the situation improves, or at least stabilizes.

Maintaining the balance of continuing to operate in the country while not being associated with the failed regime is another key challenge. Increased activity by nongovernmental organizations and the emergence of the 24-hour news cycle have increased the reputational issues that can arise from continuing operations.

In the case of Zimbabwe, the government has made increased demands for foreign exchange, supplier contracts, and employment. Companies may find themselves looking for ways to increase their political leverage by supporting the current regime. But if a company becomes associated with the regime of a failing state, it also faces the prospect of being in a weaker position once political change comes—being associated with a losing regime can clearly be bad for business.

### Coups d'État

A coup d'état implies the sudden and illegal overthrow of a government, usually by a small segment of a state's armed forces. Much more common than civil war, coups typically involve the illegal capture and arrest of the government executive. Along with the removal of key members of the government, coups often involve the simultaneous symbolic display of military force in city streets and the physical capture of critical political and economic infrastructure—most notably the executive government offices, power plants, and television and radio stations.

Unlike civil wars, which also involve a violent and ostensibly illegal challenge to a government's rule, coups are often bloodless, frequently avoiding even the death of the individuals they seek to overthrow. Often, this is achieved by the military's taking power when the head of state is out of the country, leaving the executive at a distinct disadvantage. Recent coups in Mauritania (2005) and Thailand (2006) occurred when the head of government was abroad.

This observation has led some to suggest that the immediate probability of a coup increases whenever the executive crosses the country's border. Others have analyzed coups in the hopes of finding longer-term warning signs. In *The Likelihood of Coups*, Rosemary O'Kane has sought to predict the probability of a coup by analyzing a single discrete indicator—export specialization, or the total amount of revenue derived from a single source. She has argued that this lack of diversification leads to high levels of income fluctuation and instability, creating low levels of development and reduced government legitimacy. This, in turn, increases the risk of a coup.[22]

Because of the often bloodless nature of coups, and the fact that many citizens (as well as foreign firms) experience them via television broadcasts rather than via flying bullets, coups rarely expose firms to the same levels of risk that civil wars or violent revolutions do. In many instances, day-to-day operation of foreign firms is largely unaffected. In other ideologically driven or populist-inspired coups, the political risks can be much more severe.

FAILED COUPS MAY BE WORSE THAN SUCCESSFUL ONES: THAILAND AND THE PHILIPPINES   In Thailand, the successful 2006 military coup d'état was the result of a long struggle that pitted former Prime Minister Thaksin Shinawatra against key political groups that included the monarchy, the middle class, and the military. The success of the coup can be attributed to the eventual alignment of these key institutions, a process that stretched over several years.

Initially, only the middle class and the institutions associated with it (such as nongovernmental organizations, the media, and academics) disapproved of Thaksin's rule. But as the former prime minister's power grew, his popularity began to threaten the military and the monarchy. In a brazen act that brought matters to a head, Thaksin attempted to seize control of the military by placing personal cronies from Thailand's military academy in key positions. This eventually turned senior commanders against him, culminating in the September 2006 coup.

Prior to this move by the military, there were signals that a coup was possible. The threat had been discussed and debated since the time when public protests broke out following some of Thaksin's more controversial financial dealings. A previous prime minister's public pronouncement that a soldier's loyalty was to king and country provided another strong indication of a possible overthrow.

The economic effects of the coup were limited. Markets retreated briefly following Thaksin's ouster, but because the uprising generated no violence and most believed that the coup simply exposed competition among political pow-erbrokers, the public saw little reason to fear drastic economic policy changes. Markets rebounded quickly. There is also no sign that the coup affected for-eign direct investment inflows, nor did it force investors themselves to flee the country. But subsequent warning signs of capital controls, changes to the foreign business law, and the weakening of consumer confidence appeared to cause some foreign investors to reevaluate their Thailand investment strategies.

The Thai example is notable because its economic impact has been limited and because a return to democratic rule there is virtually guaranteed. Strange as it may seem, a failed coup attempt can be more destabilizing for a country's economy than a successful one. That was the case in the Philippines, where, since the ouster of President Ferdinand Marcos in 1986, there have been at least four unsuccessful coup attempts—two against President Corazon Aquino (1987, 1989) and two against President Gloria Arroyo (2003, 2006). This tally does not include the successful 2001 "withdrawal of support" by the armed forces' com-mand, which, along with a civilian uprising in Manila (discussed earlier), forced the resignation of President Joseph Estrada. Before each of these coup attempts, warnings that military adventurism might be in the works appeared several weeks before the conspirators moved into action.

All four attempts were led by junior officers; in each case, the plotters and their forces comprised just a small fraction of the armed forces. But it was not their small numbers that did them in. Subsequent studies and surveys have shown that troops outside Manila watched developments in the capital and waited for the outcome before taking sides.

Both Arroyo and Aquino strove to ensure that senior military command-ers remained loyal to them. More importantly, unlike the successful 1986 and 2001 revolts, the broader middle class in Manila and key institutions such as the church, media, and the business community remained on the sidelines. Every extra-constitutional ouster of a government in the Philippines (and some say even Marcos's declaration of martial law in 1972) needed the coopera-tion of key middle-class institutions to provide the political legitimacy needed for success.

In each case, the coup attempt depressed equity and bond prices. The earlier Aquino coups had more unfavorable effects on the economy and foreign direct investment, because foreign investors continued to worry that possible govern-ment changes might undermine policy stability.

Coups are difficult to predict because the number of people involved is small and because they tend to depend on secrecy. But on a country level, there's still work to be done. In the case of the Philippines, coup plotters usually come from certain classes at the Philippine Military Academy. Monitoring these classes, for instance by looking at spikes in e-mail chatter among their members, is an important indicator of discontent, which in turn correlates to coup plotting. But such assessments depend on an intimate knowledge of the country, its institutions, and its people that only an expert can provide.

## Riots

If you have never experienced a riot, you might assume that the risks they create are minimal. But those that are large and sustained can be tremendously costly. They can destroy businesses and inflict huge insurance losses. The 1992 Los Angeles riots generated estimated costs in excess of $775 million in property damage alone.[23]

The May Day rioting in London in 2000, the violent demonstrations at the World Trade Organization Ministerial Conference of 1999 in Seattle, and the banlieue uprising in Paris in 2005 reveal that riots continue to create risks and headaches for businesses and governments in developed countries. In developing or emerging market states, rioting can have effects not unlike those of a civil war. The damage from the L.A. riots, for example, pales in comparison with the devastating turmoil that shook Nuku'alofa, the capital of the small Pacific island nation of Tonga, in November 2006.

The cause of the riot, ultimately involving hundreds of Tongan youths, is disputed. Some have claimed that it was triggered by a small, violent splinter group from a pro-democracy demonstration campaigning against the island nation's hereditary monarchy, the lack of elections, and a slow rate of promised reforms by the king. Others claim that the real culprits were a business mafia intent on using the democracy demonstration as a front to destroy ethnic Chinese business competition.

Whatever the ultimate cause, the outcome was clear. The rioting damaged or destroyed approximately 80% of the capital's business center, leaving the city's power infrastructure badly damaged, its newspaper offices ransacked, and the majority of its businesses looted and set ablaze. The immediate damage to local businesses was catastrophic; the longer-term effects have been even worse. Over a year later, empty buildings cast long shadows across vacant lots throughout the capital. Tonga's economy recorded zero growth in 2007, due in large measure to a lack of available funds for redevelopment. Tourism, a crucial source of hard currency and Tonga's second largest source of income, dropped 30%.[24] The state of emergency enacted after the riot remains in effect, and Tongan security forces continue to patrol the streets of the capital.

The spontaneity of these riots makes them the most difficult form of civil strife to forecast. Warning signs can appear just days or even hours, rather than months, in advance. Political grievances ignite and fuel many of these disturbances, but riots are rarely organized in any meaningful way and can surprise those who stoke them as much as those charged with containing them.

Yet we can identify political patterns underlying these events. Ethnic minority–owned businesses and residences, particularly those that are financially successful at a rate disproportionately higher than the country's ethnic majority, are often targeted for arson and looting, illustrating that much of the violence associated with riots is not always as random as it appears. Frequent attacks on Chinese business communities in Southeast Asia, as well as the targeting of over a dozen Thai-owned businesses during rioting in Phnom Penh in January 2003, are notable cases.[25]

### Mitigating Risks from Internal Strife

Companies have a range of strategies available to them to mitigate the risks associated with civil strife. These range from the extreme case of risk absorption—where a company simply lives with the risk, usually with the intent of avoiding expensive insurance costs or self-insuring—to the other extreme of risk avoidance. With risk avoidance, a firm will either divest from a project or region or delay market entry, waiting for a change in the political circumstances. Other strategies include risk transfer, risk pooling, and risk diversification. Below we outline several of these strategies and how they relate to risks of civil strife.

The case of the Chrysler Corporation in Peru in the late 1960s reveals how "international integration" can protect a firm from the vagaries of domestic instability. In late 1968, the democratically elected government of Peru was overthrown in a coup d'état led by the head of the Peruvian armed forces, General Juan Velasco Alvarado. The Revolutionary Government of the Armed Forces, as the

Velasco left-leaning regime became known, quickly launched a reorganization of the country's economy that included the rapid nationalization of entire industries. The banking and railroad sectors, public utilities, and important segments of the fishing, oil, and mining sectors experienced substantial expropriation. In some cases, the new government simply monopolized them. North American business interests were hit particularly hard due to their relatively heavy presence in Peru, and many American corporate properties were seized, including those of the International Petroleum Company, a subsidiary of Standard Oil.

Despite Velasco's sweeping seizure of foreign-owned properties and the populist appeal of taking American foreign investments, the Chrysler Corporation, using a strategy of international integration, managed to avoid becoming a nationalization target. It did so by organizing its production line in such a way that if any one country's government decided to nationalize a Chrysler factory, it could not complete production of the final product and profit from the takeover. The Chrysler plant in Peru manufactured just 50% of the total product. Completion depended on imports of crucial parts manufactured in sister factories in Brazil, Argentina, and Detroit. Since Peru's Chrysler plant could not effectively operate without the inputs manufactured from these other factories, the Chrysler Corporation's policy of international integration successfully defended the company from the political risk associated with the Velasco coup.[26]

A firm can carry out a number of options before engaging in an overseas project. First, it can and should perform due diligence on its business partners. This can be especially important in emerging markets, where the history of a local company and its political connections can be uncertain. Forging joint ventures with local equity partners can help reduce risk exposure, but the success of this strategy depends entirely on choosing the right partner.

Another technique involves minimizing local equity. By borrowing locally, a firm can create local allies with a vested interest in the success of the firm's project in the country. This strategy limits the risk of currency exchange rate fluctuations, since earnings from the local project can be used to repay local capital and interest payments. International integration—the strategy of creating interdependence between operations in various countries—is another tool of risk mitigation, as Chrysler's experience in Peru demonstrates.

In many emerging market and other developing countries, personal relationships with well-connected individuals—especially government officials—can be a tremendous asset for a company. Formal regulations in these states are often technically weak, opening the door for arbitrary governmental rulings. Officials at both the national and regional levels often have considerable personal discretion over decisions pertinent to a foreign business' operation.[27] This is why it is crucial that a firm treats a host government as both a source of political risk and potentially vitally important ally in navigating an often poorly established legal system.

Personal government contacts can also mitigate risks from civil strife. Since governments themselves are extremely interested in gathering intelligence on the potential for internal political instability, the cultivation of relationships with local officials can provide a useful hedge against the risk of civil war and other types of violent conflict. Networking with government officials facilitates information exchange and increases the firm's environmental awareness.[28]

Until the late 1990s, Shell cultivated personal contacts with government officials to shield itself from political risks while operating in Nigeria, a historically unstable country. It was the only major Western company that did so successfully from Nigerian independence through the 1990s, because the company hired and trained locals to create a pool of energy experts that later went to work for the Nigerian government. By creating personal and professional links between its staff and the Nigerian oil bureaucracy, Shell developed a competitive advantage over other foreign energy firms operating in Nigeria that allowed it to operate in a very risky political environment.[29] (This approach has had its downsides too, as it made Shell's subsequent claims to antigovernment groups that it was acting independently of the government less credible.)

"Social accommodation," a process of acting as a good neighbor who responds to the needs of a local community, offers another means of mitigating risks associated with civil strife. Accommodation usually involves such substantive goodwill gestures as the construction of schools, hospitals, playgrounds, and other facilities that directly enhance the quality of life for local residents. The informal channels that these actions create can reduce the risk that government officials and local inhabitants will resent the presence within their communities of a foreign firm. Social accommodation efforts may not provide a robust defense against broader, countrywide risks like revolution or civil war, but they can make an enormous difference when local violence erupts.

Political risk insurance can strengthen a company's position with both lender and investors. Banks, which occasionally require a company to purchase political risk insurance as a precondition to financing, may improve the lending terms once a company has this protection in place.[30] When catastrophe occurs, the right political risk policy can make the difference for a company's survival. In Rwanda, Tea Importers, Inc. relied on offsetting its damages with four separate political risk insurance policies. Without them, this small firm might not have survived.[31]

Political risk insurance can protect against risk not only from the host government but also from the home government. For instance, U.S. firms that export products that may have a dual-sue (military) application may face significant financial losses if the country that they export to comes under U.S.-imposed economic sanctions or trade restrictions. Political risk insurance offers "contract frustration" policies that are specifically designed to protect against home country risk.

Companies looking for political risk insurance can use public or private insurers. Most public insurers are export credit agencies created by a government to offer credit export or long-term foreign investments to lenders or investors from their home country doing business in overseas developing markets. On occasion, these have certain advantages over private insurers. They may be more willing to insure longer-term investments (up to 20 years) than their private counterparts. Perhaps more importantly, they have government connections that can be used to help settle disputes between host governments and foreign investors before an insurance policy needs to be enforced. One official from a public insurer noted that of the more than 850 contracts the insurer had written in the past two decades—with coverage worth more than $16 billion—its ability to use connections to leverage amicable resolutions to disputes meant that it had only paid three claims.[32] On the downside, public insurers in recent years have narrowed the types of coverage they provide. The Overseas Private Investment Corporation (OPIC), for example, insures emerging market investments but is constrained in some instances by broader U.S. foreign policy objectives. As a result, private specialist underwriters like Lloyds, Chubb, and AIG are still important suppliers of political risk insurance.

**Conclusion**

In May 1990, the *Wall Street Journal* recommended Yugoslavia as the most promising place to invest in Eastern Europe.[33] Roughly a year later, Yugoslavia began to descend into civil wars, the deadliest European violence since the end of World

War II. Yugoslavia, a country with a highly educated workforce and the most liberal policies in Eastern Europe until 1989, endured waves of ethnic cleansings, atrocities, and bloodshed, while neighbors like Hungary prospered.

We should have little confidence in economic forecasts that ignore political risk factors. The *Wall Street Journal* authors can be forgiven for missing the warning signs that few outside Yugoslavia had recognized. Yet the clues were there for those trained to see them, particularly in the nationalist trends that dominated local politics in many parts of the country throughout the 1980s. A few U.S. government officials sounded alarms at the time that Yugoslavia might be at risk of violent dissolution.[34] The promise of political risk analysis lies precisely in its ability to accurately identify early signals of potential political turmoil.

Warning signals are also critical for another by-product of social discontent: terrorism. Terrorist groups—the subject of the next chapter—often have objectives that fall short of regime change or mass insurrection, but their pursuit of specific, attainable ends can still have a dramatic impact on investors.

There is no terror in a bang, only in the anticipation of it.
—Alfred Hitchcock

Each November 5, in England and in former British colonies, celebrants light bonfires and launch fireworks to mark Guy Fawkes Night, a commemoration of the failure of the Gunpowder Plot in 1605. The plot was an attempt by a group of English Roman Catholics[1] to kill the Protestant king of England, James I, together with the English Protestant nobles and elites, by using barrels of gunpowder hidden in the cellars of the Houses of Parliament.

Terrorism, even in 1605, was not a new phenomenon. Assassinations, kidnappings, and murders are as old as history itself. In fact, the word "assassin" comes from what might have been one of the earliest known terrorist groups. "Assassin" is the Europeanized version of "Hashishin," a name (used by the enemies) of the Persia-based, mystical Ismaili Shia sect of Muslims.[2] During the 11th and 12th centuries, the Hashishin used assassinations as a weapon against their religious (both Christian and Sunni Muslim) and political enemies. Their assassins would infiltrate royal courts and palaces under different pretences, but they always killed their high-ranking victims in the same way, using daggers.[3] At the time, they were dreaded by both the Sunni caliphs and by the European Crusader states in the Middle East.[4] As the historian Walter Laqueur noted, "Their first leader...seems to have realized early on that his group was too small to confront the enemy in open battle but that a planned, systematic, long-term campaign of terror carried out by a small disciplined force could be a most effective political weapon."[5]

While terrorism is often a strategy used by the weaker party in a struggle, terror has also been used by the strong. The word's root comes from the Latin *terrere*, meaning "to frighten," and it was first coined by the government of Revolutionary France under Maximilien Robespierre. The revolutionary officials called their own rule the Terror (1793–94), and used the guillotine to purge France of enemies of the regime. Great powers like France in the 1790s and the Soviet Union under Stalin have used mass-scale extrajudicial killing as a method of cowing and eliminating internal dissidents and consolidating power—of "terrorizing" potential challengers.

What then is terrorism? By one account, there are 109 definitions of the term,[6] though many overlap. Some of the difficulty in defining terrorism stems from the fact that any act or threat of violence can technically terrorize someone else. At what point do separate or cumulative acts of terror constitute terrorism? And what makes one a terrorist, as opposed to an insurgent, a freedom fighter, or the security arm of a government?

One of the better definitions of the term comes from the U.S. Department of Defense, which defines terrorism as "the calculated use of unlawful violence...to inculcate fear; intended to coerce or to intimidate governments or societies in the pursuit of goals that are generally political, religious, or ideological."[7]

It is clear from the examples above (the Hashishin or the Stalinist-era, Soviet People's Commissariat for Internal Affairs, the NKVD) that terrorism is, at root, a strategy. As such, it "can be used by people of very different political convictions...It is truly all-purpose and value-free."[8] At the very least, we can say that the idea that "one man's terrorist is another's freedom fighter" is a cliché: terrorism is not defined by the righteousness of the terror-user's goals, but simply by whether terror is used as a strategy for the achievement of political objectives.

Given the scope of this book, we focus on political terrorism. We avoid talking about religious terrorism, inasmuch as religious terrorism does not have political goals. Examples of religious terrorism that are nonpolitical (and therefore not discussed here) include the Thugee sects of India that operated until their suppression by the British Raj in the 1830s[9] and the Japanese Aum Shinrikyo sect that carried out the 1995 sarin gas attack on the Tokyo subways. Similarly, economically motivated terrorism, such as Mafia-type racketeering, is beyond the scope of this chapter.[10] That said, often a religiously based or economically motivated group, such as a Mafia organization, does have political interests and pursues them through terrorist actions. For instance, both Al Qaeda's attacks in the West since the 1990s and certain Mafia attacks against the Italian state, like the bombing of Florence's Uffizi art galleries in 1993, had specific political goals.

Because terrorism is such a broad concept, the most sensible terrorism risk mitigation strategy for firms and governments begins with a detailed under-standing of the goals, tactics, internal organization, operational environment, and potential strengths and weaknesses of individual terrorist groups. This exer-cise can be worth the time and effort, because some situations and environ-ments that appear extremely risky may actually present lucrative commercial opportunities.

Given the extreme complexity of the topic, the aim of this chapter is to provide a basic road map for classification and management of terrorism risks—for thinking about where the real risks are and how to mitigate them. We will use three core examples—Al Qaeda, the Red Brigades, and the PLO in Jordan—for understanding terrorism and its practitioners. We consider what terrorists are after, how they are organized, their operating environments, their tactics, and how companies and governments respond to and mitigate associ-ated risks.

## Understanding Terrorism and Its Perpetrators

One of the most memorable skits in Monty Python's classic comedy *The Life of Brian*—a spoof of epic Bible-based movies, radical 1960s politics, and pretty much everything in between—revolves around the main character's attempt to join a terrorist organization called the Judean People's Front. The catch is, the terrorists themselves are not exactly sure whether they belong to the Judean Peo-ple's Front or another terrorist splinter group, the Popular Front of Judea. Add-ing to the confusion, the terrorists in question are not sure whether they hate a rival group, the People's Front of Judea, more than they hate the movie's putative oppressors, the Romans.[11]

Monty Python was on to something. Even experts sometimes struggled in the late 1980s to correctly differentiate between Italy's Red Brigades–Combatant Communist Party and the Red Brigades–Union of Combatant Communists.

When dealing with terrorism, most analysts and policy makers are interested mainly in three questions: "Who are they?"; "What do they want?"; and—ultimately—"How can we stop or mitigate terrorism?" There are rarely simple answers to these questions.

First, terrorist organizations constantly evolve in terms of their membership, goals, and tactics.[12] Take the Italian Red Brigades, an organization that significantly undermined the stability of the Italian state during the 1970s. From 1969 to the early 1980s, Italy experienced "the worst epidemic of terrorist violence in the Western world" at the time—the so-called years of lead.[13] During this period, Italy was racked by terrorist bombings, kidnappings, sabotage, and assassinations carried out by competing far-left and far-right terrorist organizations, which, though at war with one another, were united in their hatred for Italy's liberal democracy.[14]

Born in 1969 in the universities and industrial centers of northern Italy, the Red Brigades moved throughout the 1970s from industrial sabotage and labor agitation to kidnappings and bank robberies to targeted killings of government officials, businessmen, and media figures. In all, from 1969 through the 1980s the Red Brigades carried out 14,000 acts of violence. Their most notable attack was the 1978 abduction and murder of former Italian prime minister Aldo Moro. Another famous attack was the 1982 kidnapping of U.S. brigadier general James L. Dozier, the deputy chief of NATO's Southern Command.

How would one approach the question of who the Red Brigades were and what they wanted? Mapping the terrorist groups, their intentions, tactics, and memberships, depends to a large extent upon specifying a number of categories that can be compared and discussed. Understanding the environment in which they operate can offer useful insight.

## Environment

Guerillas, Mao Zedong said, are effective when they operate like fish in a sea of people. This concept also applies to terrorist organizations. Environment matters. Does the group sustain itself in a hostile environment? Does it draw support from a state or from certain population groups?

Though they drew financial support from Eastern Bloc intelligence services, the Red Brigades operated within a generally hostile environment, and like all groups that face sustained government action, they developed techniques to survive relentless pressure. This environment forced them to rely on friendship networks built in radical circles. The Red Brigades drew significant support from many Italian hardcore left activists and workers who viewed attempts by the Italian Communist Party (PCI) to move toward the political center as a betrayal. Specifically, the Red Brigades had a base in the northern Italian universities, underlining the validity of one of the oldest stereotypes about terrorists: the disillusioned intellectual. The Red Brigades and similar leftist organizations in Europe, like the German Red Army Faction or the Greek Revolutionary Organization 17 November, were forced to operate in decentralized cells that were composed of close friends and confidants. Such networks are more secure from penetration by hostile security services. Al Qaeda, after the U.S. invasion of Afghanistan, has become the preeminent modern example of such an organizational framework.

In contrast, a supportive environment can make it much easier for terrorist groups to generate resources and manpower. Before 9/11, the Taliban regime in Afghanistan provided sanctuary to Al Qaeda and other Islamist militants fighting, among others, India, Russia, Uzbekistan, and the United States. After 9/11, the loss of state sponsorship forced Al Qaeda to evolve from a centralized to a decentralized structure. Analysis of changes in the group's operating environment provides valuable insight into changes in its structure.

## Organization

During the trial of José Padilla, the U.S.-born Al Qaeda operative accused of plotting a "dirty bomb" attack within the United States, one of the prosecution's more remarkable pieces of evidence was Padilla's Al Qaeda job application: a document that proved strikingly similar to the standard employment form used by human resource departments within many large corporations, governments, and NGOs.

Like other complex organizations, terrorist groups must manage matters of governance, personnel, financing, and the raising and management of capital and labor. Organizational models are conditioned by a group's cultural heritage, political environment, and leadership. In turn, organizational models go some way toward explaining how terrorist groups behave.

Given the strength of the Italian state, the Red Brigades were largely decentralized.[15] Like most decentralized organizations, it contained a number of branches that were self-sufficient and capable of autonomous operation. Decentralized groups typically have fewer resources than bureaucratic ones and rely on fewer interconnections among units; at the peak of their popularity, the Red Brigades did not have more than around 1,000 members, of which about 100 were full-time. This is why destruction of individual nodes within such organizations can disrupt particular operations and cells but cannot inflict extensive and lasting damage on them. Only identification of the hubs that hold the system together can accomplish that. Yet decentralization has a downside for the terrorist group itself: Disagreements within the groups are especially likely to splinter the organization. That's how the Red Brigades ultimately produced the Red Brigades–Combatant Communist Party and the Red Brigades–Union of Combatant Communists.

Other terrorist organizations can be organized as strict bureaucracies, mimicking the structure of the state or the modern firm. These organizations typically want to usurp the powers of state governments or to become the leading parties within a specific state. Lebanon-based Hizbullah is such a group. Its rhetoric is religious, but its legitimacy springs from its ability to project itself as a modern Lebanese nationalist political movement that can effectively employ violence.

Still other groups operate more like cults, relying on their leaders' charisma rather than their organizational strength to draw recruits and motivate fighters. Unlike bureaucratic and decentralized organizations, charismatic groups depend on leaders who can be sources of both the group's strength and its weakness. From the 1960s to the 1990s, the Peruvian Shining Path was one of the deadliest insurgent groups in the Americas, readily engaging in terror. It was largely organized around the cult of personality of its leader, Abimael Guzmán (another disgruntled academic). When Peru's government captured Guzmán in 1992, the Shining Path declined as a threat.

Terrorist groups evolve over time, and their types of organization are typically mixed. The Red Brigades were decentralized and yet hierarchical. Al Qaeda bridges several organizational typologies, and reflects an organization's ability to mutate into different forms over time. The group was initially characterized as charismatic and bureaucratic. As its operating environment shifted from supportive to hostile, it moved away from a bureaucratic structure, but retained its charismatic character.

## What Do *They* Want?

When the Red Brigades assassinated Aldo Moro in 1978, the former prime minister was brokering an historic compromise between his conservative Christian Democrats and the increasingly mainstream PCI. The Communists, despite finishing among the top two parties in every Italian election since 1945, had been kept from government by a coalition of non-Communist parties that feared a PCI government would inspire a Communist takeover of Italy. Aldo Moro was negotiating a deal that would allow PCI to eventually come to power, in exchange for the party's full acceptance of Italian democratic processes and Italy's membership in Western organizations like NATO.

Moro was targeted because his actions made the Red Brigades' goal of a Communist revolution in Italy less likely. In this sense, the Red Brigades, like many Marxist-based terrorist organizations, operated as a classical revolutionary group, one dedicated to bringing about an ideologically radical regime.[16] Islamic fundamentalist groups frequently fall into this category, especially if they advocate the replacement of existing state structures with religiously inspired ones.

Generally, such groups are difficult to contain as long as the attraction of their ideology persists; the worldwide decline of Marxist-based terrorist groups took place only in the 1990s, when Soviet collapse undermined the global appeal of Marxist principles. But terrorist organizations need not be ideologically radical. Some can be decidedly conservative, or even pro–status quo.[17] Others, like the Irish Republican Army (IRA), are now generally reformist.[18]

Terrorist objectives are also framed by geography. Does a particular terrorist group want to change a state, a part of the state, or a large part of the world? The Red Brigades wanted to change Italy's form of government. Other groups with national goals include the leftist Revolutionary Armed Forces of Colombia (FARC) and the Salafist Group for Preaching and Combat (GSPC), which seeks to implement its Islamic fundamentalist vision in Algeria.[19]

Some groups, however, are too weak to try to take over an entire country. Subnational groups, like Spain's ETA, usually have a strong ethnic component and are seeking to carve out independent homelands from their host countries.

Finally, many subnational and national insurgent groups feature a transnational component in the form of support from a diaspora living abroad. Yet only a select few pursue transnational goals far from a specific homeland. Al Qaeda and its affiliates are the preeminent example, seeking to attack the United States and its allies wherever they are vulnerable to force them from the Middle East.

## What Are Their Tactics? And Why?

We can also identify types of terrorist groups by their actions and analyze them by their tactics. The Red Brigades tended to engage in assassinations and kidnappings of individuals, while avoiding mass bombings. Other groups, such as far-right terrorist organizations operating in Italy in the 1970s and 1980s or today's Al Qaeda, prefer attacks that generate mass casualties. The style of violence varies widely, but it is usually determined following rational calculations of how best to achieve a set of clearly defined goals.[20]

Another technique that has become more prevalent is the suicide attack. Suicide attacks are a time-honored tradition; they were employed by the Assassins in the 12th century and more recently by Japanese kamikazes during World War II.[21] The technique has been used increasingly by Islamic fundamentalist terrorists, although it has also been used by secular groups, such as the Kurdish PKK in Turkey and the Tamil Tigers in Sri Lanka.

One problematic assumption is that suicide bombing must be considered irrational because it depends on the willingness of fanatical adherents to kill themselves. Many analysts argue this is not necessarily the case.[22] In Southern Lebanon and in the Occupied Territories, for instance, suicide attacks are often carried out by poor young men without promising social prospects; in exchange for their "martyrdom operations," organizations such as Hamas and Hizbullah provide for their bereaved families, whose social standing is considerably improved. These benefits are important incentives in a society where family and honor are valued as highly as individual life.

Further, it's dangerous to presume that the leaderships of the organizations that carry out suicide attacks are clearly rational. They use suicide bombers because they believe this tactic has a significant psychological impact on the targeted states. Suicide terrorism has been on the rise in recent years because terrorists have realized that it is effective, particularly against democratic states. The threats posed by determined, intractable, and apparently irrational attackers force those who must defend democratic societies to acknowledge that suicide bombers can make for highly efficient terrorists.

Terrorism is also employed to polarize different social groups. In deeply divided societies, radical groups attempt to marginalize moderates. Sunni radicals in Pakistan launch attacks on Shiites in an attempt to promote Sunni radicalization by provoking Shiite attacks (another goal is to weaken the Pakistani government and break its morale). Some Sunni groups in Iraq have a similar agenda. The logic is that instability provoked by violence will draw people into their own identity groups and end dialogue by producing a rally-round-the flag effect. Polarization, though, can backfire on the people using it, and it sometimes makes terrorists unpopular with those they are trying to sway. Al Qaeda's atrocities in Iraq have undermined the organization's reputation with Sunni Iraqis, Al Qaeda's natural "constituency." The Red Brigades' assassination campaigns eventually drew condemnation from the majority of the Italian left wing, including many of its radical elements.

Media access is another important factor in the choice of tactics. The Red Brigades were successful for many years in part because they knew how to use the Italian media to promote their goals—often by intimidating journalists. If a terrorist group's intention is to terrorize, it is likely to go for the most spectacular or frightening actions it can conceive and implement. Success is heavily dependent on public awareness of a group's power to inspire terror. That is why, "in the final analysis, it is not the magnitude of the terrorist operation that counts but the publicity."[23]

Terrorist organizations, from Al Qaeda to the Tamil Tigers, spend a great deal of time on the transmission of communiqués, programs, and propaganda. This partly helps to explain why terrorism is more sustainable in countries with a relatively free exchange of information and personal mobility. Terrorist attacks do not tend to occur as often in closed and totalitarian societies (e.g., North Korea), because in closed societies movement of people is highly restricted and such attacks would not be reported.

Axiomatically, if terrorists aim for specific political gains or changes within a society, they need to target the social class that is politically relevant within that society. For instance, up to and during the 19th century, most terrorist activities targeted crowned heads of state or politicians. The Assassins, as we mentioned earlier, attacked mostly leadership figures. Toward the end of the 19th century in Western Europe and Russia, left-wing or anarchist terror groups, such as the Russian People's Will, began to attack members of the bourgeoisie, which they saw as the ruling class. This may also explain why the Italian Red Brigades avoided mass bombings, as their ideology would dictate attacks on the ruling classes, not the general population. By contrast, right-wing terrorist groups operating in Italy at the same time as the Red Brigades preferred to bomb trains or public places.

In the West, after World War II, mass suffrage has given every citizen a vote on how a country is ruled. Some terrorist groups, therefore, blame their grievances on the general public, which helps explain the rise of mass terrorism and mass attacks on populations. For instance, Al Qaeda is explicit in holding U.S. citizens responsible for the grievances it has with American policies. The broad point is that in democracies, more of the population is likely to be at risk of terrorist attacks. In a more authoritarian society, the elite leadership of that society is at a higher relative risk of terrorist attacks, as the attempts by Al Qaeda to assassinate figures like Benazir Bhutto or Pervez Musharraf in Pakistan show.

Yet there are some caveats to this rule, which have to do with "event terrorism" and with the symbolic value of the target. Al Qaeda has not focused on small-scale attacks on shopping malls or cinemas, places where many citizens congregate. Such attacks would be plausible and terrifying, but would not have the same spectacular impact as bringing down the twin towers. Al Qaeda aimed at what it saw as the centers of U.S. power: lower Manhattan, the heart of the U.S. financial industry, and the U.S. Department of Defense. Aldo Moro was killed because he was a former Italian prime minister, and his body was symbolically left to be found between the headquarters of the Christian Democrats and Communists in Rome.

In other words, many terrorist groups try to create mega-events rather than concerted campaigns of small-scale events. They aim for dramatic effect. This, of course, is part and parcel of trying to gain maximum attention and media coverage.

### Dealing with the Aftermath: How Corporations Handle the Impact of Terrorism

Terrorism will be with us for a long time, if for no other reason than that there will always be disaffected groups and individuals with access to weapons. In 1605, Guy Fawkes and his associates had amassed 1,800 pounds of gunpowder in their sophisticated but ill-fated attempt to blow up Parliament. It was quite an unusual feat for the era. Since then, access to weapons of mass destruction has increased exponentially. The 1995 Oklahoma City bombing and the 9/11 attacks show how relatively simple plots can inflict horrendous damage with weapons available to ordinary citizens.

There are many ways to measure the losses of 9/11. Al Qaeda's attacks in New York, Washington, DC, and Pennsylvania killed 2,970 people. The economic toll of the attack was immense: U.S. equities are estimated to have lost about $1.2 trillion in value in the immediate week after the attacks. Large financial institutions in Lower Manhattan, like Deutsche Bank and Lehman Brothers, saw buildings destroyed or damaged by the attack. At least one airline immediately filed for bankruptcy protection. The city of New York suffered enormous losses of jobs, office space, and tourism revenue.[24]

Let's look at the attacks' impact on the Bank of New York (BoNY), the world's largest custodian and settlement bank, whose facilities and communication systems were disabled on that day. Many other financial institutions suffered significant damage and disruptions, as well as terrible human costs. But BoNY suffered much of its damage because its headquarters and two additional sites were located almost literally in the shadow of the World Trade Center, a particularly obvious terrorist target given that the buildings had already been attacked by Islamic terrorists in 1993.

BoNY's three sites housed more than 5,000 of its employees and its central computer system. On September 11, the bank lost two of these offices and the equipment inside. The failure of the bank's planners to locate clearing and settlement operations further from a prime terrorist target produced operating delays that created turmoil for trading in the market and increased demand for liquidity.[25] When the building housing the communication system was evacuated following the attacks, BoNY was left with a heavy backlog of transactions that had to be "reconstructed and reconciled."[26]

During that week, BoNY was publicly reported to be overdue on $100 billion in payments,[27] creating a drain of reserves from the entire banking system. Bank of New York's settlement systems were handling half of all trade in U.S. government bonds, and the bank's emergency planners in fact had had the foresight to back up its government bond processing operations with a second computer. But the emergency system failed to function as intended because backup communication lines to clients had not been properly tested. The result was considerable confusion and extended delays.

Planners had also set up redundant telecommunications facilities in case a single line suffered damage and operations needed to continue from centers outside New York. But they discovered too late that all the lines were routed through the same physical phone facilities. The terrorist attack had inflicted substantial damage to a vital nearby switching station, leaving the bank without the bandwidth it needed for voice and data communications to Lower Manhattan.[28] Lack of location and communication diversification resulted in a more serious impact for BoNY than for its competitors.

Terrorist attacks cannot always be prevented or even anticipated. Still, precautions can be taken. For both business and government decision makers, a failure to take basic precautions can multiply the impact of a terrorist attack. Overall, large corporations face significant risks from terrorist attacks, especially when operating in dense urban areas that can easily be disrupted. Companies cannot engage in standard counterterrorism measures, but they can plan for the potential impact of terrorist attacks.

Most corporations do not plan for terrorist attacks per se. But many corporations, and especially financial institutions, plan for a range of potential business disruptions, such as building damage, failure of public utilities and transport, and telecommunication and data processing failures, as well as threats to their employees. Most of these plans implicitly cover the potential impact of terrorist attacks.

At the time of 9/11, Morgan Stanley was the World Trade Center's largest tenant. When the first aircraft struck Tower One, Morgan Stanley immediately deployed its response plan. Though WTC security officials instructed tenants in the other buildings to stay where they were, the firm's own security executives ordered all Morgan Stanley employees to immediately evacuate the second tower.[29]

Morgan Stanley also deployed its communications plan to provide relevant information to managers and employees, regulatory agencies, clients, and the media. Less than an hour after the first attack, the firm had its backup sites for essential operations and management personnel (located elsewhere in New York City) up and running. Firm executives used a dedicated emergency telephone patch network, routed through London, to communicate with other offices. Morgan Stanley lost 13 employees that day, but the firm's extensive and well-conceived planning helped prevent a far greater loss of life and assets.

The origins of Morgan Stanley's response go back at least to the first terrorist attack on the WTC on February 26, 1993, which killed six people and injured more than a thousand—this incident had persuaded the firm's executives that its response plan needed to be updated. As part of a major post-incident review, Morgan Stanley analyzed its business operations and related disaster risks and developed an integrated preparedness, response, and continuity strategy for crises. The strategy included written and web-based employee evacuation plans, business-system continuity redundancies, an enhanced on-site security presence, and an expansive emergency communication plan (covering management, employees, investors and clients, federal and state government regulators, and the media). A vital, and mandatory, component of the strategy was to practice its components frequently in preparation for another attack on the WTC and to cultivate a strong corporate culture of preparedness.

During the 1993 attack, it took more than four hours for all Morgan Stanley employees to exit the World Trade Center. On September 11, 2001, more than 3,000 people needed just 45 minutes to fully evacuate the twin towers.

### Damned if You Do, Damned if You Don't: How Governments Deal with Terrorism

Unlike corporations, governments can take actions to prevent terrorist attacks from happening in the first place. They can capture terrorists, attack them militarily, or try to address their demands. More often than not, governments try to implement a combination of these three options. But what sometimes works in one situation may not work in another.

### Policing

In 2006, terrorist plotters living in the U.K. and Pakistan planned a simultaneous suicide attack against as many as 10 commercial aircraft by smuggling peroxide-based liquid explosives on board and then detonating them with cell phones or MP3 players. In a massive British surveillance and sting operation called Operation Overt, 25 suspected terrorists, mostly Muslims of Pakistani descent, were arrested in and around London.[30] Another 17 suspects were arrested in Pakistan. The raid included 69 residences and businesses, resulting in the capture of bomb-making materials and chemicals and jihadist materials. Later, 17 of the 25 arrested were charged with conspiracy to murder and to commit acts of terrorism or failure to disclose information about acts of terrorism.[31]

The successful disruption of the liquid bombing plot was the culmination of months of surveillance and analysis by London's Scotland Yard and MI5 that began soon after the July 7, 2005, London subway and bus bombings. Informants tipped off London police about a small group of militant Muslim men in Walthamstow, London's largest enclave of Pakistani immigrants. MI5 bugged the residences and vehicles of the suspects and monitored their communication, travels, and financial transactions. Rather than finding connections to the subway and bus bombings, British authorities discovered a nascent terrorist cell and an apartment used as a bomb-making lab where these men were developing liquid explosives to smuggle through airport checkpoints. An undercover agent later infiltrated the group and provided more detailed information on the plan and dates for attack. Using counterterrorism methods called "sneak and peek" developed during the efforts against the IRA, British intelligence and law enforcement allowed plots to reach near-fruition in order to collect information and evidence for prosecution. The danger was that civilian lives might be lost should anything go wrong. According to news reports, the liquid bombing plot was disrupted a week before its planned execution.

The U.K.'s successes were in part due to preexisting government infrastructure to carefully supervise and rapidly respond to potential threats. Surveillance activities were regulated and approved by the Home Secretary, and established legal processes provided legal means to conduct covert operations to monitor suspected terrorists, such as eavesdropping and clandestinely entering private property, while providing civil protection. Finally, the U.K. was able to foster interagency cooperation and responses from senior officials to rapidly moving events related to counterterrorist activities. If anything, this example shows that acts of terrorism are often preventable through good intelligence work, analysis, and swift counterterrorist action.

The relative success that the Italian state had in reducing (though not completely eliminating) the threat of the Red Brigades does too. Despite relative state weakness, the Italian government ultimately waged a successful counterterrorism campaign that led to the defeat of the Red Brigades by the mid-1980s. A confluence of external and internal factors ultimately doomed the Red Briagdes. First there were extensive prosecutions undertaken against the group and its sympathizers. Changes in Italian law created amnesty for terrorists who began to see little future in militancy, and new mandates for counterterrorism groups, which in many cases infiltrated the Red Brigades and squeezed them to the point of collapse.

But the key factor in the Red Brigades' demise was the loss of popular support and internal coherence. Internal dissent weakened their ranks, particularly as the viability of real proletarian revolution in Italy diminished amid economic growth in the early 1980s and the birth of homegrown anti-Communist movements in Eastern Europe. In addition, within and outside the Red Brigades, leftists and workers became disillusioned with their violent methods. They were appalled by the Moro killing, as well as by the assassination of a factory worker who had informed on Red Brigades activists. The Dozier kidnapping was a last-ditch attempt to recapture the initiative, but during a massive manhunt to find the perpetrators, Dozier was freed, and the group was essentially defeated by late 1982. Although individual militants claiming to act in the name of the Red Brigades have killed Italian politicians in recent years, the group itself has not been a significant threat or political force for more than two decades. The defeat of the Red Brigades was in no small measure a matter of a changing international context that led to ideological dissent within the group.

Yet for every success there is a spectacular and tragic failure. In 2004, when the U.S. National Commission on Terrorist Attacks Upon the United States released its 570-page report on the September 11 attacks, one phrase stood out: "failure of imagination."[32] Commission members argued that the sheer scale of the assault and the ability of terrorists to use commercial planes as "weapons of mass destruction" succeeded in large measure because policy makers and security agencies had simply failed to imagine such an attack.

Treating terrorists as criminals and using standard policing measures to avert the threat of terrorism is both politically less costly than military action and typically more efficient than meeting terrorist demands. But policing action, as the British found out during their long campaign against the Irish Republican Army, has its limits as a deterrent. As has been noted many times, the police must succeed every time; a terrorist group must succeed just once.

**Military Action**

Few question the ethics of using military force against terrorists and their supporters. The question is rather: does it work? In some cases it does, as in 1970, when the Jordanian monarchy expelled the Palestinian Liberation Organization (PLO) from the country.

Jordan's conflict with the PLO began in 1967, when Yasser Arafat established Palestinian paramilitary organizations in the country. Arafat presented the PLO, organized in the wake of the stunning Israeli defeat of conventional Arab armies in the Six Day War, as the only effective weapon against Israel. Arafat chose Jordan for its large Palestinian refugee population and its proximity to the Israeli-occupied West Bank. Jordan's King Hussein, however, foresaw the threat that the PLO posed for the stability of his kingdom. Between 1967 and 1970, PLO fighters and Jordanian forces fought a series of street battles, bursts of violence kept in check only by recognition on both sides that final victory for either was all but impossible.

In the end, the PLO's objectives and the limited room for political activity afforded by Jordan's monarchical system forced a decisive military confrontation. The Palestinians' hijacking of several airplanes to Jordan provided Hussein with a justification for military action and one that assured him of the international community's support. In September 1970, Palestinian groups hijacked four international flights and brought them to Jordan. The PLO and its allies released the passengers and then blew up the planes in front of the media. Hussein used the incident to swiftly deploy his military and overwhelm the PLO. Jordanian troops routed Arafat's forces and pushed them into Syria and Lebanon. The Jordanians' action forced the PLO to abandon its goal of replacing the monarchy and of using Jordan as a launchpad for military confrontation with Israel. The PLO remained a threat to Israeli security, but Hussein's decision to use overwhelming military force against the organization eliminated the threat it posed to his political power.

The success of military force in suppressing terrorism depends on a series of interrelated factors, ranging from the number of fighting forces to the level of existing popular support for the terrorist group to whether the use of military force pushes moderates to support the terrorists. Military force can eliminate the terrorist threat in the most decisive way possible, but it can also transform small numbers of outlaws into a full-blown insurgency, fueling the recruitment of new terrorists.

### Accommodation

Another way to deal with a terrorist threat is to accommodate the terrorists' demands. This can create dangerous precedents. Countries paying ransom money for citizens kidnapped by terrorists only encourage further kidnappings. A government seen as accommodating terrorist demands also runs the risk of being perceived as "weak" on terrorism and unable to defend its citizens.[33]

Yet, accommodation, especially in conjunction with policing, sometimes works. In 1974, the U.K. government legalized the nationalist Sinn Fein party, despite its ties to the IRA and terrorism, to encourage nationalist participation in the political process as an alternative to violence. Twenty years later the U.K. government was credited with bringing an end to political violence by maintaining contact with Sinn Fein, despite disagreements within the group over the use of violence and its refusal to abandon its weapons. This approach was nearly undermined between 1982 and 1992, when Sinn Fein's participation in the political process was jeopardized by ongoing IRA violence. British counterterrorism operations and the successes of British intelligence suggested that the IRA could continue to use violence, but only to maintain the status quo rather than to achieve genuine progress toward secession. Following the cease-fire of 1994, Sinn Fein gradually managed to increase its electoral success. In the 2003 Assembly elections, it dominated the nationalist vote, appealing to nationalists in both Ireland and Northern Ireland.

In dealing with the IRA, the U.K. was able to leverage viable political institutions to gradually incorporate Sinn Fein into the political process and to reduce political violence by degrees. The U.K. used its history of representative political institutions and successful elections to convince the IRA of the merits of participating in the political process as a way of achieving its objectives. Unlike King Hussein's Jordan, which lacked political institutions with publicly recognized legitimacy, the British government was able to use popular politics as a means of incorporating a nonstate actor into state processes and of persuading it to disavow violence.[34]

## Conclusion

Revolution, civil war, and terrorism are extreme examples of social turmoil and violence, and companies can face extreme consequences as a result. But more tranquil environments can also generate substantial downside risks. In fact, cases of outright expropriation of property are surprisingly common in "nonrevolutionary" situations. In the next two chapters on expropriation and regulation, we consider these types of risks.

# Expropriation SEVEN

A prince never lacks legitimate reasons to break his promise.
—Niccolo Machiavelli

Until 1951, Iran's oil industry was dominated by the Anglo-Iranian Oil Company, the forerunner of today's BP. That year, amid growing resentment of the British presence in the oil industry, Iran's government passed a law nationalizing Anglo-Iranian's concession. The company's management failed to recognize signals that political change would soon force an adjustment in the company's relationship with Iran until it was far too late. This expropriation was driven not only by the Iranian government's demand for a greater share of the country's oil revenue but also by a growing wave of wounded national pride inspired in part by the exploitation of Iran's natural resources by foreigners.

Anglo-Iranian's management, led by Sir William Fraser, initially resisted Iranian demands for a greater share of its profits, despite pleas for compromise from the U.S. and British governments, the latter of which owned 51% of the company. By the time Anglo-Iranian was ready to make a deal, nationalist politicians, led by Mohammed Mossadeq, had shifted their demands. No longer content with a larger piece of the pie, Mossadeq called for the company to be nationalized. Mounting political violence and pressure forced the shah to sign a nationalization law in April 1951, officially voiding Anglo-Iranian's concession.

The nationalization issue helped make Mossadeq prime minister. It also was a major part of the ensuing political instability in Iran that led to both the temporary ouster of the shah and then the 1953 CIA-generated coup—Operation Ajax—which removed Mossadeq from power and restored the shah to his throne. A year later, a consortium of foreign companies was brought in to run the Iranian oil operation, though Iran owned the oil. Anglo-Iranian, while compensated for its losses, was forced to remain in the background of the new consortium. It would never again enjoy the privileged position it occupied in Iran before 1951.[1]

## Why Governments Expropriate

When it comes to expropriations, both corporations and foreign governments have an interest in avoiding surprise. In some cases, especially when dealing with government leaders, that might be impossible. But in most cases, corporations and investors do not have the luxury of claiming that they could not have known about an expropriation risk. State seizure of foreign companies and assets will remain a source of political risk for the foreseeable future. How do we understand this kind of risk? Why do governments expropriate? Where are expropriations most likely to occur?

Since the late 1980s, investors and policy makers have increasingly assumed that the risk of expropriations was waning. With the end of the Cold War there has been a general trend toward government protection and promotion of ownership and investment rights. The privatization of previously nationalized property became a core component of the process of economic liberalization in the states of the former Communist bloc and Latin America, and even in developed states like France and Britain. Developing nations have carried out more than 8,000 privatizations in recent years (1990–2003), and have raised some US$410 billion in proceeds.[2] At the same time, the number of expropriations that took place between 1986 and 1992 was lower than in comparable time frames of the post–World War II era.[3]

Yet, the risk of expropriations refuses to die. State expropriations of privately owned assets make headlines around the world these days with disturbing regularity. The Russian parliament passes a law that limits foreign investment in "strategic sectors" of the Russian economy and expropriates existing investment.

Venezuela squeezes foreign oil companies, takes land, and nationalizes electrical and telecommunications firms. Ecuador seizes the assets of Occidental Petroleum, the country's largest foreign investor. Zimbabwe's Robert Mugabe orders the large-scale expropriation of white-owned farms.

In fact, we are not witnessing a clear "convergence" process in which economic liberalization and privatization become the order of the day. If anything, the global foreign investment environment is becoming more varied and complex. Even as the number of expropriations declined between 1991 and 2004, they still accounted for about 84% of the dollars paid out in political risk insurance settlements by the U.S. Overseas Private Investment Corporation (OPIC).[4] A number of governments are still involved in outright expropriations of private property and foreign investment. The question for most investors and policy makers is: which countries are prone to expropriate, and why? As this chapter will highlight, governments have become increasingly sophisticated when attempting to interfere with property rights. Gray-area issues like "creeping expropriations," done through subtle legal and regulatory means, have become increasingly common.[5]

## Drivers of Expropriation

Governments expropriate for many reasons. "Expropriation" itself can take a variety of forms, from the creation of predatory tax regulations to the nationalization of an entire economy. The causes can be varied and complex, and understanding this allows both companies and foreign governments to better plan for handling this type of risk. The forces that induce governments to expropriate include of international politics, economics, ideology, domestic politics, and nationalism.

### International Politics

A literary masterpiece relevant to foreign direct investors is Joseph Conrad's *Nostromo*. It is the story of an English family who operates a silver mining concession in a fictitious, unstable Latin American country at the turn of the 20th century. Some of the quandaries of operating in such an environment still ring true today. Yet other things have changed: in *Nostromo* when political and social turmoil push the country into civil war, a U.S. cruiser appears offshore to ensure that Western business interests are protected—a vivid illustration of why expropriations were relatively rare before 1917.

Mexico was able to nationalize its oil industry in 1938, because the approach of war in Europe ensured that the U.S. and British militaries were in no position to threaten the Mexican government. The United States had begun to promote the "good neighbor policy" in Latin America, a move away from an earlier era of "gunboat diplomacy."[6]

The same was true for the wave of expropriations during the decolonization process that took place during the 1960s and 1970s across the developing world. Between 1956 and 1972, some studies estimate that developing countries expropriated about 25% of the total value of foreign direct investment (FDI) in developing states, or about $10 billion (1972 values).[7] With the Cold War occupying U.S. and European policy makers, Western governments had fewer available military or economic tools at their disposal to resist the nationalization of their foreign property.[8] Nor did they want to take actions that might push developing states into Moscow's embrace.

Some models of expropriation suggest that broad international events, like the wave of Communist takeovers, the decolonization process, or the Great Depression, explain why (and when) expropriations occur.[9] Although this model cannot explain why expropriations happen in some states and not others during these "waves," it does reveal that expropriations are more likely to happen under specific international circumstances.

So what are the international constraints against expropriation? What are the incentives for a country to expropriate? One obvious reason why governments engage in expropriations is opportunism: they do it because they can. Following the 1917 revolution, the Soviet Union was able to nationalize almost all private enterprise, because the country was still a great power.[10] Similarly, the governments of all other Communist countries, such as China and the Eastern Bloc states, nationalized almost all private property after taking power: China was a great power, and there was little the West could do to coerce states that were in the Soviet sphere of influence.[11]

Expropriations have declined in number since the 1970s, although the value of expropriation-related insurance claims remains high. One reason for the decline is that even in the absence of military retaliation, expropriations still carry costs for governments that engage in them. Seizure of private property usually costs the governments that resort to them access to international capital markets, loss of foreign know-how, and a steep drop in foreign direct investment.

In 2007, Ecuador's forced contract renegotiations with foreign oil companies generated a dramatic decline in foreign investment in the oil sector. Following the Ecuadorian government's move, foreign energy companies operating in the country (which included Brazilian, Chinese, French, U.S., and Spanish oil concerns) submitted investment budgets for 2008 that totaled a combined $50 million. Compare that with their combined investment budget for the previous year of $823 million.[12]

The ability to get away with expropriation depends in large part on the position of the home state in the international political economy: how dependent is the state on access to capital markets and foreign direct investment? How vulnerable is the expropriating state to retaliation by other states? In today's world of high oil prices, expropriations have occurred in Russia, Bolivia, Venezuela, and Ecuador. All these states have autocratic governments and considerable natural resource wealth (oil and gas in particular). The revenue these states earn from high global oil prices limit their vulnerability to reductions in foreign investment and to shunning by international capital markets.

The quality of relations among states is also important. Simply put, states rarely seize assets from their friends and are much more likely to expropriate firms originating from a state that is considered an enemy or rival. In today's Zimbabwe, mining and banking investments from Great Britain, which the Mugabe government sees as an enemy are at far greater risk than foreign investments from South Africa, Mugabe's most reliable foreign source of political support. In Venezuela, the Chávez government sees the United States as its main antagonist, and U.S. companies face greater risk of expropriation there than do their Chinese and Russian counterparts. In more extreme situations, when two states are at war, the risk that one country will expropriate the other's companies increases significantly.

### Economic Interdependence

Then there is the question of economic interdependence.[13] If two countries' economies are dependent on one another for stability and growth, it is much more difficult for one state to expropriate the other's properties. In 2006, when Bolivia decided to nationalize its hydrocarbons industry, the impact was mostly on Brazilian interests. Petrobras had led the investment cycle that made natural gas Bolivia's main source of tax and export revenues and was responsible for 55%

of Bolivia's total gas production. Petrobras had also invested in the construction of a pipeline that made Brazil the destination of 85% of Bolivian gas exports. More importantly, Brazil was relying on Bolivia for half of its gas needs, and natural gas was becoming increasingly important in order to avoid power shortages that might weigh heavily on economic growth (and the Brazilian government's popularity).

The move astonished Brazilian president Luiz Inácio Lula da Silva's government, which considered itself friendly toward Bolivia's president, Evo Morales. But energy security constraints limited Brazil's margin to maneuver. The Brazilian government took a cautious approach both to negotiations over the effects of nationalization on Petrobras's assets in Bolivia and the price of the gas Bolivia exports to Brazil. Brazil patiently sought to avoid any escalation and further politicization of the issue. It recognized Bolivia's right to nationalize and ruled out retaliation. Brazil opted instead to negotiate the terms of nationalization and if necessary to seek international arbitration to protect its commercial interests.

At the same time, the Brazilian government successfully pressured Morales to moderate his stance. The replacement of Bolivia's minister of hydrocarbons in September 2006, after the minister had decided to expropriate two Brazilian-owned refineries without compensation, was partially a by-product of effective pressure from Brasília. Negotiations with Bolivia were suspended, and high-level Brazilian government officials convinced the Bolivians to step back and stop taking unilateral measures. If Bolivia adopted a hard line, Petrobras could leave Bolivia, posing serious operational and financial challenges for Bolivia's gas revenues. The outcome of the negotiations process was a compromise solution that significantly increased taxation on the sector, but allowed Petrobras to maintain commercially viable operations in the Bolivian gas fields that supply Brazil. Brazil also managed to avoid a significant increase in the price it was paying for the Bolivian gas. Strong economic and political ties between the two countries helped mitigate the impact of expropriations.[14]

### Economic Drivers

A number of economic factors also affect the likelihood of expropriations. One is an overtly statist economic policy. In 1975, Great Britain expropriated the (already bankrupt) British Leyland Motor Corporation, which was perceived as having a strategic value for Britain and for labor relations.[15] This followed an earlier spate of nationalizations in Western Europe, where after World War II, governments under the influence of Socialist and/or Keynesian economics attempted to either set up state-controlled "natural monopolies" in certain sectors such as energy and telecommunications or to take over strategic manufacturing industries.

Another rationale for expropriating property, particularly in developing states, has to do with structural economic inefficiencies, such as a government's inability to collect taxes, tackle corruption, service its debt, or maintain financial discipline. In difficult budgetary conditions, expropriation (usually surrounded by nationalist or ideological rhetoric) can provide a government with a quick infusion of cash. Not surprisingly, some analysts point out that there is a relationship between lack of economic growth and expropriations: Governments can expropriate firms as a response to economic problems, which they can then blame on foreign firms.[16]

Others note that governments are more likely to expropriate commodity-producing industries when commodity prices are high.[17] The recent expropriations in the oil and gas industries in Russia, Venezuela, and Bolivia make sense in this context.

A number of technical factors can influence a government's economic motivations for expropriating investment. One is the ability of the expropriating country to market[18] and sell the seized investment. This is one of the reasons extractive industries are often especially prone to expropriation: it is relatively easy to sell oil, gas, and other commodities.

The availability of the right technology and managerial talent can make a difference, as well. Governments have economic reasons for avoiding the expropriation of firms in high-tech sectors—bureaucratic mismanagement can kill such industries. In high-tech fields, governments more typically try to push for intellectual property transfers and highly restricted operating environments; these may amount to "creeping expropriation" but are rarely examples of "outright expropriations."

For some governments, whose interest is more in gaining greater tax revenue and control of cash flows than in the domestic political capital gained, "creeping expropriations" are a more common tactic. In 2004, China announced a set of regulatory policies in its domestic automotive sector that banned "the sale and transfer of manufacturing licenses by bankrupt or failing manufacturers"[19] to either domestic or foreign investors. The rules also required investors setting up new automotive plants to invest at least $240 million and to invest in research and development, which would then become Chinese-owned intellectual property. By prohibiting automotive companies from selling their licenses and imposing intellectual property requirements, the Chinese government limited the ability of foreign corporations to viably operate as private enterprises in China's automotive sector.

Do expropriations make intermediate-term economic sense? That's another question, and not one that we will address in detail. In brief, however, most developing countries that have nationalized entire industries have not achieved robust and sustained levels of development. Following the nationalization of its oil industry and the creation of the state-run PEMEX oil company, Mexico expected to become a wealthy country. That didn't happen. Nationalization provoked a significant drop in foreign direct investment: by 1940, foreign investment in Mexico had fallen to a quarter of its 1920 level.[20] The loss of foreign know-how undermined new oil exploration efforts. Oil revenues declined, and national debt increased.[21] Mexican governments of the 1940s and 1950s had to reverse many of Cárdenas's economic policies and to encourage new investment in the oil industry, though they did not reverse the creation of the state-run oil monopoly. Similarly, Khrushchev's threat that the nationalized state-run economies of the former Soviet Bloc would "bury" the West was not realized. That said, there are some cases where nationalization did not result in showstopping economic inefficiencies: expropriated French car companies and certain European national airlines were able to operate in a relatively efficient manner for decades.

### Ideology and Domestic Politics

Ideology has historically been a key driver of expropriations. This was the case not only for Communist states (Cuba, the Soviet Union, etc.) but also for a number of socialist or statist-minded developing countries like India, Sri Lanka, and Mexico—and, in the 1940s and 1950s, for developed countries like Britain and France. With the end of the Cold War and the retreat of communism, ideology has significantly diminished as a driver of nationalizations, though it remains a factor in places like Venezuela, where the Chávez government's stated goal is to create a socialist society.

Expropriations driven by ideology are relatively predictable, because those who build political movements on demands for the nationalization or expropriation of private property are usually not shy about broadcasting their intentions. When Iran's Mossadeq government nationalized Anglo-Iranian's vast oil industry concessions, the writing was already on the wall. Chilean politicians debated nationalization of that country's copper-mining industry for years before the government finally pulled the trigger in 1971.

Some assume that governments expropriate investments for the "public good," to restore the national wealth to the nation's people. Political motivations for expropriation are often far more selfish. Expropriated property can be used to build popular support and political capital, to placate interest groups and constituencies, or simply to enrich public officials.[22] To predict when domestic politics will play a role in expropriation, it helps to identify the sources of a particular government's political power. An understanding of who benefits from expropriation can tell us much about how a government will treat questions of property rights. For some governments, the political benefits of expropriation simply outweigh the economic costs and international penalties[23]—especially if valuable natural resources are involved.

In the early 1970s, Zaire and Zambia nationalized all foreign investments in their copper and mining industries, transforming the countries into two of the largest copper producers in the world (based on their reserves). Both governments, in charge of weak and newly independent states, saw opportunities to use the revenue created by expropriations to pay off friends and foes alike—and to line their own pockets.[24] But patronage is not limited to extremely corrupt or failing states. In many cases, such as in Mexico or in Britain (where a newly elected Labour government nationalized the coal, steel, and other sectors in 1945), expropriating governments draw significant electoral support from labor movements. Expropriation and state ownership can be used to placate key constituencies.

The risk of expropriation is also related to treatment of property rights. Risk analysts sometimes gauge expropriation risk by looking at how domestic capital is invested. Investments in emerging markets and developing states generally provide higher rates of return than investments in developed states. As a result, investors based in these markets should have a strong incentive to invest at home, especially since they can expect to understand the economic dynamics within their own countries better than foreign competitors. But if domestic investors invest heavily abroad (think of Russian moguls buying English real estate or soccer teams), this is usually a good indicator that property rights are not consistently enforced at home and that domestic investors lack confidence in their government's commitment to protect private property. In Brazil, on the other hand, wealthy domestic investors are keeping their money at home much more than they did several years ago.

This does not mean that democracy is always a good predictor of the climate for expropriations. Property rights are generally better protected in advanced democracies than in developing authoritarian states. But especially in young democracies, property rights may be in a state of flux. This was the case following the partial privatization of Telekom Srbija by the Milošević regime in 1997. The privatization was undertaken to provide cash for the corrupt Milošević regime's drive to buy elections and to stay in power. Once the Milošević regime fell, the democratically elected governments that followed charged that these privatizations had been politically motivated. Similar privatization challenges have emerged in recent years in Poland and Ukraine. The first step in this process is often "renationalization." Privatizations carried out in countries plagued with political instability are at significant risk of being renationalized or renegotiated once a new government—with a new set of political motivations and interests—takes charge.

Yet while stability of property rights and economic openness are useful in understanding how a government will likely behave, they are not enough. Revolutionary governments, like the Chávez government in Venezuela, do not typically expropriate property immediately after assuming power. They often work first to create political stability and to consolidate their political standing. Chávez did not begin to nationalize the petrochemicals or telecoms industries until four or five years after coming to power, when his regime's political position was secure. So while political stability typically diminishes risks of expropriation in a consolidated democracy, under certain types of ideologically based regimes, a newly enhanced stability may dramatically increase these risks.

## Nationalism

Nationalism is an important factor in expropriation. Take Russia, where political appeals to national pride have increasingly become a means of bolstering the government's domestic popularity and of strengthening the Russian state. In policy terms, this has meant an increased risk of expropriations in industries that the government labels "strategic." Russian political elites and the broader public view the 1990s (when privatizations were the norm) as a period of national vulnerability and shame, one in which unscrupulous foreign and domestic business interests defrauded the state and plundered much of Russia's natural wealth. That's why the state's efforts to reassert control of these assets enjoys broad public support: Russians accept that state expropriations are necessary to restore the country to great power status.

The trend in Russia toward state control in certain sectors has advanced mainly through ad hoc regulatory and judicial pressure. The most widely publicized case—the dismantling of the oil company Yukos—was carried out using the tax authorities, and was sealed by a judiciary that consistently ruled in the state's favor. More recently, the Shell-led consortium operating the Sakhalin-II energy project succumbed to attempts by Gazprom, Russia's state-sanctioned gas monopoly, to take a controlling stake in the project after a sustained campaign of pressure from Russian environmental and other technical oversight agencies. The French firm Total and the Anglo-Russian firm TNK-BP have come under similar pressures. The Russian government has also worked to establish state-controlled umbrella holding companies in key sectors such as nuclear power, aircraft production, shipbuilding, and arms production. The Kremlin will likely remain open to strategic partnerships with foreign firms in these areas, and may even conduct IPOs of state holdings, but control will remain firmly in government hands.[25]

There is often an historical dimension to firms' vulnerabilities. Nationalism most typically becomes a factor when foreigners are seen to dominate a local economy and when local politicians exploit this perception by blaming foreigners and foreign influences for local poverty, gaps between rich and poor, worker exploitation, and other social ills. In the mid-20th century, as most Asian countries decolonized, many foreign firms were identified with former colonial regimes as a pretext for the expropriation of their assets.[26]

Fanning anxiety over foreign influence in the economy can help a government maintain its popularity and legitimacy. "Foreigners" need not come from foreign lands or represent foreign governments; they can be people labeled as "internal foreigners," members of economically powerful ethnic minority groups, such as prosperous Han Chinese in Thailand, Indonesia, Malaysia, and Burma[27] or white South Africa, whom some accuse of profiting from economic and social privileges at the expense of the black majority. Often this results in expropriation of domestic investment—"indigenization" campaigns that redistribute property from the economically powerful minorities to the politically powerful majority. Idi Amin's confiscation of nonnative Ugandans' properties provides an early example.

Paradoxically, expropriations of local ethnic minority business can favor foreign investors, as the government may try to replace local know-how and capital with foreign investments. Yet ethnic tensions and populist strains of nationalism—with slogans like "Mexico for Mexicans" or "Poland for the true Poles"—usually increase a country's political risk. Even if favorable to foreign direct investment, chauvinist governments can create other potential risks, such as domestic instability.

### Predicting Expropriations

Think of expropriation as the mirror opposite of privatization. Both actions represent a change in government policy on property ownership. What triggers one or the other? One model[28] suggests there is a cycle of expropriation and privatization. Governments seize properties to address economic woes, promote domestic political goals, stoke nationalism, or realize an ideological vision. More often than not, expropriations eventually produce significant economic inefficiencies, increased levels of corruption, and higher levels of national debt. A need for new access to foreign investment and capital markets then forces these governments to restore their credibility in international economic and financial markets—in part, by privatizing industries that have in many cases been nationalized. In the longer term, however, privatization can inflict social pain by destroying jobs and creating new opportunities for corruption. This development provokes public anger and empowers a new class of populist politicians ready to satisfy public demand for social justice with calls for the renationalization of key industries. This cycle has played out in various forms and at various speeds in several developing states in Asia and Latin America. The Venezuelan government privatized its oil industry in 1976. Chávez completed the process of renationalizing in June 2007.

For the foreseeable future, we will live in a world in which the trend toward privatization continues. Expropriations in many countries are more likely only after privatization has been implemented and operating for a while, and governments and consumers can assess its relative effects.[29] Yet, we are also beginning to see the signs of a populist anti-privatization backlash in countries rich in national resources as well as in states that have gone through financial crises, like Argentina. In recent years, governments that draw support from the "losers" in economic transitions (and privatizations in particular) in post-socialist countries have threatened to reverse or renegotiate privatizations and asset sales to foreigners. Will this eventually produce a wave of expropriations? It's hard to say. But the risk will be with us for many years to come.

Another way to analyze these risks is to determine the relative bargaining power of the foreign investor. If a government cannot operate an industry without outside know-how, it is less likely to intervene in it. National governments generally prefer national companies. This is why so many countries—like France, South Korea, and China—have "national champions" in specific industries. Yet most governments welcome foreign investment if it helps create new jobs, build local economies and gives local workers access to foreign know-how and technology. In fact, many governments offer attractive terms on taxes, tariffs, and other subsidies to attract foreign investment. As the relationship begins, bargaining power usually rests with the investor.

But as a foreign investment becomes operational, the government's bargaining power increases, giving it greater incentive to impose new taxes or regulations—or even to contemplate expropriation. Just as governments generally prefer domestic corporations to foreign ones, companies invested in foreign markets have little incentive to walk away from the money they have invested and the infrastructure they have built. From the position of the corporation, this is an "obsolescing bargain,"[30] meaning that its bargaining position becomes weaker as its investment in a country matures and begins to generate profits. Often, the very profitability of a foreign investment can lead the government to question whether the corporation is "exploiting" the country.

The idea of an "obsolescing bargain" fits the story of Anglo-Iranian in Iran. In 1933, Anglo-Iranian secured a very profitable concession to exploit oil in Iran, whose terms were supposed to run for some 60 years. But the terms were simply too favorable, and the Iranian government tried a number of times to renegotiate the contract. When Iranian left-wing nationalists took power in 1951, they judged that the bargaining power of Anglo-American had declined to the point that expropriation of its assets was feasible. In this case, however, the Iranian government misjudged the changing geopolitical situation. The British government in particular was prepared to retaliate, and did so by freezing Iranian assets and by imposing a blockade of expropriated oil shipments in 1952. The United States was at first reluctant to back its ally in overthrowing the Iranian government and favored negotiations. However, when the Eisenhower administration was elected in 1953, given the context of the Korean War and increasing Cold War tensions, the United States began to favor the British position. This was in no small measure exacerbated by Mohammed Mossadeq's government ties to the Iranian Communists (Tudeh Party). The Mossadeq government had miscalculated, thinking that the world and Britain could not function without Iranian oil, and that Iran could withstand the political and economic pressure of two great powers.[31] Unfortunately for Mossadeq, that turned out not to be true. He was overthrown by a British and U.S.-supported coup in 1953.

### Expropriation Risk Mitigation

*Spreading Risk*

United States–based Kennecott Mines offers a prime example of a company that developed a strategy to stave off the worst effects of nationalization. In the 1960s, Kennecott began to believe that its copper investments in Chile faced a real risk of expropriation. The center-left government of Salvador Allende followed through on some of its more extreme policy pronouncements, including nationalizing selected industries. By 1971, when the Allende government nationalized the El Teniente copper mine (in which Kennecott had a significant stake), Kennecott already had created a self-defense strategy. It eventually lost control of the mine, but it managed to extract a heavy price from the Chilean government in return.[32]

Kennecott in the 1960s was interested in expanding its mining holdings, but remained wary of making new investments that the state might eventually seize. The company thus embarked on a plan that minimized its risks by engaging other parties to share in them. The company did not finance the project itself, but sold a majority stake in the mine to the Chilean government—the sale proceeds partially funded the expansion—while keeping management of the mine under its control. Kennecott took out loans and insurance from U.S. government institutions and arranged financing through other foreign investors. By the time the expropriation was finally ordered, the company had laid the groundwork for legal action to gain further compensation.

These combined actions created an international network of interests that would be upset by any Chilean move toward nationalization and saddled its

government with some of the responsibility for the consequences of its decision. Thanks to this strategy and the network of interdependence that it created,
Kennecott was not the only interested party upset with Allende. The Chilean
government eventually agreed to compensate Kennecott for the loss and took on
the obligations to customers of Kennecott's former Chilean subsidiary.

## Joint Ventures

Joint ventures (JVs), when set up appropriately, can help protect foreign investments, especially if they are forged with a domestic partner. Integrating domestic
players into a foreign investment's supply chains and distribution systems has
the significant benefit of increasing the bargaining power of the foreign investor: government interference would have a negative effect on domestic economic
interests, which most governments would like to avoid.

The ideal structure of a joint venture and its aims can vary from country
to country. For instance, in Russia, foreign firms operating in strategic sectors
can meet certain obligations to gain lucrative strategic stakes and partnerships,
even if outright control is severely restricted. These include establishing channels for the transfer of desired technology and expertise to Russian specialists;
guaranteeing markets for Russian products; and assisting Russian firms in key
projects.

In this respect the experience of the aircraft maker Boeing is instruc-
tive. The U.S.-based company has long been active in Russia and maintains a
large Russian-staffed design and research bureau in Moscow. It is the major
buyer of Russian titanium, and works closely with Russian companies on the
production and marketing of the Sukhoi Superjet, a priority project for the
Russian government, which hopes it will make Russia a major player in the
global civilian aircraft market. Planned sales of Boeing aircraft to Russian
state carrier Aeroflot have occasionally been vulnerable to political tensions
between Moscow and Washington. Still, Boeing enjoys a durable relationship
with the Russian government and faces limited political risk to its business
there.

Joint ventures are not without risk; for example, a local JV partner with
government support can expropriate an investment. In addition, governments
sometimes make demands that a foreign firm cannot afford to satisfy, like transfers of intellectual property that would put the foreign investor at a competitive

disadvantage. In case of a regime change, having a previous JV with a business connected to the old regime can increase the risk of expropriation.

Another risk is reputational. A JV in a country with a poor human rights record, or with a partner that engages in questionable business practices, can burden a firm with enormous public relations problems within its home market. For instance, contracting local partners that used child labor was a serious issue for Western companies such as Nike in the mid-1990s. So while JVs can significantly reduce the risks of expropriations, this depends on the nature of the partner and requires significant due diligence both on the business conditions and the political stability of the country involved.

Another way to reduce the risk of expropriation is through structuring foreign investment contracts that work around the "obsolescing bargain" by reducing a government's incentive to expropriate. In the oil, gas, and other extractive industries, "profit-sharing" contracts have been developed that give foreign investors control of operations while ownership remains with the host nation. These kinds of contracts have been used both to ensure that governments do not nationalize companies to earn windfall profits when commodity prices increase and to avoid the politically thorny issue of resource nationalism.[33] These contracts are not foolproof: governments can and do change the terms. As we discussed above, this was a problem in Ecuador in 2007.

In manufacturing and in infrastructure building, some foreign investments have been structured as "build, operate, and transfer" contracts, whereby a foreign investor builds a greenfield plant (a brand-new facility), operates it for a number of years under specific tax and regulatory terms, and then transfers the operation to national or local ownership. This type of contract allows investors to earn a profit while ensuring that local governments have little incentive to interfere with an investment they will eventually inherit.

### Government Engagement, Financing, and Legal Recourse

Many developed states use bilateral investment treaties (BITs) to protect their investments abroad. These treaties protect against both direct and "creeping" expropriation and ensure that if an investment is expropriated, full compensation is paid. BITs also usually protect intellectual property and contractual terms. The number of such treaties has increased, and there are currently about four times as many BITs as there were a decade ago.[34] The United States and Canada have negotiated some of the most stringent BITs in terms of protecting against expropriations.

In addition, some countries have laws that allow their governments to retaliate if their companies' foreign direct investment is expropriated. In the United States, there is legislation that reduces U.S. aid to countries that expropriate without full compensation. There is also legislation that the U.S. government can use to ensure that its representatives in multilateral financial institutions like the IMF and World Bank veto loans to countries that expropriate U.S. investments. Yet, these rules are rarely enforced. The U.S. government has discretion to waive penalties against the expropriating government if a waiver serves U.S. "national interests."

Companies can also use creative financing to protect themselves against state seizure of their assets—by structuring an investment so that expropriation would damage that government's standing in capital markets. Kennecott's involvement in the Teniente mine reveals a variation on this strategy. Some companies use financing from local banks, increasing the default risks that expropriation poses for the host country's banking system. Other companies structure financing through international consortiums, using the backing of multilateral or governmental development agencies from several different countries. Any government that would seize that company's assets knows that it would risk making enemies in several countries at once.

Still other companies protect themselves with insurance and legal arbitration. These are usually considered last resorts, because they represent a corporation's public recognition that it cannot avoid the risk or negotiate it away. Both insurance and litigation are fraught with expropriation-related questions: What constitutes expropriation? How can laws and contracts be enforced? What constitutes fair compensation? Exxon and Conoco now find themselves in what will likely prove a long legal battle with the Venezuelan government over how much they will be paid for expropriated assets. Should Venezuela pay book value or the much higher market value?

Another reason that "creeping expropriations" are such a tricky problem: Legal distinctions between legitimate government actions and regulations meant to loosen investor control of their assets are exceptionally fine. This is the case with bovine spongiform encephalopathy (BSA), better known as "mad cow disease." In the mid-1990s, following an outbreak of this mass hypochondria–inducing affliction, the British government banned the use of meat from cow heads.

Few could argue that this wasn't sensible public policy, because the food industry's use of cow heads and spines had triggered the outbreak. But the companies that remove bones from cattle heads and sell the meat for processing into other food products faced a big problem: Though they had spent large sums of money to comply fully with British food-safety standards, their business had suddenly become illegal. The British government compensated companies like Pinnacle Meat Processors for some of their unsold stocks, but did not compensate them for the loss of equipment—or goodwill. Pinnacle Meats sued the British government in the courts of the European Commission of Human Rights, claiming that its business had effectively been expropriated.

The court found that the British government had the right to impose new health standards even if it meant significant losses for some companies.[35] This case had all the features of a "creeping" or indirect expropriation, but there was very little that Pinnacle Meats could do about it, underscoring the fact that governments continue to have considerable leeway in imposing taxes, regulations, and exercising their policing powers.

## The Future of Expropriations

Governments have a long history of interfering with private property. In 1429, the Mamluk sultan of Egypt expropriated the right of Egyptian traders to deal in spices in order to grant himself a royal monopoly.[36] The spice and pepper trade was enormously profitable at the time, and Egypt controlled some of the main trade routes between its European consumers and the Far Eastern production centers.[37] Historians continue to dispute the long-term effects of this expropriation, but it probably contributed to both Egypt's economic decline and its eventual conquest by the Ottoman Empire. Within 50 years of the sultan's decision, European states began to sail around Africa and trade directly with the Spice Islands, cutting out the politically and economically unreliable Egyptian middleman. In search of spices, Columbus sailed west to reach the Far East and found himself in the Americas.

Governments will continue to interfere in private property rights—though the forms of interference will change over time—and natural resource–rich countries will continue to prove exceptionally risky operating environments.

The combination of the developed world's thirst for resources and developing-world populism lurks just beneath the surface of many of today's expropriation stories. Many Russians believe that the West took advantage of Russia's post-Soviet weakness during the 1990s to strip the country of much of its natural wealth. NATO and the European Union fueled Russian anger by extending membership to countries along Russia's borders. Then global oil prices tripled. Flush with windfall profits, President Vladimir Putin developed a newly assertive foreign policy, feeding the sense of anti-Western grievance of many Russians to build on his government's domestic popularity.

Venezuelan president Hugo Chávez has long stoked Latin American resentment toward Washington to bolster his popularity. In the name of resistance to "imperialism," he began in 2004 to demand that U.S. and other foreign oil companies pay his government higher taxes and royalties. Meeting little resistance from multinationals operating within a supply-hungry global marketplace, he continues to push for more, using the new profits to tighten his control on domestic political power. Presidents Rafael Correa of Ecuador and Evo Morales of Bolivia have followed much the same model.

Governments facing internal challenges to their legitimacy are among the most likely to resort to expropriation, seizing foreign assets in the name of their peoples to enhance their nationalist credentials. In some cases, this strategy will make a bad economic situation much worse. Zimbabwe's president Robert Mugabe, in power since 1980, once presided over a relatively trade-friendly government. But by the late 1990s, his failure to tackle unemployment and to lift millions of black Zimbabweans from poverty threatened his political survival. To profit from lingering racial tensions and rebuild his popular support, he ordered a large-scale state seizure of white-owned land.

The strategy worked for Mugabe—but not for Zimbabwe. The country's economy, once among Africa's strongest, contracted by more than 30%, because the government's arbitrary and politicized treatment of property rights drove investors from the country. Inflation spiraled, the stock market plummeted, and the country's economy is now in ruins. Russia, Venezuela, and other resource nationalizers are highly unlikely to suffer such dire consequences any time soon. High oil prices will continue to buoy their economic growth rates. But Zimbabwe's fate offers warnings for all these countries.

Zimbabwe's downward spiral explains why South Africa's government has taken such pains to assure foreigners that it will not follow Mugabe's lead. As investment dollars move elsewhere, problems develop—even for the oil-rich nationalizers. Russia continues to suffer from infrastructure problems that make it extraordinarily expensive to move energy to market. All of its energy exports to China, for example, continue to move by rail, a costly and inefficient way of doing business.

In Venezuela, the state oil firm PDVSA once pumped substantially more oil than it does now. A strike in 2002 and 2003 by oil workers, angry over Chávez's heavy-handed policies, induced the president to fire thousands of them—including a large percentage of the company's most experienced and talented engineers. The company has not recovered. Venezuela's problem is not limited to oil. In 2002, Chávez ordered that land be redistributed to squatters and the unemployed, who would then grow the food needed to feed Venezuela. But the haphazard way in which the program has been implemented has damaged Venezuela's economy. The country is now more dependent on food imports than before, because farmers, fearful that their land could be seized at any moment, have been unwilling to plant crops they may not be allowed to harvest.

Though most corporate decision makers (and the financial press) consider expropriations the most dramatic form of risk that companies face, regulatory risk can pose greater (if more subtle) threats to the profits (and sometimes the survival) of companies doing business overseas. That's the subject of our next chapter.

# Regulatory Risk

## EIGHT

You have to learn the rules of the game. And then
you have to play better than anyone else.
—Albert Einstein

As any good investor knows, the commonly used adage "buy when there is blood in the streets" applies not only to literal times of bloodletting but also to metaphorical ones. It is best to buy cheap assets in the wake of some crisis. With this in mind, in August 2003 the Dallas-based private equity firm Lone Star Funds believed it had found an unusually promising investment deal in South Korea. The country's macroeconomic conditions were sound, but twin economic shocks—the 1997 Asian financial crisis and a 2002 credit card crisis— had inflicted heavy damage on local businesses in the financial and industrial sectors. Overwhelmed by bad debt, thousands of Korean firms faced insolvency. Lone Star determined that the Korea Exchange Bank (KEB), the country's only foreign exchange bank, provided a great opportunity to enter the Korean financial market.

Many other Korean firms were sold, merged, or simply left to collapse, but Lone Star bought KEB for $1.3 billion, injecting new capital into the troubled financial institution and assuming management control. Under Lone Star's guidance, the bank was restructured and put on a path to profitability.

At the same time, the Korean financial sector and the economy in general began to recover, generating substantial profits for private equity investors who had entered the market a few years earlier. For private equity firms, this story looks (so far) like a textbook example of intelligent investment. Invest in distressed assets like KEB, manage them back to health, and then (hopefully) sell them at a significantly higher price during a period of promising economic growth.

Yet with the economy recovering, South Korean attitudes toward foreign investors began to sour. Local media began to run stories alleging that foreign investors were reaping enormous and unfair profits. Local attitudes toward foreign private equity investors shifted from gratitude toward economic saviors to anger at greedy profiteers.

In 2005 Lone Star decided to sell its KEB stake, offering its majority share holdings to a Korean bank, Kookmin Bank, for $6 billion. Lone Star decided to use its Belgian subsidiary to transact the bank sales to take advantage of a bilateral tax treaty to recoup $4.5 billion in profit from the sale tax-free. There was nothing illegal or unethical about the move. After all, without going into arcane details of tax law, tax treaties are meant to be used, and Lone Star did have a Belgian subsidiary.

Yet given the state of public opinion, the decision triggered a storm of public outrage—and multiple government and regulatory investigations into Lone Star. These investigations were extensive; they did not limit themselves to the proposed sale of KEB to Kookmin, but examined the legality of Lone Star's original deal to buy KEB. Even the Korean government officials who had approved the sale were questioned.

Thus began a sweeping government effort to find fault with Lone Star and to prevent the company from recouping this profit. Government prosecutors ultimately charged the executives of Lone Star and Korea Exchange Bank with illegal acquisition of the bank, collusion, stock manipulation, and tax evasion, locking the financial firms into multiple drawn-out legal battles.

Korean financial regulators blocked any approval for Lone Star to sell its management control of KEB as long as court proceedings continued. The court battles have already derailed two deals to sell KEB, first to South Korea's Kookmin Bank and then to Singapore's DBS, and is currently threatening to disrupt a third with HSBC.

The Lone Star case illustrates the kind of treatment that foreign firms can encounter in overseas markets. The problem may be getting worse. Ironically, some of the countries that have benefited most from globalization (including the United States) have exhibited a growing tendency toward government action against foreign firms. A closer look suggests a number of concerns driving the developed world's reaction against globalization: fear that national identity will fade, anxiety over immigration, growing unemployment in formerly dominant sectors, and the rise of new economic powers (e.g., China and India). In the developing world, corruption, weak governing institutions, and concern for protecting noncompetitive indigenous industrial sectors still drive much of the discriminatory actions against multinational corporations.

Most countries have begun resorting to more subtle forms of discrimination against multinational corporations, in order to avoid the economic, legal, and diplomatic retaliation that accompanies blatant interference. The most pervasive and subtle forms of government interference with trade and foreign investment can be broadly labeled "regulatory discrimination." Especially for corporations that invest in multiple countries, monitoring and complying with the varying regulatory environments across the globe can be both complicated and costly. Because they are so prevalent, and also difficult to observe and mitigate, regulatory risks pose as least as great a threat to multinational corporations' operations abroad as do terrorism, natural disasters, country risks, and other economic risks.[1]

Varying government agencies use regulatory, legalistic, procedural, and prosecutorial means to favor domestic firms over outside companies or inflict additional costs on foreign corporations, as in Lone Star's case. We briefly discussed in the chapter on expropriations how it is often difficult to distinguish between legitimate government concerns regarding regulation and actual use of regulatory measures as a politically based instrument meant to discriminate against specific investors, corporations, NGOs, or other governments operating within a country.

One trouble with regulatory risks is that they involve governments that have both the sophistication and the need to actively regulate their economies and societies. This is partly because more sophisticated economies need to be integrated into the global economy if growth levels are to be maintained for the longer term. At the same time, these governments have the legal and regulatory capacity to selectively interfere with foreign investments and trade in a way that favors domestic interests without attracting too much negative publicity. In countries with relatively strong and stable state institutions, traditional political risks like expropriations, civil strife, and breaches of contract remain of some concern, but the more significant risks usually come from more subtle forms of discrimination.[2]

### Analyzing Regulatory Risks

To understand regulations and their implications, most corporations need experienced legal counsel. Without compliance departments, most companies and organizations would be unable to deal with the web of complexity created by most regulatory frameworks. Yet without understanding the political background that drives a government toward regulatory changes, it is very hard to pinpoint the source of regulatory risks.

Poland's regulatory climate provides a useful example. Since the fall of its Communist regime in 1989, Poland has enjoyed a foreign-investor-friendly reputation. Yet between 2006 and 2007, a populist government led by the Law and Justice Party (PiS) embarked on a significant change of course. Ideologically, PiS was a statist party, motivated by a deep suspicion of any devolution of centralized power and a philosophical opposition to privatization and deregulation. PiS's leaders viewed both of these processes as fostering corruption and the entrenchment of post-Communist elites, unless they were closely monitored by police, prosecutors, and other organs of state control.

PiS therefore focused on creating a new Anti-Corruption Office (ACO) and a revamped Financial Supervisory Commission (FSC). Neither regulatory body was autonomous. The FSC, while superficially resembling the U.K. single market regulator model (where one regulatory body is in charge of all capital markets regulation), was actually quite different, in that it merged the previously autonomous insurance, banking, and securities watchdogs into a single board, four of whose seven members could be replaced by the prime minister (three) or the president (one). Poland at the time was run by the identical twin Kaczyński brothers (Jaroslaw served as the PiS prime minister and Lech as Polish president), and it was clear that the new regulatory body would follow the government agenda.

But most of the party's agenda was fueled by resentment. The Kaczyński brothers reached the pinnacle of political power by arguing that most of the large privatizations enacted during the decade and a half that followed the fall of the Communist regime (especially in the financial sector) were either botched or completely corrupt. This was a crucial element of PiS's legitimizing myth, which presented Lech and Jaroslaw Kaczyński as tough "sheriffs" who would drive the crooks from their privileged positions and impose clean government.

In addition, PiS was deeply tied to certain factions of the labor movement. As such, it had a strong electoral incentive to politically favor state employees and their unions. Most of the party's policies were thus aimed at strengthening the control of the state and appointing loyalists in regulatory posts and state-owned enterprises, regardless of competence. This was coupled with a near-total halt to the privatization of large state-owned enterprises during 2006, and an emphasis on increased scrutiny of foreign direct investments.

The PiS government lasted just two years. Foreign direct investment inflows remained strong during the period, but anecdotal evidence suggests that perceptions of political and regulatory risk kept some investors sidelined or looking for opportunities elsewhere. To give one example, many companies were irritated by the PiS's vetting law, which required all board members of publicly listed companies to disclose any ties with the Communist-era secret police (and perhaps other foreign intelligence agencies as well—legal interpretations differ). All of those vetted (under some definitions, up to 700,000 professionals, including many foreign executives) faced the prospect of providing an exhaustive disclosure of personal financial assets, updated yearly.[3]

There are a number of angles in this story that are worth a second look. First, the political orientation of the government matters a great deal. Populist governments (left or right) with ties to large labor movements that use anticorruption platforms to build popular support generally favor regulatory changes that can make doing business more difficult.

Second, the strength and autonomy of local regulatory institutions—and their ability to withstand government pressure—matters, as well. In Britain or the United States, the government cannot decide on political grounds which bank or corporation should receive regulatory scrutiny or face closure. In part, this is because these countries have enacted laws that explicitly separate regulatory bodies from the executive branch of government, especially in the financial services sector. In South Korea, Poland, and Russia, regulatory institutions have far less independence from the government's political and policy agendas.

## Domestic Political Agendas

From the 1960s to at least the 1990s, rising East Asian economic powers like Japan, South Korea, and Taiwan implemented economic development policies that emphasized symbiotic government-business relationships. Collectively, they created an economic "incubator" environment for local firms in many strategic sectors until the companies became competitive in international markets. This came to be known as the "developmental model." In Japan, for example, for much of the postwar era, the ruling Liberal Democratic Party (LDP) offered firms contracts or preferential regulatory environments in exchange for financial support and resources for the LDP's electoral/political machines. These exchanges of policy and a supportive regulatory environment were the basis for the extraordinarily pro-producer economic environment that successive LDP governments refined from 1955 onward. In many sectors, firms were restricted from competing with one another on price, limits on product variety were imposed, and market entry was circumscribed. In combination, these policies created what were essentially government-enforced cartels, sometimes formal and sometimes informal. Institutionally, regulators in this environment were highly centralized, and cross-functional comprehensive agencies played a powerful role in designing industry strategy. The regulatory bureaucracy was (and is) relatively free from political (notably, legislative) oversight, so that there is little public accountability or transparency, but also little political meddling. Outsiders were at a distinct disadvantage when trying to enter such sectors.[4]

In developing countries, the chosen economic policies almost always play a large role in determining the kind of regulations that are imposed. For instance, China's authoritarian politics, coupled with an emphasis on developing a high-tech manufacturing base, ensure that China often uses regulations to abrogate Western intellectual property rights. In 2004, the Patent Re-examination Board of the State Intellectual Property Office of the People's Republic of China revoked both Pfizer's patent protection for chemical compounds used in Viagra and GlaxoSmithKline's patent for a diabetes drug. This opened the opportunity for China's 12 pharmaceutical companies to develop competing alternatives to these popular drugs. Many outside observers saw this move as part of the Chinese agency's dedicated effort to nurture China's still immature pharmaceutical sector at the cost of foreign patents and profits.[5]

In countries with competitive political systems, analysis of elections and incoming governments' agendas can provide a good sense of the regulations that foreign firms can expect to face.[6] The election of President Evo Morales in Bolivia in December 2005 quickly shifted the government's political disposition and threatened foreign investment. The Bolivian Congress passed an energy law that imposed an additional 32% tax on production on top of existing

18% royalties and required all companies to renegotiate contracts with the state within six months or face expulsion. The government also nationalized natural resources and took charge of sales. The state would pay foreign companies for their services by offering up to 50% of the value of production. The new Bolivian government did this to capture greater energy-related revenues from the hydro-carbon sector, which helped pay for its social welfare programs.

Electoral politics and public sentiment are important issues for regulatory regimes in both emerging and developed states. There is some risk of increased discriminatory regulation in the United States in the coming years. Job losses in the manufacturing sector and heightened anxiety over national security have intensified debates over trade policy and foreign investment in American assets. Lawmakers in both political parties have responded to growing public demand for protection by crafting legislation intended to slow the pace at which trade deficits mount, American jobs move overseas, and foreign firms acquire U.S.-owned companies and other assets.

No commercial relationship generates more friction in Washington than trade relations with China. Between 2000 and 2006, bilateral trade flows grew from about $116 billion to just shy of $343 billion. China needs U.S. consumers to spend freely, as the United States is China's largest foreign market. About one-fifth of China's exports are now destined for the United States,[7] and Americans draw about 40% of their consumer goods from China.[8]

But some in the United States charge that low-cost manufacturing in China kills American jobs and that state manipulation of China's currency aggravates an exploding bilateral trade deficit that pushed past $256 billion in 2007.[9] Some American companies operating in China insist that Beijing refuses to enforce protections of their intellectual property rights.

Hence the potential political impact on trade relations of cough syrup. In May 2007, at least 100 Panamanians died after ingesting cough syrup containing a chemical that can produce kidney failure, which had been shipped from China by manufacturers looking to cut corners and maximize profits. The U.S. Food and Drug Administration responded by yanking thousands of boxes of Chinese-made toothpaste made with the same chemical from U.S. store shelves. Around the same time, hundreds of American pets died after eating Chinese-manufactured pet food contaminated with a toxic chemical. In June 2007, the U.S. government ordered the recall of nearly 450,000 tires imported from China because of concerns they might shred during highway driving. Every toy recalled by the U.S. Consumer Product Safety Commission in the first half of 2007 was made in China.

Imagine the impact on U.S.-Chinese political and trade relations—arguably the most important bilateral relationship in the world—if dozens of Americans suddenly died after ingesting toothpaste or cough syrup imported from China. American lawmakers would waste no time in attacking the Chinese government for corruption and criminal negligence.

Panic often drives regulation. The U.S. Sarbanes-Oxley Act of 2002 was imposed in the aftermath of a series of scandals and bankruptcies at companies such as Enron and WorldCom. By many accounts, the Sarbanes-Oxley Act is a problematic piece of regulation. An oft-cited study by Financial Executives International (FEI) estimated that in 2006, total average cost for compliance with the core elements to the act (Section 404) was $2.9 million per company.

The U.S. Congress enacted Sarbanes-Oxley to prevent fraud. Yet the new law has plainly made it harder and more expensive for some types of medium-sized corporations to comply with financial disclosure regulations. An increasing number of foreign companies have chosen not to list their stocks on U.S.-based stock exchanges, preferring to list in Europe or other places with fewer complex disclosure rules. This in turn has impacted the competitiveness of U.S.-based financial markets, with costs for the U.S. economy. It is a cautionary tale of how politicians faced with media-fueled public demand to "do something" often have incentive to impose regulations whose implications are not fully thought out or understood.

Foreign policy priorities and national security challenges also influence regulatory treatment of overseas firms. The Exon-Florio Amendment and the Committee on Foreign Investment in the United States (CFIUS)—examples of U.S. regulatory oversight that can make foreign investment in sectors related to "national security" more difficult—illustrate how foreign firms often face a level of scrutiny that domestic firms do not. Exon-Florio was meant to provide an objective, nonpartisan mechanism to review and, if the president finds it necessary, to restrict or prohibit foreign investment that may threaten U.S. national security. But the more onerous review process has also created an extra step in the acquisition of U.S. firms that has thwarted some foreign firms and driven others away.

The Israeli company Check Point Software Technologies Ltd. gave up its $225 million deal to acquire U.S. software company Sourcefire Inc., a network security company whose clients include U.S. intelligence agencies, once Check Point's leadership realized that CFIUS would conduct a second round of investigations into the firm before ruling on the deal. Before a ruling was announced, the company broke off the deal. CFIUS has since blocked the acquisition of U.S.-based 3Com by the Chinese firm Huawei Technologies and Bain Capital. The U.S. view of China as a long-term rival that refuses to fully enforce intellectual property rights protections for U.S. and other non-Chinese companies leads the U.S. government to carefully scrutinize any acquisition by Chinese firms in the national security and critical infrastructure realm.

**Emerging Statist Players**

Regulatory agendas could also become more aggressive in core emerging market countries. A growing number of successful, global multinational corporations are based outside the G-7 "wealthy" countries. This dynamic could potentially put the governments of these countries at odds with their G-7 counterparts, particularly if they decide that their companies are not receiving fair treatment and access to markets in developed countries—and that they are in a position to do something about it.

Today's fastest-growing emerging market countries—China, India, Russia, Brazil, Mexico, Turkey, and others—have produced a new generation of multinational companies capable of competing in foreign markets with established international firms. According to a May 2006 report by the Boston Consulting Group, the 100 fastest-globalizing EM-based companies generated combined annual revenue of $715 billion in 2005. These firms are growing at an average annual rate of 24%, "ten times as fast as the GDP of the United States, 24 times that of Japan, and 34 times that of Germany." Collectively, they are expected to double their international revenue by 2010.[10]

Some of these companies are state-owned or controlled, and many of the private ones have very close ties to their home-country governments. Their growing influence is most obvious in the energy sector; as much as 90% of the world's oil and gas reserves are now controlled by national oil companies. In many cases, the interests of these state-related energy multinationals are closely aligned with those of their governments. Whether those interests diverge over the next several years as more of these enterprises seek capital via overseas stock market listings remains to be seen. But over the next generation, these increasingly competitive companies will shift the balance of international corporate power away from established multinationals. The governments of these emerging market countries, flush with the revenue generated by these companies' successes, could eventually decide that the current global economic system does not serve their interests and challenge its legitimacy. For example, the rise of state-owned multinationals will almost certainly drive changes in the World Trade Organization's rules on subsidies and the ways in which charges of unfair trade practices are resolved.

A number of such countries—including Russia, India, and China—have intensified their regulatory scrutiny of inward foreign direct investment and merger and acquisition activity based on political and national-security grounds.[11] Regardless of the pretext, these measures are often intended to shield uncompetitive domestic industries and firms and to protect lucrative natural resources. These pressures are pushing governments to consider a variety of measures to tighten assessment of foreign direct investment flows, including introducing legislation fencing off perceived strategic sectors—such as defense industries and critical infrastructure—from foreign bidders.

### Local Politics

Politics need not have international or even national implications to influence the regulatory climate, because in many countries—particularly federal states like Germany, the United States, and India—local and regional governments wield significant influence over taxation rate agreements, business permits and other elements of regulatory power. Given that these governments are elected, they face significant media, public, and interest group pressures that come into play when regulation is enacted and implemented.

When Wal-Mart took steps in 2007 to enter the Indian retail market, it faced a mixed reaction in the country. A partnership signed in August 2007 with local company Bharti Enterprises to enter the wholesale market was met with a strongly negative reaction from antiforeign direct investment groups, retail associations, and local retailers afraid of the loss of their livelihoods at the hands of giant retailers. Borrowing from Gandhi's 1947 "Quit India" campaign, these groups launched a "Quit Retail" protest against the deal in August 2007.

Wal-Mart will continue to move into India, but local concerns are likely to factor into the pace and scale with which it penetrates the market. For foreign direct investors, understanding regional and local political dynamics in the areas where they operate can be as important as understanding the national political climate. This understanding can work both ways: many organizations in India do want the retail market opened up to larger corporations and foreign direct investment. The interest of different Indian states to foreign direct investment also varies widely.

Federal officials are often the main boosters for increased foreign direct investment, but regional and local authorities have the same incentive to see outside groups invest in their areas. For foreign investors, this interest creates opportunities, but it also comes with responsibilities and risks—many related to local employment, tax payments, and technology infusion. Local officials often expect that foreign direct investment will directly benefit them and their political allies. Failure to understand the various expectations of officials at the outset and to shape investment plans accordingly can lead to problems over the long term. Federal officials will sometimes intervene on investors' behalf, but in many cases they have good reason to side with the local leaders.

Another element of risk for foreign investors: state and local governments change, and these changes sometimes empower political leaders with very different attitudes than their predecessors toward foreigners and their money. The Ford Motor Company discovered in 1998 that a new government in Brazil's Rio Grande do Sul state had revoked the previous administration's offer of tax incentives. The new governor then took heavy criticism from those communities that would have benefited from a Ford facility, especially after Ford reached agreement with another state to build its plant there.

Beyond governments, nongovernmental entities—advocacy groups, unions, and trade organizations, among others—are often important players in the foreign investment process. The same issues that sometimes unite these groups in opposition to the actions and plans of some domestic companies—labor issues, pro-competition or protectionist activism, environmental concerns, and protection of impoverished or ethnic minorities—can provoke them to take similar stands against foreign investors. Their ability to make their case with sympathetic lawmakers at the local and federal levels can give them considerable sway over investment decisions.

## Politicized Regulatory Institutions

In September 2006, the Russian Federal Service for the Oversight of Natural Resources called for a halt of construction for the Shell-operated Sakhalin-II liquefied natural gas project. The environmental regulatory agency cited damage to salmon-bearing rivers, excessive logging, and irreversibly disrupted ecosystems on Sakhalin Island that would cost billions to repair. Shell denied the violations, but the Russian government used threats to revoke the company's environmental license to pressure Shell to hand over management control to Russia's state-owned Gazprom.

Was the Russian government using regulatory bodies for political purposes? Shell's suspicions were confirmed when President Vladimir Putin attended the Moscow signing of the new agreement that transferred management control from Shell to Gazprom and announced that environmental problems with the Sakhalin II project had been inexplicably resolved. Because individual regulators often enjoy a certain level of discretion to determine whether firms are in compliance, some regulatory authorities have abused this power to apply pressure on foreign companies. The more relevant point is that the Russian Federal Service for the Oversight of Natural Resources is, like many Russian regulatory institutions, strongly influenced by the Kremlin.

Firms that have interests in countries with weak institutions, whether these are courts or regulatory bodies, are much more exposed to political risk. Self-interested regulators discriminating against foreign actors constitute one scenario. When regulators have considerable discretionary power over the economy with little oversight, there is always the temptation to abuse that power for private gain. They are especially vulnerable to opportunistic businesses that are willing to pay for political favors to get ahead. This can happen through direct payoffs or, more broadly, where the entire regulatory authority is skewed to favor certain local interest groups—a phenomenon called "bureaucratic capture."[12] The payoffs can range from direct monetary payments for favors to more subtle forms, such as promises of lucrative jobs after retirement.[13]

In Mexico, entrepreneur Carlos Slim successfully "captured" his country's telecommunication sector and the officials who oversaw the industry. In 1990, Mexican president Carlos Salinas announced his decision to deregulate and privatize Mexico's telecommunication sector as part of a broader market-oriented reform program. Teléfonos de México (Telmex), which held a monopoly over telephone services, went up for privatization. Slim successfully purchased the fixed lines, with a guarantee of exclusivity in the long-distance call market for six years. With this steady stream of revenue, Slim subsidized the local calling market and undercut the price of his competitors, thanks to effective lobbying efforts. He controlled the telecommunication agencies by putting allies in key leadership roles. Former Telmex executives oversaw the design of the company's concession title, and his company's lawyers carefully reviewed the Telecommunications General Law during the drafting to ensure Slim's interests were protected. With his influence, Slim also suppressed the Federal Competition Commission's efforts to liberalize the telecommunication market in federal tribunals (particularly between 1997 and 2002). On the back of this skillful lobbying and "bureaucratic capture," Slim built a regional telecommunications empire.

Another source of regulatory discrimination can be a regulatory authority that is dysfunctional because it lacks the talent, the training, the institutional infrastructure, and/or authority to effectively manage the economy. In other cases, such as China's, the authorities and division of labor are poorly delineated between agencies, creating a situation in which many organizations are competing for influence and sometimes moving at cross purposes. In the Chinese telecom sector, in addition to one regulatory body inside the Ministry of Information Industry (MII), there are at least four national and many local government bodies that play a role in the regulation process.[14] Fragmented and competing, the multiple regulating organizations inevitably create new sets of regulatory risk.

In Peru in 1999, the Engelhard Corporation purchased Peruvian gold and exported it to a U.S. refinery, thereby becoming eligible to receive Peru's value-added tax (VAT) refund. Although its refund was legitimate, the Peruvian tax authority refused to return the company's funds even when auditors and the country's courts ordered repayment. Rather than repay, the tax authority seized more than $30 million in Engelhard's assets and tax refunds without any evidence of wrongdoing. On April 28, 2004, the Constitutional Court ruled that Engelhard's rights had been violated. The Peruvian authorities appealed the Constitutional Court ruling. On May 28, the Fifth Civil Chamber of the Superior Court was assigned to decide the appeal. The Superior Court had 20 business days to make a decision. To date, the Superior Court has not ruled or even rendered oral arguments in the case.[15]

This is how competing government institutions can produce chaos. The Peruvian government's tax authority is known for frequently violating legal foreign contracts and unlawfully or retroactively changing tax assessments. In many cases, Peruvian courts have ruled against the tax regulators' decisions. But the tax authority has circumvented court rulings and used the appeals process to prevent the courts and foreign businesses from interfering with the agency's rulings.[16]

### Foreign Firms' Vulnerability to Regulatory Discrimination

Different types of firms have different types of regulatory vulnerability. A bank and a meatpacking corporation face radically different regulations (and regulatory costs), no matter where they invest. They also face entirely different levels of risk that a government will interfere (through regulatory or other measures) in their operations.

A dominant approach to studying firm vulnerability is Obsolescent Bargaining Theory. Raymond Vernon, a leading proponent, argues that when a host government and a multinational corporation sit down to bargain, the government has resources that it cannot access unless and until an multinational invests in them and provides assistance.[17] This is why governments are initially at a relative disadvantage: The corporation has the flexibility to go elsewhere in search of more favorable investment terms.

To attract these firms, the government offers the firm incentives (like tax breaks and infrastructure support) to mitigate investment risks. Once the investment has had a period of successful operation, however, the perceived risk to the firm drops and the host country begins to ask why the multinational corporation is generating such large profits. The multinational's valuable technology has now been transferred or made available in the open market, and locals have successfully adopted many of the foreign firm's management techniques.[18] In the meantime, national priorities may have changed. New political leaders may have assumed power. Voters may have developed new expectations about the fair division of labor and profits between a foreign firm and local communities. The political landscape has changed, but the corporation has now invested substantial amounts of capital into a money-making project that it wants to continue running.[19] The advantage has now shifted to the government, which can use its newfound leverage to renegotiate contracts, impose higher taxes, expropriate assets, or seize income streams from the firm.[20] The implication is that a firm, once heavily invested in a host country, has little leverage to do anything except move its production elsewhere. But this will not be a rational and cost-effective decision until the cost of discrimination exceeds the cost of moving.

This conceptual approach to firm vulnerability is not without problems. A closer look suggests that the relationship between host government and foreign investments is not necessarily this asymmetric. First, the basic assumption of obsolescent bargaining theory, that international firms have heavy up-front sunk costs and are immobile once invested in the host country, may apply to mining or infrastructure companies, but is not so well suited to light or technology-based manufacturing industries. The investments are not so large that it would be difficult for these firms to move production if they face regulatory threats.[21] In addition, in some industries (e.g., software and manufacturing), technology, managerial skills, and know-how are often complex and may be beyond the capacity of local workers to absorb. Therefore, the shift in leverage toward the host government may take far longer.

Product-based industries are more nimble and flexible than extractive industries and can more easily counteract government discrimination to mitigate risks and costs. Manufacturing firms "have a good deal more flexibility and control than extractive investors....They can move to a new activity such as export, begin more complex manufacturing, add more value locally, manufacture new products, or incorporate additional technology to counter government requests."[22]

Obsolescent bargaining theory also assumes that multinational corporations are powerless once invested in host countries. But corporations, knowing that host countries may have poor property rights, interventionist tendencies, or weak rule of law, often actively lobby politicians and use their influence to pressure governments to develop regulations and laws to protect their foreign investments.[23] Moreover, investors rarely face governments alone, but increase their leverage by pooling their efforts with domestic and international partners (coalitions of investors) that have a vested interest in maintaining a supportive business environment.[24] Thus, firm vulnerability can also be gauged by how linked international firms are to domestic partners, influential companies, other foreign investors, and international organizations (e.g., World Bank, IMF) with leverage over the host country.

Yet many governments, fully capable of accepting loans from international institutions, will resist pressure from them on the treatment of foreign investors. One recent study found that there is a specific risk of negative policy and regulatory changes impacting foreign investments, especially in electricity and infrastructure, in countries where multilateral institutions are involved in lending.[25]

Many multinational institutions lend to countries with the explicit requirement of macroeconomic policy reforms, such as balanced budgets and reduced inflation. These types of reforms are often politically costly and considered illegitimate. In Latin American countries where the IMF pushed for liberalization during the 1990s—especially in states with populist political leaders like Venezuela, Ecuador, and Argentina—many argue that this pressure amounts to unwelcome meddling in their domestic politics. The study we cite[26] looked at 1,400 private investments in 85 countries between 1990 and 2001 and found that in countries where the influence of multilateral investment agencies and their requirements for reforms are seen as illegitimate, there is a higher propensity for policy changes that negatively impact foreign investors.

### Mitigating Regulatory Risks

The Russian government's attitude toward its country's oil sector has undergone a radical change. For a decade, the government had been content to allow private domestic and foreign operators to exploit Russia's oil and gas wealth. But in mid-2003, it began to shut down this access in favor of greater state control, and foreign operators interested in acquiring domestic oil companies faced unprecedented scrutiny. As in the case of Shell's Sakhalin Island project, regulatory agencies became the Kremlin's weapon of choice.

The Russian government still recognized the need for foreign capital, technology, and expertise to help develop new oil and gas deposits in the country, as well as to help with Russian companies' expansion abroad. Sensitive to these concerns, ConocoPhillips sought a minor stake in the oil market. It initially pursued a 7.6% stake in Lukoil, with the option to buy more shares—ConocoPhillips now owns 20% of the Russian company. This was shy of the 25%-plus-one share required to exercise veto power over company decisions. Additionally, the company kept a line open to the government, making sure officials were informed of its intentions. ConocoPhillips CEO Jim Mulva met with President Vladimir Putin in 2004 as the deal was being discussed and gained Putin's public approval of the share purchase. In sum, one important mitigation strategy is to partner with either state-owned corporations or private companies that have good relations with the government, making sure that senior decision makers are kept in the loop.

Another mitigation strategy is to use the Build-Operate-Transfer model, especially in the case of infrastructure projects. The private international firm takes control of a project, builds it, and operates it over a period of time to recoup its costs. The government (or domestic utility distribution company, in the case of a utility project) agrees to buy the output from the project at some fixed and pre-agreed price. Then the project is transferred to the government or to a domestic partner. This arrangement has been used to build large infra-structure projects, such as water treatment plants in Australia and Malaysia, as well as sewage treatment plants in Chile and New Zealand. It has gained wide popularity because it shares the risk between the local government and the international partner, and all participants have a vested interest in the success of the project.

In addition to local allies, there are international financial partners that can provide leverage for foreign investors and better protect investments vis-à-vis host governments. With global finance critical to even the most isolated states, the backing of these key international players may offset a government's tendency to misbehave for fear of losing access to international financial markets. The problem with regulatory risks, of course, is that they are not as easy to prove as other, more evident political risks, such as direct expropriation or civil war. In other words, claims of regulatory discrimination often end up in court. Courts can take a long time to render unchallengeable verdicts and are generally an option of last resort.

In the end, national governments' attitudes toward "national champions" still matter a great deal. In February 2006, the German utility E.ON launched a takeover bid for the Spanish utility Endesa. The bid was quickly approved by the European Commission, the EU's primary competition authority.

The Spanish government, eager to keep Endesa in Spanish hands, responded by passing a law that granted its national regulator more powers to block take-overs by foreign companies. The commission protested that this new law violated European Community law by granting the national regulator powers that it should not have. The Spanish government also actively sought to persuade Spanish firms to buy Endesa, or to take minority stakes in the company, and attempted to hive off the assets of most importance to E.ON. The German firm opted to abandon the deal.

The Spanish government's active involvement in trying to influence the commercial terms and the parties to the transaction is not uncommon in Europe. In a highly publicized matter the year before, Banca d'Italia chief Antonio Fazio allegedly sought to prevent the Dutch bank ABN-AMRO from acquiring Banca Antonveneta by assisting an Italian firm, whose chief executive he was close to, to buy the Italian bank.

The complex regulatory structure that gave Italy's national bank wide-ranging regulatory jurisdiction provided Fazio with a useful tool. The special Spanish law intended to block the E.ON takeover amounted to an attempt to create a similar option for Spanish officials. Hungary has created a law designed to prevent outside takeover of its leading energy company, MOL.

The use of arcane regulatory tools or the passage of transaction-specific laws represents an effort to shape transactions to advance certain political objectives. While Western European countries are hardly emerging markets, competition policy there is still in flux as the European Commission continues to try to bolster its institutional capacity. The commission depends heavily on political support from member states to implement its rules. Thus, the politics of competence building affect how significant a role the commission can play in countering the sort of actions seen in Spain and Italy. This in turn becomes an important commercial variable.

In the ABN-AMRO–Banca Antonveneta case, the commission took a hands-off approach, hoping to prompt a political shift in Italy without giving domestic political figures an opportunity to attack the commission. In the Spanish case, where the law was enacted after the proposed takeover, the commission was more aggressive. In March 2007, the commission decided to refer the matter to the European Court of Justice—a far weightier step.

In April 2007, E.ON formally ended its effort to buy Endesa, and instead announced that, along with the Italian energy firm Enel and the Spanish construction consortium Acciona, it would acquire a minority stake. By contrast, Antonio Fazio was eventually forced to resign over disclosures that emerged in the course of the deal, and ABN-AMRO was eventually successful in its acquisition strategy.

Ultimately, regulatory changes can create opportunities as well as risks. When new regulations are drafted, a company well positioned to understand the who, what, when, and why behind a proposed change can use these insights to develop a competitive advantage. In Brazil in 2007 the Lula government began to strengthen the autonomy of telecommunication, power, and oil and gas regulatory agencies. It appointed more professional technocrats and signaled that it was prepared to accept legislative changes to the regulatory agencies that made them less susceptible to government interference. Measures included separate funding for the agencies and more public transparency.

Why the change in the Lula government's approach to regulation? Strong economic growth has increased the risk that Brazil's economy is expanding faster than its roads, ports, electricity grid, and energy infrastructure. As a result, bottlenecks may limit the pace of future economic growth. The popularity of Lula and his government depends on their ability to deliver a rising standard of living for the country. This future prosperity will depend on greater investment, much of it from abroad, in Brazil's infrastructure. The government is finally taking steps that potential foreign direct investors have been wanting for a long time—ensuring that the regulatory agencies relevant for key infrastructure projects are better funded and staffed and more autonomous. While Brazil is on a positive regulatory trajectory, taking advantage of improving environments like this requires a great deal of attention to the currents of regulatory politics. Some countries and subregions are improving, others are getting worse. The larger point is that they are almost all dynamic in one direction or the other.

## NINE

# Reporting and Warning

Information is a source of learning. But unless it is
organized, processed, and available to the right
people in a format for decision making,
it is a burden, not a benefit.
—William Pollard

The year 1683 represents the high-water mark of Ottoman expansion, the second
Siege of Vienna[1]—the last time the Ottoman Empire had a real chance of con-
quering Central Europe.

The failure of the Ottoman Empire to conquer Vienna, the capital of the
Habsburg Empire, signaled the slow decline of the Ottoman Empire. The
Ottomans were never again to mount a genuine threat to a European power. Yet
the Ottoman failure to take Vienna was a close call.

There are many reasons why the Ottomans nearly succeeded at Vienna. The
Habsburg Empire, the main European power facing the Ottoman armies, repeatedly ignored warnings of pending invasion and were caught unprepared when
it came.

There had been ample warning that the Ottomans would soon attack. The
first signs were the increasingly aggressive demands by Sultan Mehmed IV during negotiations ostensibly meant to extend a peace treaty between the two
empires. The sultan employed this as a strategy intended to provoke war. Yet the
Hapsburgs and their emperor, Leopold I, failed to recognize the threat. There
were clearer signs of trouble. Reports began to circulate that the Turks were
keen on trying again to take Vienna. The Habsburg envoy to Constantinople,

the Ottoman capital, was informed that the Hungarian vassals of the Ottomans had been told to prepare for war.[2] Other European leaders began to warn the Austrians of the growing danger. Frederick William, the Elector of Brandenburg (and Duke of Prussia; a key political and military leader in Europe), sent emissaries to Leopold to persuade him to take the Turkish threat seriously. Pope Innocent XI, had warned of the threat from the Ottoman Empire since his ascension in 1676. In 1678, a papal emissary advised Leopold to shore up his defenses on the Ottoman border regions. The pope's man was dismissed.[3] The Austrian envoy in Constantinople, Albert Caprara, reported to Leopold his discovery that a recently returned Turkish emissary from Vienna had sketched the layout and fortifications of Vienna and given them to the Sultan.[4] In fact, not only had the Ottomans prepared an army of more than 100,000 to campaign in Austria, they had begun to prepare an invasion years before by carefully repairing the roads and bridges in their territory that led toward Vienna. The Hapsburg court missed or ignored every one of these warning signs.

By the fall of 1682, about one year before the siege began, the Austrians finally began to get the message.[5] The walls of Vienna were strengthened as effectively as possible, given the short amount of time involved. The city filled its storehouses in preparation for a possible siege and to support the Austrian army in the field. Yet many still refused to believe that the Turks could move so quickly to the city, and discounted reports that indicated otherwise.[6]

When the Turkish army advanced on Vienna, the Austrians were caught woefully unprepared. The city's defenders lacked both manpower and supplies. The Ottomans missed taking Vienna "by a hairsbreadth,"[7] following mistakes by the Turkish army and, more importantly, the just-in-time arrival of a relief force led by the king of Poland. Chasing the retreating Turkish armies the Austrians managed to capture much of the Ottoman baggage train. Inside, they found a substance that had been ground into a blackish powder and which they assumed was some form of horse fodder. It was coffee, the spoils of a barely won war. Almost overnight, coffeehouses began to spring up, and legend has it that this failed siege was the start of Vienna's now famed coffeehouse culture.

Why did the Habsburg Empire fail to heed warning after warning—a mistake that nearly passed Vienna to Ottoman control? First, Leopold I surrounded himself with advisors chosen for their rank and loyalty rather than for their education, experience, or erudition. The court was also burdened with a highly complex and convoluted organizational structure prone to bureaucratic infighting.

Petty squabbling among various nobles and potentates bothered the court with constant and needless distractions.

Second, fears of French king Louis XIV's aggressive policies against Habsburg holdings and allies to the west diverted attention from the Turkish threat. Third, arrogance and bias proved a stubborn combination. Though warned directly of a possible attack, Caprara found the idea preposterous. How, he wondered, could a second-rate force like the Ottoman army threaten a capital as grand as Vienna?[8] A more thoughtful student of history might have warned him that the Turks had almost taken Vienna 150 years earlier and that the Ottoman threat to Central Europe had not receded in the interim.

Blindness to a catastrophic threat is an old and common story, and it illustrates an important point. Indentifying a risk and providing timely analysis of it are not enough. The risk must be understood by someone who can do something about it. The most elegant story about the inability to see an evident threat comes from Greco-Roman mythology. In the story of another siege, that of Troy by the Greeks, the god Apollo granted Cassandra, the daughter of Troy's king, a remarkable gift: he allowed her to see the future. Yet, because Cassandra spurned Apollo's subsequent attempts at seduction, the gift came with strings attached. The spurned Apollo cursed Cassandra, so that no one would ever believe her prophecies. When Cassandra warned the Trojans of their impending doom, her warnings were ignored. As old as Homeric legend, the problem is as immediate as "Bin Laden Determined to Strike in US," the title of an intelligence briefing that President George W. Bush received just 36 days before the 9/11 terrorist attacks.

For a government or corporation, risk warnings can come from anywhere: external parties, media, business partners, enemies, and hopefully, more often than not, from parts of the organization that are tasked with analyzing and monitoring risks. Why do so many fail to act when warned of impending doom? It is not always (or even usually) because they are incompetent or negligent. Rational people generally listen to rational warnings. Yet sometimes a rational warning can appear absurd.

Social scientist Herbert Simon coined a useful term: "bounded rationality." Our ability to hear, deliver, judge, and act on facts rationally is limited by the ingrained biases and perceptions that allow us to cope successfully with the daily grind of doing business. Ultimately, communicating a threat successfully depends on risk selection:[9] Which warnings do we choose to consider and which do we ignore?[10] Biases abound, and we do not always recognize them. As part of an organization or a culture—as a human being—we are conditioned to hear certain things and to filter others out.[11] The fundamental question is whether it is possible for those facing risks, political or not, to avoid the Trojans' fate.

## Organizational Biases

One main type of bias is bureaucratic or organizational. Bureaucracy is often used as a pejorative term, but the word is also often used to mean rational and efficient organization.[12] Bureaucracy made the Industrial Revolution possible by standardizing the human processes needed to run large corporate and governmental enterprises. Bureaucracy allows modern corporations and governments to function. It provides clear lines of authority, separation of private from public interests, written and consistent rules, staff training, and meritocratic hiring based on competence. It can reduce organizational risk and run an organization "according to calculable rules."[13] The Austrian establishment's failure to heed warnings of the 1683 Ottoman attack on Vienna owed much to its lack of bureaucratic structure. The royal court was staffed with incompetent cronies. In other words, bureaucratic and organizational standards can be a good thing. Contrary to what many have come to believe, it is "thinking inside the box" that helps most organizations run smoothly.

Yet, the other side of bureaucracy, even when it operates at its best, is the often harsh limitations it imposes on human thought and behavior. Paradoxically, by trying to force the world to operate in a uniformly predictable and robotic way, bureaucracies run a constant risk of missing the forest for the trees.[14] Nothing shows this better than the many warning signs the U.S. government missed before 9/11:

> Most of the intelligence community recognized in the summer of 2001 that the number and severity of threat reports were unprecedented. Many officials told us that they knew something terrible was planned, and they were desperate to stop it." (9/11 Commission, p. 262)

Al Qaeda–associated Islamic terrorists had in the 10 years prior to 9/11 tried to crash planes into tall buildings (in Paris, for example) and had previously attacked the World Trade Center. The U.S. government's domestic security agencies had even considered an airplane attack scenario.[15] More shockingly, in the summer of 2001, FBI field agents in Minnesota and Arizona[16] explicitly raised warning signs about some of the would-be hijackers and plotters' specific plans to hijack airplanes for attacks. The bureaucratized nature of the government system ensured that these specific warnings never reached the top of the decision-making chain.

An important factor in this failure: U.S. government bureaucracies could not separate signal from noise. The 9/11 Commission noted in its report the extremely high volume of data coming in to intelligence agencies during the spring and summer of 2001 from a variety of sources that warned of threats to U.S. and overseas targets. Amid speculation about domestic and foreign targets for attack, the pieces of intelligence available were not put together to identify the actual threat.

Organizational bias comes in many flavors. In most corporations, standard ways of doing business can mean that certain types of risk information are commonly missed. It should go without saying that if you are a firm investing abroad in different countries, you should differentiate between the different risk profiles of the countries in which you operate (or plan to). Russia and Switzerland create very different sets of political risk, but some multinationals fail to make this simple distinction.

A 2000 study of British construction firms looking to enter the Russian market revealed a general recognition that political risk could impact their performance. Russia was (and still is) a country where political risks matter a great deal.[17] Yet when considering a number of different risk factors, the firms in question did not treat Russia differently from other markets.[18] The study emphasizes that the firms ranked the *same* factors to be of similar importance in all the foreign markets they operate in.[19]

Why this blindness to an obvious distinction? The corporate culture and history of this particular industrial sector valued opportunistic approaches to choosing projects abroad rather than long-term strategic planning.[20] Different types of organizations have different types of goals and means, and can have fundamentally different risk cultures, meaning different managerial approaches to (and appetites for) risk.[21] Hedge funds, for instance, have far greater appetite for risk-taking than do savings and loans institutions. The U.S. Army has a fundamentally different view toward risk than the U.S. Department of Agriculture does.

In the case at hand, British construction firms have been successful at expanding by using opportunistic strategies. There is nothing wrong with that in principle, but when expanding abroad, this organizational bias has led these companies to highly value information that is itself ad hoc or opportunistic. Such information, coming from informal contacts such as expatriate staff and business contacts, can be useful. It often provides more color than country-based analysis can. Yet a preference for informal information encourages these firms to discount formal data sources[22] on political risk. The end result is that the firms in question treat risks posed by different countries as if they were the same.

This goes to a deeper question: Which threats should one fear? Within any organization, corporate or governmental, decision makers are bombarded with a steady stream of risk warnings. Which threats are real?

Given the sheer amount of data available, spotting trends or identifying specific risks to an investment can be difficult. Decision makers have to be able to efficiently and intelligently filter information to separate the important from the trivial. United States officials are subject to enormous (and growing) amounts of information from various sources: signals intelligence from electronic sources, human intelligence from operations personnel, open source information, and analysis work done by intelligence officers. This mountain of data may be hiding a legitimate threat to U.S. interests.

Finding the real threats requires, in part, thinking through dangers ahead of time and drawing on that experience. The 9/11 Commission criticized intelligence and counterterrorism officials for not doing scenario planning involving the hijacking of airliners for suicide missions. On the other hand, the report also notes that counterterrorism head Richard Clarke testified that he did not warn of this particular scenario because it "would have been just one more speculative theory among many, hard to spot since the volume of warnings of 'al Qaeda threats and other terrorist threats, was in the tens of thousands—probably hundreds of thousands.'"[23]

Conflicts of interest can create problems, as well. There are conflicting interests within organizations that impede the perception and reporting of risks. Should an advisor to Saddam Hussein in 1991 have counseled him to bow to U.S. demands and withdraw his army from Kuwait? Consider what he knows about his boss. Saddam believes he is the greatest Arab leader since Saladin. He doesn't respond well to bad news. Those who have given him bad news in the past have regretted it. Assuming this advisor values his good health, a fair assumption, he has a conflict of interest that might well prevent him from delivering a bit of analysis that accurately reflects his best thinking on the matter. This is an extreme example, but any leadership (governmental or corporate) that tends to punish the bearer of bad news can expect to hear mostly what it wants to hear.

Conflicts of interest can happen in endless variations. The perception of a conflict of interest partly explains why Stalin ignored Churchill's and Roosevelt's warnings in 1941 that Hitler was preparing to invade the Soviet Union.[24] The Soviets believed the warnings were false, motivated only by Britain's need to gain a powerful ally in its fight with the Nazis. Stalin's perception of a conflict of interest in the British warning contributed to his decision to discount what turned out to be a very real threat.

How risks are publicized and understood in the media can also be impacted by real or perceived conflicts of interest. In the spring of 2006, Dubai Ports World, a state-owned enterprise based in the United Arab Emirates, sought to buy the British firm P&O, which managed port operations in six U.S. ports. Dubai Ports met resistance from U.S. lobbying groups and politicians. Some of these politicians feared that a state-owned Arab firm's operation of U.S. ports would threaten U.S. national security. Others simply used the controversy to score political points with their constituents. Following a tidal wave of media coverage, the U.S. Congress blocked the deal, citing concerns that a foreign firm might help terrorists infiltrate the country.

Organizations charged with ensuring that foreign investments do not compromise national security, such as the Treasury Department and the Committee on Foreign Investment in the United States (CFIUS), approved the bid. CFIUS then informed Dubai Ports that there were no outstanding issues with its application—nothing to signal the political firestorm that news of the sale would soon ignite. The ports in question, in New York, Miami, Baltimore, and other cities, were already being managed by a foreign entity, and objections to the Dubai Ports deal were based solely on the firm's nationality, not the technical aspects of the transaction.[25]

Dubai Ports World eventually divested itself of P&O's American contracts. Many of the politicians involved in blocking the deal simply used the event to enhance their national security bona fides and to score political points at the expense of those who had supported it.[26] In other words, a clear assessment of a threat to national interests conflicted with the electoral interests of some members of the U.S. Congress. Ultimately it was *the perception and reporting* of the potential risk that undermined Dubai Ports.

Conflicts of interest in many organizations can partly be explained in terms of "negative feedback." For many business and corporate organizations, policies and actions are often developed and implemented by the same people who are in charge of delivering reporting and warnings to the top management.[27] So if you had been the decision maker in charge of a policy that is not working, are you more likely to deliver the bad news to top management or to make excuses, temporize, or say that your organization needs more resources for the policy to work?[28]

### Cultural and Ideological Biases

Cultural prejudices run deeper than organizational or conflict of interest biases. Some cultural biases are in fact so deeply held that they are difficult to fully comprehend. Take the issue of risk selection. Humans face many perils but focus on only a few of them. In some ways, this relates to the issue of noise; for example, how do we as a society choose to fear terrorism more than car accidents? The answer is often that we do not; cultural norms help determine what we fear.

In premodern times, there was a strong presumed connection between morality and risk events.[29] Catastrophic risk events like earthquakes, plagues, and wars were attributed to the "wrath of the gods." Human transgressions of moral codes brought swift punishment. Most religious traditions include dozens of parables along these lines. "The Cheyenne believed the scent of a tribe member who had murdered a fellow tribe member would drive away the buffalo and thus spoil the hunt."[30] Modern anthropological research points out that these ancient perceptions of causal links between catastrophe and human misbehavior were not random. By creating taboos out of certain types of unacceptable behaviors, ancient societies were engaged in a form of early risk management. Murder is considered bad in all societies, but social values determine how it is discouraged. The Cheyenne valued the buffalo, their main economic resource. Associating murderers with risk of an unsuccessful hunt (i.e., an economic risk) served as a social check on the risk of a high murder rate.

We are not that different from the Cheyenne when it comes to *how* we decide what risks to fear, and why. Fears of global warming, of a terrorist attack, or even of expropriation are all inherently tied to our cultural and ethical norms. That does not mean that these risks are not real. But *risk selection,* the act of choosing which risks a society chooses to mitigate (from a broad spectrum of risks we actually face), is often determined not rationally but socially. This is inherently an issue of politics *and* perception.[31] Things that we consider risky are based on those values that we want to protect (e.g., democracy at home and abroad, the value of our investments, or the planet's health).

The media, politicians, and the broader public all engage in attempts to define what is risky, creating a constant competition to determine what is perceived as a risk and what is not. Often, what becomes socially accepted is riskier than other things that are seen as serious risks. "University of Chicago economist Steven Levitt...calculated that having a swimming pool in one's backyard is a hundred times more lethal for a child than having a gun somewhere inside one's home. Yet no gun control advocacy group has called for banning swimming pools."[32] Guns are culturally associated with crime and fatalities. Swimming pools are not. Culture and perception of danger plays a significant role in explaining why guns are more tightly regulated than swimming pools.

One type of cultural bias can be historically based. In most countries there are ingrained biases against foreigners. When U.S. firms have to operate in certain countries, they often have to deal with anti-American sentiment. This has long been the case in Latin America, where U.S. intervention in domestic politics has a long and painful history. During the 20th century, the United States significantly intervened in the politics of Haiti, the Dominican Republic, El Salvador, Cuba, Guatemala, Mexico, Chile, Panama, Granada, Nicaragua, and Guatemala, among others. Some of these interventions have been portrayed (fairly or not) as attempts to bolster U.S. business interests.[33] Washington has generally respected the sovereignty of Latin American countries in recent years, but painful historical memories and perceptions remain, especially when politicians in these countries fan anti-Americanism for political gain.

In the United States, at least until the early 1990s, there has been a bias against Japanese investment in U.S. assets. One study found that between 1984 and 1991, use of the word "unfair" in the American media was six times more likely to be associated with Japan than with other countries having significant investments in the United States, countries like Canada, France, Great Britain, or Germany.[34]

The reasons for this cultural bias are anyone's guess, but they probably reflect racial prejudice, anxiety over the competitive strength of Japanese businesses, and historical memories of Pearl Harbor and World War II. As a practical matter, this bias complicated life for Japanese companies operating in the United States. Japanese corporations, aware of the bias, made smaller investments than their competitors from other countries and tended to operate through joint ventures.[35]

A related bias is ideological. Identifying friends and enemies through ideological lenses can create significant analytical and warning errors. In chapter 4, we argued that before Brazil's 2002 presidential election, most Wall Street economists feared that victory for the leftist contender, Luiz Inácio Lula da Silva, would yield an unpromising business climate for foreign investment. These analysts were wrong. Following Lula's victory, he adopted an orthodox set of pro-market policies that quickly reassured capital markets participants. With hindsight, it was clear that ideological biases were at play. The economists who produced these forecasts were almost all Brazilian, and from political circles in which Lula's Workers' Party (PT) was considered hostile to markets.[36] Their own ideological blinders trumped their analysis of the facts. What these otherwise well-regarded analysts overlooked was that Lula's views toward markets had moderated and were also bound to be constrained by the nature of Brazilian market exposures.

Fear, culturally motivated or not, can make the accurate reporting of risk, especially to large audiences, almost impossible. Following 9/11, the U.S. airline industry fell on hard times. In 2001, U.S. airlines posted net losses in excess of $7 billion, and the industry continued to lose money until 2005, shedding about 168,000 jobs—about 38% of its pre-9/11 total.[37] At least four major carriers— Delta, Northwest, US Air, and United Airlines—filed for bankruptcy or bankruptcy protection.

There were many reasons for the industry's troubles, chief among them a public perception that air travel was far riskier than it really is. The average American faces much greater risk inside an automobile than in an airplane.[38] In the United States, there were 42,119 deaths on rural interstate highways alone in 2001. Compare this with the 433 deaths in aircraft accidents between the years of 1992 and 2001.[39] Between 1992 and 2001, it was 65 times more dangerous to drive the length of an average flight than to fly.[40] In 2007, there were no deaths from U.S. commercial scheduled or commuter flights.[41]

The social amplification of risk, or "starting a panic," is driven by many things: culture, ideological fads, public visibility, stigma, and, in particular, fear of catastrophe. Fat tail risks pose a particular dilemma. Corporations are right to worry that they might be vulnerable to the impact of a large-scale terrorist attack, a revolution in an emerging market country, or a civil war. History reveals that these things happen more frequently than most would assume. But anxiety over these issues can provoke an unneccessary overreaction.

The challenge is to balance accurate reporting with reassurance, especially in the face of media and public pressure. The results are often less than ideal. This is the logic that brought us Bert the Turtle, the animated star of a 1951 U.S. government civil defense film on emergency preparedness. Early in the 10-minute film, Bert is attacked by a monkey holding a firecracker on a string—the suicide bomber of an earlier, simpler time. Recognizing the danger, Bert "ducks" into his shell, sparing him from the blast that consumes the monkey and the tree he is sitting in. Next, the film's narrator explains to children how to recognize the flash generated by an exploding atomic bomb and urges them to seek safety as Bert did—by a method known as "duck and cover."[42]

Sometimes simple commonsense government plans can help avoid panic. Mayor Giuliani's reassurances to New Yorkers in the aftermath of September 11 were more effective in reducing anxiety and the social amplification of risk than other measures like shows of force from security personnel.[43] Similarly, we might add, Roosevelt's fireside chats and Churchill's speeches probably did more to calm the U.S. and British publics during times of crisis than any public relations campaign could have.

## Cognitive Biases

According to Richards J. Heuer Jr., "Cognitive biases are similar to optical illusions in that the error remains compelling even when one is fully aware of its nature. Awareness of the bias, by itself, does not produce a more accurate perception. Cognitive biases, therefore, are exceedingly difficult to overcome."[44] In the spring of 1998 it was clear to virtually all independent observers that Poland's famous Gdańsk Shipyard was going to be declared formally bankrupt, and that its assets would be sold to an outside investor. The shipyard's employees had played a critical role in the Solidarity movement that faced down the Communist government in the 1980s. Lech Walesa, the company's most famous employee, had been elected Poland's president. But by the mid-1990s, the Gdańsk Shipyard's unique history had become a unique burden.

As Poland's other two main shipyards, in Gdynia and Szczecin, transformed rapidly and adapted to the global market environment, Gdańsk did little to reform. Thanks to its "special" connections with Solidarity's leaders, many of whom moved into prominent positions in the democratically elected governments after 1989, both the workers and managers in the shipyard felt they could play by a different set of rules. In the early years of transition, they were right. They secured more state subsidies and maintained high levels of employment. But by the mid-1990s, having failed to adapt to the market changes taking place all around them, they found themselves burdened with empty order books and a bloated staff.

As reality tightened its grip and the Polish government moved to push the firm into the market, its employees continued to believe they could count on unconditional support from both politicians and the public. They had neither. Yet, even the week before the firm was declared bankrupt, managers and trade union leaders expressed complete confidence that the status quo would hold. Their counterparts in the other two Polish shipyards found this preposterous. The fate of Gdańsk had been sealed for years, but its employees were simply unable to imagine what was obvious to the rest of the country.

The Gdańsk Shipyard case is an example of a very common form of cognitive bias—wishful thinking. Cognitive biases involve the processes by which the human mind absorbs and processes information. They affect all of us. Our psychological makeup and personal disposition have a significant impact on what we perceive. We will resist any temptation to delve into psychology, but look instead at a few of the practical ways in which risk reporting depends on the way we think.

Consider the personality types of the analysts and reporters of risk. In chapter 1 we outlined how "hedgehogs" and "foxes" approach their work differently. Winston Churchill proved, among other things, that hedgehogs sometimes get it right. Churchill was warning of the threat posed by Hitler's Germany in 1934, when most of the British establishment remained focused on disarmament. He was roundly ignored, both for domestic political reasons (assertive foreign policy remained unpopular with voters) and because his views were seen as alarmist and unsophisticated. At the time, much of the British leadership considered Hitler a man they could do business with.

A hedgehog can sometimes cut through existing cultural and organizational biases to deliver an important warning, but there are cases where this approach can backfire. Before the 2003 U.S. invasion of Iraq, the CIA acted as foxes in their analysis of the existence of weapons of mass destruction (they were not convinced). Some analysts within the Defense Department acted as hedgehogs, insisting that refusal to accept that Saddam Hussein represented an imminent threat could prove catastrophic for U.S. national security. The hedgehogs carried the day, providing justification for the invasion, for better or worse.[45] Style, in other words, in political analysis and especially in reporting, can often be substance.

Another common type of cognitive bias is that of "mirror imaging," or assuming that those we assess think, behave, and understand their interests as we do. In 1977, the U.S. intelligence community detected signs that South Africa was developing a nuclear bomb.[46] Many intelligence analysts dismissed these reports, because they did not match their sense of South Africa's national interests. Apartheid-era South Africa was engaged in a number of conflicts, against the African National Congress (ANC) and guerrilla groups operating in neighboring states, such as Angola and Mozambique. Many in the U.S. intelligence community posed a simple question: Why would South Africa need nuclear weapons? They have asked the question with greater urgency after discovering that they had been wrong.

Mirror imaging is also often apparent in foreign direct investments. Corporate planners think that the government of an emerging market "sees" the world in the same economic, market-driven terms that they do. Just because something appears reasonable or rational to one group does not mean that it appears the same to someone else. Expropriation of private property, as it recently occurred in Venezuela under Hugo Chávez or in some African states during the 1960s and 1970s, may seem economically irrational to many outsiders. But it will only come as a shock if analysts project their own rationality on that of the leadership of those states, which operate under a different set of incentives, constraints, and perceptions.

Even a good analyst can misinterpret warning data. A common cognitive mistake is to confuse detail for accuracy. An experiment carried out in 1982 asked a group of more than 100 experts what they thought was more likely:[47]

1. Suspension of U.S.-Soviet diplomatic relations in 1983, or
2. Suspension of U.S.-Soviet diplomatic relations in 1983 *and* a Russian invasion of Poland in the same year.

Being experts, the survey groups (correctly) estimated the likelihood of both events as low. Yet, the experts who thought that *both* an invasion and diplomatic suspension were likely (#2) actually outnumbered those who thought that *only* a diplomatic suspension was more likely (#1). This is astounding, because it ignores a fundamental law of probability. It is always less likely that events 1 *and* 2 will both occur than that event 1 will occur. There is a human tendency to assume a higher probability of occurrence for statements or data that are more specific or detailed.[48]

Humans generally prefer the tangible to the abstract. When it comes to political risk, they will often trust a piece of quantitative data more than a piece of qualitative data. They assume that "numbers don't lie." In fact, one reason risk management departments ignore political risk is that they have trouble translating into quantitative terms.

People also tend to believe data that confirms their expectations.[49] Usually, troubling data has a higher belief threshold that it needs to pass before it is accepted, especially if the data in question would require a costly change in policy or a high-risk decision. Again, this often ties into biases related to organizational structure and conflicts of interest, showing that one type of bias in reporting tends to engender others. In the worst-case scenario, one can end up as Saddam Hussein did, surrounded by aides who generated fictional data to explain the previous week's fictional data.

For these reasons, reassuring data on countries' basic economic fundamentals can make other threats seem more obscure."[50] In the case of Venezuela, Hugo Chávez had made noises about increased government control over the economy (especially over the oil sector) since well before becoming president in 1999. This was a risk that would impact all foreign companies involved in the extractive industries. But this was a difficult issue for many investors in Venezuela, as they had sunk costs in the country and little motivation to move operations elsewhere. In 1999, in the context of relatively low oil prices and what were seen as economic structural constraints on any Venezuelan government's ability to interfere with foreign investments, many investors chose to believe that Chávez's statements were simply rhetoric for public consumption.

Generals are often accused of fighting the last war; this is yet another type of ingrained cognitive bias. We have discussed throughout this book how understanding history can help corporations and policy makers avoid past mistakes, but there are instances when using historical analogies and scanning the horizon for specific past events actually induces decision makers to make new mistakes, by ignoring the present.

One (nonpolitical) example: the East Asian financial crisis of 1997. Most business and regulators knew at the time that financial crises *do* happen and that their effects are most unpleasant. The last significant one in memory, the Latin American debt crisis, had taken place in the 1980s. Many Latin American states had borrowed large sums of money to finance infrastructure projects in the 1970s. Most of this was government debt, and the borrowing was possible because credit was relatively inexpensive during the 1970s. But these debts ballooned[51] and by the early 1980s, states like Mexico, Brazil, and Argentina faced significant balance of payment problems. Mexico eventually defaulted, and others followed. As a result, by 1997, most regulators and commercial lenders were careful about monitoring and reporting government-held debt. But they were fighting the last war. The East Asian financial crisis, which began with a run on the Thai baht in 1997, was created by significant imbalances in lending to private institutions, not governmental debt. At the time, those figures were not systematically monitored.

Organizations and decision makers tend to remember the lessons they have learned selectively. They remember traumatic events with searing clarity, and a "never again" mentality can sometimes appear to trump the observation of emerging risks. The problem here is "hindsight bias."[52]

To take a military case, the French constructed the Maginot Line, an elaborate set of trenches and fortifications, during the 1930s to halt any repeat of Germany's invasion of France during World War I. Its construction was driven by a "never again" mentality: French casualties between 1914 and 1918 were staggering, about 1.6 million people dead and more than 4 million wounded of a total population of about 40 million. Only trench warfare had prevented an even greater catastrophe. But German tactics had changed drastically since 1918 to emphasize rapid advances spearheaded by tanks and motorized troops. In 1940, the French were caught entirely unprepared. Despite the time and effort spent building the Maginot Line, France fell to the advancing Germans in less than two months.

Those in the business of forecasting future events know that dire warnings get more attention than predictions of benign outcomes, which means that analysts have a built-in incentive to warn of worst-case scenarios. But when the most dire predictions fail to materialize, these analysts can fall victim to a "boy who cried wolf" syndrome. This can happen even when warnings are accurate; U.S. intelligence warned of an impending Japanese attack on Hawaii both on October 16 and November 27, 1941. When the Japanese attack on Pearl Harbor took place on December 7, the second warning was taken less seriously, because the first one had been inaccurate.[53]

This question is at the crux of Cassandra's quandary: what if a prediction of doom is accurate? How can you accept such a prophecy? Human beings aren't very good at processing the unusual.[54] If someone told you that the world (as you knew it) would end tomorrow, you would probably question his sanity. You would probably be right. Predictions of apocalypse are not all that uncommon. So far, none have proven true.

Yet, worrying about the unlikely is not at all a waste of time. Events that appear catastrophic happen more often than most of us think. Modern-day Cassandras abound. To take just a few notable examples, there were clear warnings before the German invasions of Belgium and Holland in 1940 and of Russia in 1941, of Pearl Harbor, 9/11, of the Rwandan genocide, and of the spate of nationalizations that Hugo Chávez launched in Venezuela. All were, for one reason or another, ignored by those who could have done something about them.[55]

### Seeing through the Fog

Let's return to the Siege of Vienna in 1683. If you could travel back in time to 1682–83 and take the place of Leopold I, the Habsburg Holy Roman Emperor, would you have acted differently? It is very easy to insist you would have reacted differently to the now obvious warnings that the Ottoman armies would lay siege to your capital. It's all too easy to second-guess the decisions of others with the benefits of hindsight. But if you faced the same constraints with the same body of knowledge that Leopold and his advisers had, you might well have responded as he did.

Identifying biases that hamper the understanding of risks and threats, as we did in our previous discussion, is a cautionary tale. Cautionary tales allow decision makers to be on the lookout for certain reporting and analytic assumptions. Yet this does not answer the question of *how* to avoid reporting biases. Even today decision makers operate under the same kinds of pressure as Leopold, with organizational, cultural, and cognitive biases all adding layer upon layer of complexity to the whole business of deciding which are the key risks to mitigate. How, then, to prepare to be able to understand when a risk is actually real?

Often, corporations and governments receive fair warning of a risk and choose to discount it. If this is based on rational calculations and the risk is simply understood and accepted, then risk warning can be said to have been successful, no matter what the outcome is. For instance, in 2007, the Iraqi government of Nouri al Maliki attempted to use its sovereign control over Iraq's oil resources to combat the growing autonomy and power of the northern Kurdish regions of the country. The Iraqi government had been working hard to portray itself as the only legitimate authority for oil production contracting, and to that end required registration of international oil corporations wishing to do business in Iraq.

The Iraqi government threatened to deny SK Energy, a South Korean oil firm, sales from the state-run SOMO unless it canceled oil exploration contracts signed with the Kurdistan Regional Government (KRG), setting a deadline of January 31, 2007. SK Energy refused to meet the deadline and cancel its agreement with the Kurdish Regional Government. SK was thus prohibited from doing business with the Iraqi central government. Existing sales of 90,000 barrels per day of oil exports to South Korea by SOMO were promptly canceled and the stock sold to other firms.

SK Energy and the South Korean government both lobbied the Iraqis to reverse their decision. Yet the Iraqis were determined to make an example out of SK Energy to discourage similar activities by larger firms, a move which was thought to have been partially successful in preventing larger oil corporations from doing business with the KRG. For SK, however, the benefits from its deal with the KRG outweighed the loss of business with the central Iraqi government. SK made a reasonable choice based on a specific warning.

So how does an organization begin to think about how it delivers and understands information about key risks? Part of this is about creating the right organizational structures, and part of it is about customizing the information for its intended audience so it can avoid the biases that can impact reporting.

As our previous chapters have discussed, political risks change quickly. At the moment, most corporations engage in at least a cursory reporting of political risk. A recent survey of 106 companies found that although 69% of companies analyze political risks for new investments, only 27% of companies monitor political risk once the investment has been made. What this suggests is that, on the whole, corporations generally believe that political risks are static and that monitoring is not worth the effort.[56]

One way to deal with risks, including political ones, is to create clearly defined structures to report and address risks both internally to management and to other stakeholders. In June of 2005, Credit Suisse was targeted by Greenpeace for its funding of a massive Royal Dutch Shell energy development project on Sakhalin Island, off the Pacific coast of Russia. Protesters picketed in front of the firm's Zurich headquarters, its U.S. offices in New York City, and its office in Moscow, where activists presented bank representatives with a list of demands and suggestions for investments in Russian renewable energy firms.[57]

Greenpeace, the Rainforest Action Network, and other organizations were (and still are) concerned that the project will damage the habitat for the gray whale, which spawns and feeds in the waters surrounding Sakhalin. To draw attention to this cause, the protesters used traditional techniques of picketing, flyer distribution, and the coordinated blocking of access to the construction site on the island itself.[58]

In the past, Credit Suisse, like most financial institutions, did not have to worry about political risks at home attaching to its investments abroad. Credit Suisse is an investment bank, and its impact on whales in the Sea of Okhotsk is arguably indirect at best. Yet as investments have become increasingly global in scale, ethical issues abroad can become thorny political issues at home. Investments in emerging markets that touch on transnational issues such as the environment, human rights, labor ethics, and money laundering are increasingly the third rail of political risk. Regulatory scrutiny, boycotts, and demonstrations *at home* due to factors related to investments *abroad* are becoming an increasingly common category of political risks. Ultimately, a global institution like Credit Suisse faces a world in which the quantity of political actors that can affect their operations is expanding and diversifying, while lines of authority are less clear.

At the same time, a multinational firm also needs to be able to report these risks and their severity internally to management before they become a public relations nightmare. Nike suffered such a disaster in 1996, when *48 Hours*, the U.S. news program, broadcast an investigative report on the appalling working conditions in Vietnamese factories producing Nike products. Remarkably, Nike's management claimed it was unaware of these abuses, implying that this was the first time they had heard about it. This led to accusations that Nike tried to hide behind the subcontractor relationship—and, ultimately, resulted in a product boycott by global activist groups.

In order to avoid these kinds of risks, Credit Suisse created a unique system of in-house risk reporting that addressed political risk as part of the firm's overall reputational management. This effort included monitoring both internal and external activities, assessing collected data, and lobbying.[59] The bank employs a Public Policy department that facilitates the monitoring system and coordinates delivery of risk reports. It also uses a formalized reporting structure for assessing reputational risk, known as the Reputational Risk Review Process (RRRP), which is used to inform an internal Reputational Risk Policy.[60] The review process is used with senior managers, with senior reputational "risk approvers" involved in all areas of the bank's activities.[61]

To manage its external reputation, Credit Suisse targets its use of lobbying and public awareness to where they will be most beneficial. The bank also works proactively to shore up its image and demonstrate its role as a responsible and charitable Swiss organization in its home country, while also emphasizing its global credentials at events such as the World Economic Forum.[62]

External, reputational risk is one area where transparency and clear reporting are important. Shareholders and regulators are two other constituencies with whom communication must be well managed. A lack of reporting and transparency can transform itself into political and regulatory risks. The importance of transparency and reporting to corporations is hard to underestimate. Some of the largest corporate fraud scandals of the last 20 years, such as those involving Barings, Arthur Andersen, and Daiwa, had to do with the failure of internal and external lines of reporting. In all three cases, top management may not have been aware of rogue activities at branches away from the headquarters. And in all three cases, the companies failed to properly report their troubles to shareholders and to regulators. As a result, Barings and Arthur Andersen went out of business and Daiwa had its U.S. banking privileges revoked.

Internal as well as external reporting of risks is more often than not hampered by bureaucratic and organizational biases. One way to improve the flow of accurate information is to break down institutional walls and information silos.

In the wake of what were seen as intelligence (and reporting) failures surrounding 9/11, the United States created the Department of Homeland Security and the position of Director for National Intelligence in order to be able to better "connect the dots" between different pieces of intelligence.[63] The idea was that by combining and centralizing reporting functions and through the better employment of information technology, the issues that plagued reporting on terrorist groups before 9/11 could be avoided.

In financial risk management, the Committee of Sponsoring Organizations of the Treadway Commission (COSO), a private-sector initiative that focuses on designing ways to avoid fraudulent financial reporting, emphasizes that it is not the risk managers who usually report risks in corporations, but the "frontline" employees and staff.[64] For most organizations, a crucial question then follows: how can they create sets of incentives for risk reporting from lower-level employees?

In the case of 9/11, the U.S. government was not able to get risks from on-the-ground operatives and effectively pass them up the organizational chain. It is fundamentally an issue of corporate governance, and illustrates the need to find and cultivate managers who understand the value of the process and will listen to the reports produced, not simply treat the reporting process as a regulatory headache. This is true for both corporations and governments.

Risk reporting also requires transparency. When it comes to credit or operational risks, most large financial institutions are increasingly required to comply with the reporting and transparency rules of the Basel Committee on Banking Supervision's Basel II Accords.[65] Basel II seeks to more closely link the capital requirements of banks to their risk exposure and sensitivity to loss. Key to this was the consideration of a new category of "operational risks" as well as traditional credit and market risks. Operational risk under Basel II is defined as "the risk of loss resulting from inadequate or failed internal processes, people and systems or from external events."[66]

Basel II has three main "pillars" that financial institutions need to implement. While the first pillar deals with risk calculation and analysis methodologies, the other two deal specifically with regulatory reporting and with shareholder/market disclosures of risks. Thus, Basel II requires semiannual reporting by financial institutions on their exposure to credit, markets, and operational risk, as well as on their use of innovative financial instruments.[67]

Particularly when firms become involved in assets that are not traded in "deep and liquid" markets, transparency is crucial in informing investors and regulators of possible measurement error in valuations.[68] Yet political risk is not explicitly covered under Basel II, and it is not likely to be in the future. What this means is that there is no requirement for most corporations to consistently monitor and report on the political risks they face. As we saw with the example of British construction firms operating abroad, this can lead to an ad hoc approach to gathering and reporting data on political risk.

Financial institutions have found that one way to get staff to make accurate, timely reports on risks has been to use a carrot-and-stick approach. Usually the risk-management and auditing functions have wide-ranging abilities to report to top management on all other departments' compliance with risk management. Compensation and promotion for all employees can then partially be based on effective risk reporting.

Another way in which organizations ensure that conflicts of interest are properly kept in balance is through creating competing checks and balances in reporting. During the Cold War the Central Intelligence Agency and the Defense Intelligence Agency used to check each other's reports to the U.S. Congress to ensure reporting accuracy.[69]

Financial institutions typically have risk committee and audit functions whose purpose is similar: to reduce biases in reporting and ensure that executive management hears accurate reports. The Sarbanes-Oxley Act of 2002 requires that most corporations satisfy an extremely high level of disclosure. The internal audit department annually assesses all risk-management processes and procedures and their implementation. This is a significant expense, but the audit office's role is valuable. In a sense, it acts as a constant "red team."

In addition to developing appropriate corporate structures, methodologies, and procedures for reporting political risks, firms and governments need to develop cultures that encourage effective risk reporting. Many corporations, especially in the financial sector, have begun to implement comprehensive Enterprise Risk Management (ERM). ERM is a form of holistic risk management that breaks down information silos across the organization and standardizes the ways in which risks are analyzed, reported, and ultimately addressed. Yet ERM processes often do not cover political risks, which, at least in the private sector, are often underreported and assumed away.

## Reporting and Trust

One last and fundamental issue in reporting any type of risk is how well it is presented and communicated. To be heard, reporting needs to be customized for its audience. So understanding how the decision makers absorb information is crucial. Ronald Reagan had difficulty paying attention to structured briefings on issues of international security and arms control; he did not easily relate to the hypothetical examples being presented. Bill Clark, Reagan's second national security advisor, realizing that Reagan processed information better through anecdote and visualization rather than spoken hypothesis, put together briefings based around movies from the Defense Department. He had the CIA put together "movie profile documentaries" about world leaders the president was scheduled to meet.[70]

Emotions and mental imagery are linked,[71] and emotions underlie decision making when confronting risk and uncertainty. People react to risks more strongly when they can visually imagine the consequences of a possible outcome.[72]

Some ways to better present information are visual. Risk heat maps, commonly used in the risk management industry, have been used to successfully present political threats. There are color-coded risk matrices that graphically represent and organize risk exposures. For decision makers who may not be experts in each business area, well-constructed heat maps can be effective risk reporting tools because they are in an easily understood and intuitive format. A heat map might break down risk exposure by class of risk, business-unit exposure, quantity of assets exposed, or expected frequency of loss events.

Political risk management constantly faces this issue of presenting relevant data. For financial traders, political risk reports will represent one of many inputs that go into making a buy/sell decision. Traders are by definition pressed for time and have short attention spans. Analysts are often detail-oriented; they would like nothing better than to explain at length the history and in-depth analytics of why the government of some country or other is just about to change its currency regulations. So the challenge is not only having the right analysis, but also the right reporting format. With financial traders the right format is typically a note or a phone call that can be understood in under a minute. In communication with financial clients, then, the conclusion of the analysis should come first, and the analysis follows, the opposite of how an academic would deliver a paper.

For this to work, for someone to consider a conclusion before seeing the proof, there needs to be a fundamental level of trust. Which is perhaps the most important factor in reporting any kind of risk. Cassandra's warnings to the Trojans failed because, as Dryden put it in his translation of Vergil's *Aeneid*, "all heard, and none believed."

# Conclusion: Mitigating Political Risks in an Uncertain World

> There are risks and costs to a program of action.
> But they are far less than the long-range risks
> and costs of comfortable inaction.
> —John F. Kennedy

On June 23, 1757, at Plassey, about 100 miles north of Calcutta, India, the British adventurer Robert Clive led a force of about a thousand British troops and 2,000 Indian locals into battle against the 50,000-strong army of Siraj-ud-Daula, the last independent ruler (*nawab*) of Bengal. Clive won an overwhelming victory thanks in no small part to treachery among Siraj's commanders. Whatever the circumstances, the defeat of 50,000 troops by 3,000, with just 73 killed and wounded, represents a remarkable military achievement. But historians remember the battle of Plassey mainly as the beginning of British rule in India, which ended only with India's independence in 1947.[1]

From our perspective, the battle's main interest is that it represented an early corporate attempt at risk mitigation. Clive and his 3,000 troops were at Plassey not in their capacity as soldiers of King George II or even as British subjects. They were fighting as employees of the Honourable East India Company (HEIC), a joint-stock corporation headquartered in London.[2] Thus, British rule in India began when a London-based trading corporation, run by a board of directors representing its shareholders, took over the country.

The HEIC's venerable and colorful history began in 1600, when members of the Levant Company, an enterprise trading in spices imported from the Middle

East, decided to cut out the Middle Eastern middlemen and procure the spices from their original source in today's Indonesia.[3] The company's early years were economically uncertain, but once spices and tea from the Far East and India began to arrive in England, it grew into a profitable enterprise. In 1740, some 17 years before Clive's rout of the Bengali ruler, the HEIC was still a commercial enterprise that imported and exported goods from its factories at Bombay, Madras, and Calcutta and was not terribly bothered by the internal politics of India.[4]

What led to Plassey, and ultimately to the establishment of the British Raj, was the fact that business became intertwined with politics. For one thing, the British HEIC had significant competition from other European companies. Great Britain had not been the only European power to set up an East India Company—the Danish, Dutch, and French created similar entities to trade with the Far East.

Competition among the different companies for trading monopolies, granted by the local Indian princes and potentates, was fierce. It led to the companies' involvement in India's fractious politics, which in turn led to the risk of trading posts being taken over by the local rulers or potentates. In a particularly direct form of risk mitigation, most East India Companies began to develop their own private armies and navies and to provide allied local potentates with European arms and training. And they were not shy about using them.

As a result, by the late 1740s, both the British and the French East India Companies were in full control of key Indian coastal cities, like Calcutta and Madras (British) and Pondicherry (French). Often, they were busy employing their armies to either besiege each other's possessions or to fight local Indian princes. In fact, it was precisely the successful takeover of Calcutta, not by the French but by Siraj-ud-Daula, that sparked the Battle of Plassey. Siraj's early form of "expropriation" of HEIC land and property was met by force of arms. This proved a very successful way of dealing with risks—so successful that by 1815 the HEIC had become the most significant military power on the Indian subcontinent.[5]

The story of the HEIC reminds us that though political risk managers used different tools in the past, risk mitigation itself is not new. Neither is risk mismanagement, both at the corporate and governmental levels. Thucydides recounts how, at the start of the Peloponnesian War, the Athenian state faced the stark question of whether to defend a smallish state, Corcyra (now Corfu), against its parent city-state, Corinth. Corinth was one of the great powers in the Greek world and a key ally of Sparta, Athens' deadly rival. The Athenians would never have considered defending Corcyra, a severe violation of the norms governing relations between Greek city-states, were it not for one unfortunate fact: Corcyra had developed the second-largest fleet in the Greek world, after Athens.

Athenian power grew from the prowess and size of its fleet. The risk that Corinth (and therefore Sparta) might seize control of the large Corcyran fleet posed a mortal threat to Athens' hegemony in the Greek world. Yet intervention meant violation of international law of the time. Athens' enemies could use its attack as a precedent and a justification to involve themselves in the affairs of Athens' own colonies. To make their choice, Athenian leaders undertook a tortured process of political risk analysis and deliberation.

Tragically for Athens, the final decision to help Corcyra sparked the conflict that ultimately destroyed Athenian power—a reminder that actions meant to mitigate one set of risks can sometimes generate a new (and often more dangerous) set of risks. Preemptive action has always generated risks of unintended consequences.

Political risk management of centuries past extended beyond state-to-state relations into the business and commercial worlds. The East India Companies of the early modern period were not a fluke; they evolved from the development of trading rules, corporate structures, and insurance, all meant to lessen the risks of long-distance commerce. Trade insurance that covered the political risks of the time (looting and pillaging) existed as early as the Code of Hammurabi (2250 B.C.).[6] The ancient Roman Republic indemnified private traders who transported supplies for the Roman legions against capture by enemies,[7] a process we can consider a distant ancestor of today's export-import guarantor agencies like U.S. Ex-Im Bank, the U.S. Overseas Private Investment Corporation (OPIC) and Japan's JBIC.

The late medieval and Renaissance eras produced a broad expansion of sea trading with faraway regions in the Middle East, Africa, Asia, and the Americas. Such trade required the pooling of capital for what were risky (and extremely profitable) business ventures. Entrepreneurial businessmen invented the concepts of limited liability and corporate shareholding to rationalize and mitigate the risks faced by traders engaged in shipping ventures—including political risks like piracy and expropriation.[8] The governance structures of the East India Companies were not so different from those of today's corporations. The British East India Company was a joint-stock operation. The Dutch East India Company was a limited liability company traded on the Amsterdam Stock Exchange—the first modern stock exchange, created precisely for trading in Dutch East India shares.[9]

So, while risk and risk management may be relatively new concepts—since pre-17th-century mercantilists did not have a probabilistic concept of risk—risk functions have been performed for centuries.[10] Risk, as we have detailed is the likelihood of a negative outcome multiplied by its impact. Faced with a particular risk, an organization can try to minimize or eliminate the likelihood the event will occur or simply prepare to absorb the event's impact. A corporation can try to minimize the risk that a host-country government will expropriate its investment in that country. It can also try to reduce the financial impact of any expropriation by buying insurance or by downsizing its business in that country.[11]

With HEIC's experience in the subcontinent in mind, let's jump to June 1992, when another aggressive firm, the Enron Corporation, signed a memorandum of understanding with the government of the Indian state of Maharashtra to build the largest gas-based power plant in the world.[12] The Dabhol Power Company (DPC) was conceived by the Indian central government in the early 1990s as one of a series of key projects that would help India overcome its growing power shortages. Enron expressed an interest in leading the project, estimated at $3 billion, which was to be implemented in two phases.

The Power Purchase Agreement was signed in December 1993, and financial closure for the project in March 1995 relied heavily on a guarantee from the Government of Maharashtra as well as a counter-guarantee from the Government of India. Soon after the memorandum of understanding was signed, the Maharashtra State Electricity Board (MSEB) sought the view of the World Bank on the project, which argued that it was too large and expensive. It was suggested that the MSEB would have trouble paying for the power generated, and that the terms of the agreement were skewed in Enron's favor.

A number of activists and other groups filed suit against the project, insisting that it was too expensive and might damage the local environment. Also, at the time that financial terms for the project were reached there was a change of government in Maharashtra, and the incumbent Congress Party was replaced by the opposition Bharatiya Janata and Shiv Sena parties. The new state government alleged that the high project cost was inflated by bribes and kickbacks worth millions of dollars to the previous government. These charges, though never proven, became widely accepted among local residents, and the project was mired in controversy. The new Maharashtra state government then decided to cancel the project, but under pressure from Enron and an international arbitration ruling was instead compelled to renegotiate the terms of the agreement.

Despite the renegotiation, the MSEB found it difficult to pay its bills to the DPC. By the end of 2000, it began to delay payments. In early 2001, the DPC invoked both the state and central government guarantees. The governments refused payment, claiming that the bills were disputed by the MSEB. The DPC then claimed political force majeure and resorted to the conciliation and dispute resolution process. Loans to the project began to dry up and DPC had to lay off employees. India's image as an international investment destination suffered, and a number of large project proposals were shelved. Further arbitration claims were filed against the Indian government, and in 2005 a complicated settlement was reached through which the Indian government made some financial settlements but eliminated its guarantee.

India's federal government favored the project—and remained neutral when things began to fall apart. The opposition that killed the plan came from the local level—from the state government and community activists—and internationally, from the World Bank. "Macro" political risks, those at the national level, were effectively managed. "Micro" risks, which can impact a sector, a region, or even a single corporation, killed the project.

What might Enron have done to mitigate these risks? It seems ridiculous to imagine a corporation today acting like the East India Companies of old, with its own fleets and regiments meting out punishment to unfriendly host countries or competitors. Yet the HEIC and Enron faced the same fundamental problem: how do you mitigate an impending risk? Do you try to reduce its likelihood? Or do you prepare to minimize its impact?

The first step is to understand the situation on the ground. As we have illustrated throughout this book, risks are hard to manage unless they are understood. An understanding of local political dynamics could have helped Enron engineer a better outcome. India has a vocal civil society and media, and there was a strong public perception that Enron had pushed the deal through unfairly. In addition, the company did not win the contract through a transparent public tender (bidding) process. Better management of these problems could have reduced the likelihood that the risk event would occur—by making it more difficult for political parties to exploit public anger over the deal. Similarly, Enron could have better understood the true balance of legislative power between the federal and local governments.

Enron did prepare in advance for the impact of a potential breach of contract. It won guarantees for the project from the Indian federal and state governments. It obtained some $231 million in political risk insurance and $160 million in lending from the U.S. Overseas Private Investment Corporation.[13] As companies are advised to do when investing in politically risky infrastructure, Enron allowed Indian lenders and other large multinationals to invest in the project.[14] Yet the case ended up in court, with the Maharashtra state, the domestic lenders, the foreign lenders, and the U.S. and Indian governments all fighting to secure the best possible deal. Legal action is ultimately likely to recoup just a fraction of original costs. As Enron's experience demonstrates, it is much better to prevent such a costly political risk event from occurring than to simply prepare for its worst effects.

### Reducing the Probability of a Risk

There are four main strategies for reducing the likelihood that a risk event will occur. Risk managers can try to eliminate the threat, minimize its likelihood, isolate the event, or avoid the risk altogether.[15]

Obviously, where possible, the ideal way of dealing with a particular risk is to eliminate it. Enron would have saved itself a lot of money if it could have persuaded those who won control of Maharashtra's state government to honor the Dabhol power plant contract.

Some threats cannot be eliminated. The United States and its allies have been trying since at least 1998 to capture or kill Osama bin Laden. The United States is not the only government that has struggled to capture individuals hiding in remote locations with active support from local allies. In 2006, Italian police captured the *capo di tutti capi* of the Sicilian Cosa Nostra, Bernardo Provenzano, who had been hiding in remote parts of the Sicilian countryside for 43 years. Despite its reputation, Sicily is better policed than the Afghan-Pakistani border, where bin Laden is thought to be hiding.

Terrorists, like mafiosi, are notoriously hard to eliminate. They pose risks that, as we discussed in Chapter 6, can only be minimized. It is impossible, even for a government with excellent counterterrorism capabilities, to eliminate all possibility of a mass terror attack. Governments can try to police certain groups and to ensure that surveillance is tight enough to catch groups that are not known. The latter measure comes at a cost, and most democratic societies struggle to develop a consensus view of the wisest trade-off between liberty and security.

In the corporate world, many organizations have little choice but to try to minimize the likelihood of risk events. Royal Dutch Shell has been remarkably successful at managing the political risks it faces in Nigeria.[16] For the last 50 years, Shell has run a profitable energy business in Nigeria's rich oil and natural gas fields. Nigeria today accounts for 16% of Shell's 2 million barrels per day of global oil production. The company operates the Shell Nigeria Exploration and Production Company and an LNG joint venture with the government. With so much risk exposure, Shell faces constant threats to its business and production, including failure by the government to adequately fund joint ventures, local political-military conflicts, and government instability. These are the problems that have plagued Western companies operating in Nigeria since 1960. Yet, Shell has leveraged its ability to manage these risks into a competitive advantage.[17]

Another way to manage risk: Isolate it. Between the end of the Gulf War in 1991 and the 2003 U.S. invasion of Iraq, three successive U.S. administrations had used economic sanctions to isolate Saddam Hussein's regime, and to ensure that he could not rebuild his weapons of mass destruction program or again invade his neighbors.[18] When it comes for foreign direct investment, corruption at the governmental level is a pervasive form of political risk, which at best, can be isolated, as it can never be entirely eliminated and its minimization is perilous (e.g., it is better for most companies not to engage in bribery at all). One way for U.S. companies to avoid getting entangled with corruption has been to cite U.S. law, and in particular the Foreign Corrupt Practices Act that prohibits U.S. companies from engaging in any form of corruption. Colgate-Palmolive has used this approach in China with some success.[19] While this may reduce some business opportunities that would require bribery, generally making one's code of ethics public and enforcing it can help insulate a company from the issue of corruption.

Lastly, risk can be avoided completely.[20] The problem is that the ability to do so can be sharply limited. Many organizations cannot simply pick up and move. For a Western oil corporation, like Conoco or Exxon, with operations in Venezuela, the election of Hugo Chávez generated a broad range of risks. Yet Venezuela has too much oil to ignore, and companies already operating there when Chávez rose to power had spent huge sums on the infrastructure needed to extract oil from such a geographically challenging location. To simply walk away from such a sizable investment is easier said than done.

Finally, those hoping to reduce the likelihood that a known risk event will occur must face the problem that there are many other things they do not know. As detailed in earlier chapters, there are many risks that organizations, states, and individuals cannot see, much less avoid, because they are unknowable, too complex to mitigate, or simply misunderstood. In 1985, there was no shortage of international relations experts, Russia specialists, and Kremlinologists. Yet, virtually no one predicted the imminent collapse of the Soviet Union. In the mid-1990s, very few analysts foresaw the East Asian financial crisis.

## Reducing the Impact of a Risk

Enron and Robert Clive did not (or could not) prevent a risk from occurring. Both had to deal with the impact of an event, whether a breach of contract for Enron or the Bengali takeover of HEIC's Calcutta possessions. In previous chapters, we discussed at length how different companies and organizations have tried to reduce the impact of an event that either happened or was near-certain—from how Morgan Stanley's contingency plans helped the company deal with the impact of the 9/11 attacks to how the Chrysler Corporation in the 1960s managed to avoid expropriation in Peru by a revolutionary government.[21]

Needless to say, it is important to develop resilience to potential crises—as Morgan Stanley did before 9/11. Contingency plans ensure the capacity to survive a shock; this is an important tool for both corporations and states. How that can be accomplished depends on what is at stake. Crisis preparation can range from business continuity planning to the development of lobbying capacity and local on-the-ground partnerships to structuring financing, investments, and supply chains in ways that minimize the potential impact of a risk—as Chrysler did in Peru.[22] It is increasingly likely that capital markets will develop derivative products for political risk that will provide hedging capabilities where insurance does not exist.

## Holistic Risk Management

Understanding the risks is clearly important. Mitigation of these risks, whether through reducing their likelihood or through building resilience to buffer their impact, ultimately depends on leadership and governance from the top. Risks cannot be addressed in a vacuum. Successful government and private organizations find that comprehensive risk approaches with the full support and buy-in of executive leaderships address risks more effectively than do haphazard approaches.

One approach to managing risk is developing governance structures based on Enterprise Risk Management (ERM),[23] the main framework for risk management that most corporations and financial firms are currently implementing. It emphasizes the responsibility of management as well as staff in analyzing risks to see how they could impact the organization and ensure that there is a strategic view on risk management and mitigation that is actively implemented. Further, ERM is a form of holistic risk management that formalizes efforts to break down information silos across organizations and to standardize the ways in which risks are analyzed, reported, and addressed.

Yet, most organizations face barriers when implementing ERM,[24] including a lack of experts with knowledge of all areas covered, questions about the credibility of current methods, a lack of industrywide standards, and with the challenges of maintaining analytical objectivity and independence. For political risks, these barriers are particularly acute. There are very few corporations, or for that matter governmental or civil society organizations, that actually take a strategic and systematic approach to political risk.

Too many corporations and organizations ignore political risks until it is too late. These risks are either assumed to occur rarely (or to someone else) or to be entirely unpredictable. In both cases nothing could be farther from the truth. As we argued at the beginning of the book, too many economists consign politics and political risk to a kind of statistical rounding error. Risks faced by a firm operating in a specific country are assumed to be mostly economic or financial or to have mainly to do with that country's ability to meet its debt obligations. Politics are assumed to matter rarely, as if political interests were incidental to the formulation and implementation of economic policy.

Robert Clive and his employer, the HEIC, in the mid-1700s and American oil corporations in Venezuela after 1999, faced the economic consequences of dramatic political decisions. But almost all corporations and organizations face some form of political risk. Those who operate in a market or any regulatory environment are subject to the rules of a political game. Often, the assumption is that political risk primarily affects organizations operating in unstable and risky countries. Yet the time and money spent by corporations operating in the United States to comply with anti–money laundering laws (some of which are a direct result of the 9/11 terrorist attacks) or with the arcane rules of the Sarbanes-Oxley Act were the direct result of political choices and decisions.

Looking ahead, political risks are likely to become more, not less, relevant to both governments and corporations. Globalization, economic integration, trade and capital mobility, and the free exchange of ideas across borders have not rendered politics obsolete. There is no "end of history" just behind the horizon. War, terrorism, expropriation, violent changes of government, politically motivated lawmaking, and civil strife are not going away. Governments will continue to change both national and international regulatory regimes, often dramatically. Government responses to the 2008 banking crisis are perhaps the most notable recent example of this.

Increasing numbers of corporations and organizations now recognize that politics matters at least as much as economic fundamentals for market outcomes in many countries around the world. But just as there is a growing recognition that political risks are important and have a significant and regular impact, many still presume that political and policy outcomes are too difficult to predict to be effectively mitigated.

Yes, in politics there are real black swans. There is much that we cannot know, whether because of chains of events that are too complex for us to understand or because ingrained bias prevents us from seeing the truth.

Politics is notoriously hard to quantify. Unlike economic risks, political risks also tend to be more heterogeneous: their causes vary greatly. The way politics impacts economic assets can be equally varied, from a government imposing currency controls, to a mob rioting and burning down a business, to a panic starting among traders. Another complicating factor is that political risk affects not only economic assets, but also the decisions and policies of governments and nongovernmental organizations. And, as we discussed early on, it is often hard to put a link between cause and effect.

But there is also a great deal that *can* be known. This book represents our attempt to illustrate how the world of politics can be illuminated. Actions of governments, insurgents, and even rioters can be analyzed with a good deal of precision. Identifying the interests at stake and those who hold social and political power reveal a lot about how certain political risks will develop. The classic detective story question "cui bono" (i.e., "who benefits?") often reveals a great deal.

Understanding where decision-making power lies reveals much about the risks those powers can produce. In a country like Saudi Arabia, where informal power structures are dominant, attempts to negotiate with the government via formal ministries may not get you very far. Attempts to win government tenders in Germany by trying to map a particular government official's network of family and friends will not help much either. Context matters.

Politics as a social phenomenon and politics as an area of inquiry are not a unitary field. What holds today may not hold tomorrow. An analytical tool that works in one circumstance may not work in another. Politics and the risks it poses constitute a broad subject, not reducible to one universal theory. Understanding where and how to test different theories has a great deal of value.

Similarly, the ability to keep an open mind while being both rigorous and creative is necessary in order to successfully mitigate political risks. Gunboats are no longer tools of the political risk management trade for most corporations, although recent developments make this statement less definitive than it sounds. In 2007 the Russian Duma passed a bill to allow Gazprom and Transneft, two large utility companies, to raise their own private armed security forces in order to protect their gas lines.[25] Similarly private military companies have increasingly been involved in providing protection for economic and strategic assets in unstable places around the world. In 2008 post-Saddam Iraq, the U.S. government was estimated to have contracted over 25,000 private security firm employees to complement the work of the U.S. armed forces in that country.[26]

For most companies however, the use of force as mitigation for political risk has been replaced by far more complex methods. Financial options and derivatives, insurance policies, complex legal agreements, commercial treaties, and diplomacy, whether corporate or governmental, provide new levels of complexity and nuance to the possibilities for managing political risks. Being able to manage political risk successfully depends on a company or government's ability to consider different information sources and different theories and methods, and at the same time remain able to question its own assumptions and biases. Balancing this combination of skills is, at the end of the day, as much art as science.

# Notes

## Chapter 1

1. There are a number of variants and uses of the term "fat tail," and our characterization and use of the term are by no means exhaustive. In the finance world, the term often refers to asset price distributions that are not "well behaved" (normal) and where returns can be either much better or worse than one might typically observe. In other words, in some markets extreme price movements between alternative equilibrium price ranges are actually much more plausible that a "thin-tailed" normal distribution would predict. Other variants of fat-tailed distributions have been recognized in fields ranging from marketing to natural disasters and weather prediction. Our use of the expression is limited to politically influenced events and outcomes that are worse and more likely than if the outcomes were normally distributed. So in a sense our variant of the term refers to something that looks more like a bimodal distribution than a normal distribution, with the fat-tail portion of the probability distribution being a "bump" on the downside. Another way that we use the term "fat tail" is to describe situations where seemingly unrelated events really are connected by some common, but hard to notice, link.
2. Chartis Research, as quoted in "Credit Risk Technology Market to Grow to $8bn by 2010," *Finextra*, June 16, 2006, http://www.finextra.com/fullstory.asp?id=15459 (accessed June 25, 2008).

3. Deloitte Consulting, *Global Risk Management Survey: Accelerating Risk Management Practices,* 5th ed., 2007.

4. Most of the writing on political risk, as well as the analysis, tends to be crisis-driven; for instance, a lot of academic writing on political risk in the '70s, around the time that many developing-world countries began to nationalize foreign assets. Then there is significant writing in the mid-1980s, when other types of political risk, surrounding the Latin American debt crisis, began to surface. The field also expanded around the time of the 1997–78 Russian and Asian financial crises.

5. Another way of saying this is that risk is the likelihood of "any event or action that may adversely affect an organization's ability to achieve its objectives and execute its strategies" (Alexander J. McNeil, Rüdiger Frey, and Paul Embrechts, *Quantitative Risk Management: Concepts, Techniques, and Tools* [Princeton, NJ: Princeton University Press, 2005], p. 1).

6. Risk, by being measurable, is different than uncertainty, which is the possibility of an event occurring that cannot be quantified in probabilistic terms. Risk, in other words, is quantifiable uncertainty (see Frank H. Knight, *Risk, Uncertainty, and Profit* [Boston: Hart, Schaffner & Marx; Houghton Mifflin Company, 1921]).

7. P. J. Villeneuve and Y. Mao, "Lifetime Probability of Developing Lung Cancer, by Smoking Status, Canada," *Canadian Journal of Public Health,* Vol. 85, No. 6 (Nov.– Dec. 1994), pp. 385–388.

8. In fact, when one speaks of the Russian Revolution this is further complicated by the fact that there were two sets of events that took place in 1917, the February (or "bourgeois") one that established the Provisional Government and the October or Bolshevik revolution that brought Lenin to power. This only highlights the difficulty of analyzing such complex political and historical events as revolutions.

9. It is worth mentioning that the 1575 default was one of at least four that took place during Philip II's rule (1556–1598).

10. See A. W. Lovett, "The Castilian Bankruptcy of 1575," *The Historical Journal,* Vol. 23, No. 4 (Dec. 1980), pp. 899–911; John A. Marino, "Creative Accounting in the Age of Philip II? Determining the 'Just' Rate of Interest," *The Historical Journal,* Vol. 36, No. 4 (Dec. 1993), pp. 761–783; James Conklin, "The Theory of Sovereign Debt and Spain Under Philip II," *The Journal of Political Economy,* Vol. 106, No. 3 (June 1998), pp. 483–513.

11. Jonathan Israel, *The Dutch Republic: Its Rise, Greatness and Fall, 1477–1806* (Oxford, UK: Clarendon Press, 1998), p. 185.

12. Linwood T. Geiger, "Expropriation and External Capital Flows," *Economic Development and Cultural Change,* Vol. 37, No. 3 (Apr. 1989), p. 536.

13. Amy L. Chua, "The Privatization-Nationalization Cycle: The Link between Markets and Ethnicity in Developing Countries," *Columbia Law Review,* Vol. 95, No. 2 (Mar. 1995), p. 231.

14. Chua, "The Privatization-Nationalization Cycle," p. 225.

15. For a more detailed discussion of what defines politics and political action see the Appendix on political risk methodology.

16. For more in-depth commentary on political risk analysis, research methodology, and practical applications, please see www.eurasiagroup.net/publications.

17. The expression "The fox knows many things, but the hedgehog knows one big thing," which was used by Isaiah Berlin for the title of a famous 1953 essay "The Hedgehog and the Fox," is attributed to ancient Greek poet Archilocus by Erasmus' renaissance-era collection of classical proverbs, *Adagia*. See http://www.let.leidenuniv.nl/Dutch/Latijn/ErasmusAdagia.html (accessed August 23, 2008).

18. Philip Tetlock, *Expert Political Judgment: How Good Is It? How Can We Know?* (Princeton, NJ: Princeton University Press, 2006).

19. *The 9–11 Commission Report: Final Report of the National Commission on Terrorist Attacks Upon the United States, Official Government Edition* (Washington, DC: U.S. Government Printing Office), p. 264. (Internet download version: http://www.gpoaccess.gov/911/).

20. Mary Douglas and Aaron Wildavsky, *Risk and Culture* (Berkeley: University of California Press, 1983).

21. Anthony Giddens, *Modernity and Self-Identity: Self and Society in the Late Modern Age* (Cambridge,UK: Polity Press, 1991).

22. For a sample of the literature on the "risk society" see Ulrich Beck, *World Risk Society*. (Cambridge, UK: Polity Press, 1999); C. Coker, "Globalisation and Insecurity in the Twenty-first Century: NATO and the Management of Risk," Adelphi Paper no. 345 (London: The International Institute for Strategic Studies, June 2002); Anthony Giddens, *Modernity and Self-Identity* (Cambridge, UK: Polity Press, 1991); Martin Shaw, *New Western Way of War: Risk Transfer and Its Crisis in Iraq* (Cambridge, UK: Polity Press, 2005); Keith Spence, "World Risk Society and War Against Terror," *Political Studies*, Vol. 53 (2005), pp. 284–302.

23. Nassim Nicholas Taleb, *The Black Swan: The Impact of the Highly Improbable* (New York: Random House, 2007).

*Chapter 2*

1. Upon landing on the Yucatán peninsula and making contacts (and fighting) with the local petty Mayan chiefdoms, Cortés's expedition gained knowledge about the Aztecs and their wealth. More importantly, it was in the Yucatán that Cortés was able to pick up the key interpreter who would facilitate his contacts with the Aztecs. See Bernal Diaz, *The Conquest of New Spain* (New York: Penguin, 1963), pp. 80–98.

2. Estimates of the population at the time range from as low as 4.5 million to 30 million; however, a range of 21.5 million to 25 million is believed to be correct. See Robert McCaa, "The Peopling of Mexico from Origins to Revolution," in Robert Steckel

and Micahel Haines (eds.), *The Population History of North America* (1997), table 2 (http://www.hist.umn.edu/~rmccaa/mxpoprev/table2.htm).

3. For a detailed description of the battle between Cortés's expedition and the Aztecs, see Victor Davis Hanson, *Carnage and Culture: Landmark Battles in the Rise of Western Power* (New York: Anchor, 2001), pp. 222–230.

4. It is not known for sure how many other Indians perished in the epidemic started by Cortés's men in 1520. Estimates of the total population of Mexico around this time range up to 30 million. Cartwright (1972) says nearly half of the native population of Mexico died of smallpox in less than six months. According to Magner (1942), when the terrifying conflagration ended after a few months, an estimated 2 million to 3.5 million Mexican Indians had died. Crosby (1967) suggests that central Mexico's population had declined from about 25 million just before the conquest to about 16.8 million ten years later, from all causes. At a minimum, at least half of the Aztecs who caught smallpox died of it (D'Ardois, 1961). Donald R. Hopkins, *The Greatest Killer: Smallpox in History* (Chicago: The University of Chicago Press, 2002), p. 207.

    "A fair-minded cross-examination of the broad range of primary sources for the epidemic of 1520 leaves little doubt that smallpox swept throughout the Central Mexican Basin, causing enormous mortality. The epidemic ranked with the deadliest disasters that native annals customarily recorded. Whether the fraction of smallpox deaths was one-tenth or one-half, we have no way of knowing, but from my reading of the texts discussed here, the true fraction must fall within these extremes, perhaps near the mid-point." Robert McCaa, "Spanish and Nahuatl Views on Smallpox and Demographic Catastrophe in the Conquest of Mexico," *Journal of Interdisciplinary History*, Vol. 25, No. 3 (1995), pp. 397–431.

5. Hanson, *Carnage and Culture*.

6. Ortwin Renn and Andreas Klinke, "Systemic Risks: A New Challenge for Risk Management," European Molecular Biology Organization, EMBO Report, Vol. 5 (Suppl. 1), 2005, http://www.pubmedcentral.nih.gov/articlerender.fcgi?artid=1299208 (accessed June 23, 2008).

7. Secretary Donald Rumsfeld and General Richard Myers, Department of Defense News Briefing, February 12, 2002, http://www.defenselink.mil/transcripts/transcript.aspx?transcriptid=2636 (accessed June 24, 2008).

8. Press Release, "Arla Affected by Cartoons of Muhammed," Arla Foods, January 26 (2006), http://www.arlafoods.com/appl/hj/hj202com/hj202d01.nsf/O/3DE8AAFDECABBA97C12571020061F1C1 (accessed June 24, 2008).

9. Eric Pfanner, "Danish Companies Endure Snub by Muslim Consumers," *New York Times*, February 27, 2006, http://www.nytimes.com/2006/02/27/business/worldbusiness/27image.html (accessed March 2, 2008).

10. Leon Gettler, "Denmark: Cartoon Backlash Builds but Some Can Still Beat the Boycotts," *Asia Media*, UCLA Asia Institute, February 14 (2006), http://www.asiamedia.ucla.edu/article.asp?parentid=39070 (accessed June 24, 2008).

11. See: Nassim Nicholas Taleb, *The Black Swan: The Impact of the Highly Improbable* (New York: Random House, 2007), pp. 248–249.

12. For some technical discussions of "fat tail" risks, especially as applied to the financial sector, see Andre Lucas, "A Note on Optimal Estimation from a Risk-Management Perspective under Possibly Misspecified Tail Behavior," *Journal of Business & Economic Statistics*, Vol. 18, No. 1 (Jan. 2000), pp. 31–39; Eric L. Talley, "Cataclysmic Liability Risk Among Big Four Auditors," *Columbia Law Review*, Vol. 106, No. 7 (Nov. 2006), pp. 1641–1697; Yexiao Xu, "Small Levels of Predictability and Large Economic Gains," *Journal of Empirical Finance*, Vol. 11, No. 2 (Mar. 2004); for some lighter articles, see "A Tale of Fat Tails," *Economist*, October 9, 1993; "Too Clever by Half," *Economist*, January 24, 2004.

13. Nassim Nicholas Taleb, *The Black Swan: The Impact of the Highly Improbable* (New York: Random House, 2007), p. xvii.

14. Ibid., p. 149.

15. Ibid., p. 11.

16. In the latter case, historical record was actually useless or worse; in the past the hijacking of planes usually resulted in negotiations, not in suicide attacks—in fact, one reason that the passengers did not fight in any of the flights except for Flight 93 (where they found out what happened to the other planes) is that they operated under the assumption that the hijacking would end through negotiations, as in the past.

17. Taleb, *The Black Swan*. See chapter 10, "The Scandal of Prediction," pp. 138–164.

18. Ibid., p. 11.

19. See Taleb, p. xxiv: "Almost everything in social life is produced by rare but consequential events."

20. As opposed to major graft and corruption, which can actually be a serious political risk.

21. For arguments about how long-term corruption leads to state collapse see Chris Allen, "Warfare, Endemic Violence and State Collapse in Africa," *Review of African Political Economy*, Sept. 1999. See also J-F. Bayart, S. Ellis, and B. Hibou, *The Criminalization of the State in Africa* (Oxford, UK and Bloomington, IN: James Currey and Indiana University Press, 1999). For a classic work on the effective lack of state control in many African countries see Robert H. Jackson, *Quasi-States: Sovereignty, International Relations and the Third World* (New York: Cambridge University Press, 1990).

22. Galima Bukharbaeva, "Uzbek Bank Closure 'Political,'" Institute for War & Peace Reporting, RCA No. 362, March 25 (2005), http://www.iwpr.net/?p=rca&s=f&o=238747&apc_state=henirca2005 (accessed June 24, 2008).

23. Ibid.

24. Ibid.

25. Ibid.

26. Richard K. Betts, "Surprise Despite Warning: Why Sudden Attacks Succeed," *Political Science Quarterly*, Vol. 95, No. 4 (Winter 1980–1981), pp. 551–572.

27. Michael Pearson, *The Sealed Train* (New York: Putnam, 1975), http://www.yamaguchy. netfirms.com/789740l/pearson/pearson_index.html (accessed June 24, 2008).

28. "Monte Carlo simulations" refers to a number of computational algorithms that use randomly generated numbers to approximate an outcome. They are used to estimate the results to problems with a high degree of uncertainty. This is done by generating iterative random data samples; each successive approximation is used to come closer to the result. One way to think about it is that it is similar to a game of Battleship. A number of random "hits" are taken. Based on where these "hits" land, one can estimate the position of the opponent's battleships.

   Due to the large number of data used, Monte Carlo simulations are usually computer-aided. The method was designed by Stanislaw Ulam, a physicist working for the Manhattan Project in the 1940s. The method has wide applications in scientific and engineering fields, and also in finance and risk management, where data inputs are often uncertain.

   Extreme value theory (EVT) is a statistical discipline that tries to estimate the probability of extremely rare events. It is thus directly applicable to the estimation of tail risk, and especially of "fat tails." It has traditionally been used in the insurance/actuarial industry to calculate the chance of catastrophic disasters, but increasingly it is used in risk management, especially as more and more risk managers are beginning to recognize that statistical models based on normal distributions tend to discount "fat tails."

29. Staffan Mörndal and Martin Lindeberg, "Managing Political Risk—A Contextual Approach," Linköping University, January 17, 2002, pp. 20–21, http://www.ep.liu.se/ exjobb/eki/2002/iep/012/ (accessed June 24, 2008).

30. Renn and Klinke, "Systemic Risks."

31. Robert Jervis, "The Future of World Politics: Will It Resemble the Past?" *International Security*, Vol. 16, No. 3 (1991–1992), p. 40.

32. In quantum mechanics, the field of physics that studies motion and interaction at the subatomic scale, the Heisenberg uncertainty principle states that an observer cannot know the position and velocity of a subatomic particle, such as an electron, at the same time. The impossibility of such knowledge stems from the nature of the objects being examined. To judge the motion or position of a subatomic particle, it must interact with a means of measurement, such as another particle. Yet because of the scale of the phenomenon being observed, this interaction also affects the particle being measured, altering its location or momentum. So what is in Newtonian physics a relatively simple calculation becomes, when studying a much smaller scale, an impossibility.

33. "Surviving the Markets," *Economist*, August 16, 2007, http://www.economist.com/ opinion/displaystory.cfm?story_id=9646451 (accessed February 29, 2008).

34. Tom Engelhardt, "In Iraq, the Fix Is In," *Los Angeles Times*, December 14, 2006, http:// www.latimes.com/news/opinion/la-oe-engelhardt14dec14,0,2334181.story?coll=la- opinion-center (accessed June 24, 2008).

35. Fred Kaplan, "War-Gamed. Why the Army Shouldn't Be so Surprised by Saddam's Moves," *Slate Magazine*, March 28, 2003, http://www.slate.com/id/2080814/ (accessed July 15, 2008).

36. Kaplan, "War-Gamed."

37. Peter Cornelius, Alexander Van de Putte, and Mattia Romani, "Three Decades of Scenario Planning in Shell," *California Management Review*, Vol. 48, No. 1 (2005), p. 95.

38. Pierre Wack, "Scenarios: Uncharted Waters Ahead," *Harvard Business Review*, Sept.–Oct. 1985,

39. Ibid., p. 73.

40. Ibid., p. 76.

41. Ibid., p. 80.

42. Ibid., p. 82.

43. Leslie E. Grayson and James G. Clawson, "Scenario Building," UVA-G-0260, University of Virginia (1996): 6, http://ssrn.com/abstract=909927 (accessed April 10, 2008).

44. Shell recognized the oil crisis and its implications for what it was because its scenario analysis, prior to 1973, looked at the possibility of high oil prices and an oil crisis. "While most of the refining industry needed years to decide that something really fundamental had happened, Shell moved immediately, switching investments well ahead of their competitors. As a consequence of this industry inertia, refining capacity in the industry ran into considerable oversupply, with disastrous consequences for profitability. However, due to Shell's early adaptation of alternative policies they suffered much less from overcapacity and outperformed the industry by a long margin" (Kees Van der Heijden, *Scenarios: The Art of Strategic Conversation*, 2nd edition, [New York: John Wiley and Sons, 2005], p. 6).

    Parts of Shell that were not involved in the scenario process, such as their maritime transport unit, made the same mistakes as the whole refining industry, and their profitability suffered accordingly (ibid., p. 7). For instance, the coordinator of Shell's manufacturing had suggested in the early 1970s that some of Shell's refiners be upgraded to produce lighter oil. This proposal was shelved as too expensive, in light of the low oil prices at the time. However, Pierre Wack's scenario exercise showed that oil prices could rise significantly, which would have made upgrading very profitable. When the oil crisis happened and prices began to rise, Shell was able to quickly begin upgrading its facilities to take advantage of the higher oil prices (ibid. pp. 140–141).

45. Wack, "Scenarios," p. 146.

46. Cornelius et al., "Three Decades of Scenario Planning in Shell," p. 101.

47. "Grand scenarios" do not depend heavily on past experiences, history, or data. This is a good thing, because in the long term, due to the issues of duration, complexity, and bias, past events are not reliable (they cannot identify "fat tails"). Scenario analysis deals with uncertainty by plotting different plausible outcomes. One example of

"grand scenario"–type planning comes from the U.S. National Intelligence Council (NIC). The NIC runs various scenario projects, which usually extend out 15 years from the time they are written. The NIC's scenario-based risk identification outlines trends and drivers and extrapolates scenarios from each of them (or some combination of them).

Developing such scenarios is tricky business. For one thing, it is an exercise in trying to identify future outcomes based on a limited number of factors. Another difficulty is identifying how these scenarios could affect an entity as complex as the United States. A lot is subjective, and the analysis of how those scenarios would play out is predicated on country-specific knowledge, knowledge of international relations and political theory, and historical analogies. So scenario analysis requires a significant amount of creativity as well as a knack for the plausible. Its great advantage is not necessarily in its accuracy (although that is a welcome quality) but in forcing corporations and policy makers into imagining alternative futures in a uncertain world and getting them to think how they would or could respond to drastic change.

48. An orderly and democratic election that would not be adverse under Gurr et al.'s definition, such as the 1995 Quebec referendum on independence, can nonetheless have adverse effects on economic assets. For the effect of the referendum on Quebecois companies' stocks, see Marie-Claude Beaulieu, Jean-Claude Cosset, and Naceur Essadam, "Political Uncertainty and Stock Market Returns: Evidence from the 1995 Quebec Referendum," *Canadian Journal of Economics*, Vol. 39, No. 2, (May 2006), pp. 621–642.

49. Orson Welles, *The Third Man* (film), http://www.britannica.com/EBchecked/topic/592615/Thirty-Years-Peace.

50. Andrew S. Grove, "Intel Keynote Transcript: Academy of Management, Annual Meeting," August 9, 1998, http://www.intel.com/pressroom/archive/speeches/ago80998.htm (accessed June 24, 2008).

51. Bracken, "How to Build a Warning System," in Bracken, Bremmer, and Gordon (eds.), *Managing Strategic Surprise: Lessons from Risk Management & Risk Assessment* (New York: Eurasia Group, 2005), p. 29.

52. Ibid., pp. 29–30.

53. Ibid., p. 30.

54. Ibid., p. 31.

55. Ibid., pp. 31–32.

56. Ibid., pp. 32–33.

57. Sandy Markwick, "Trends in Political Risk for Corporate Investors" in Theodoer Moran, ed. *Managing International Political Risk*, Blackwell, Massachusetts: 1998, p. 52.

58. Bracken, "How to Build a Warning System," in Bracken, Bremmer, and Gordon (eds.), *Managing Strategic Surprise: Lessons from Risk Management & Risk Assessment* (New York: Eurasia Group, 2005), p. 33.

59. Anglo American, "Report to Society 2006: Corporate Social Investment," http://www.angloamerican.co.uk/static/reports/2007/sc-social-investment.htm (accessed June 24, 2008).

60. Steven Horwitz, "Making Hurricane Response More Effective: Lessons from the Private Sector and the Coast Guard during Katrina," Mercatus Policy Series, Policy Comment No. 17, George Mason University (March 2008), pp. 3–4, http://www.mercatus.org/repository/docLib/20080319_MakingHurricaneReponseEffective_19Mar08.pdf (accessed June 24, 2008).

61. Michael Barbaro and Justin Gillis, "Wal-Mart at Forefront of Hurricane Relief," *Washington Post,* September 6, 2006, D01.

62. Ibid.

63. Ibid.

64. Horwitz, "Making Hurricane Response More Effective," p. 4.

65. See, for instance, Mikkel Vedby Rasmussen, "Reflexive Security: NATO and International Risk Society," *Millennium: Journal of International Studies,* Vol. 30, No. 2 (2001) pp. 285–309.

66. Take the welfare state. It is in itself a form of social risk insurance that was built from the late 19th century onward. It is noteworthy that in the 19th century the one state that developed the concepts of social welfare systems most extensively was Bismarck's militaristic German Empire. Domestic social safety nets were a form of risk mitigation used by Germany to stave off the possibility of revolution. Welfare systems then generate their own problems and risks: they impact economic growth, create special interests, and can lead to divisive politics—witness the difficulty that politicians have had making even modest reforms to these systems.

67. The United States ostensibly invaded Iraq in 2003 because the Iraqis *could* have possessed weapons of mass destruction. While Saddam's regime had used chemical weapons against the Kurds and the Iranians, he had never used them against the United States. There was no indication that he would, but the invasion was based on the precautionary principle that a regime change might prevent Saddam Hussein from giving such weapons to terrorists.

68. Yee-Kuang Heng, "The 'Transformation of War' Debate: Through the Looking Glass of Ulrich Beck's World Risk Society," *International Relations,* Vol. 20, No. 1 (2006), p. 79.

69. Quoted in Heng, "The 'Transformation of War' Debate," p. 77.

*Chapter 3*

1. Halford John Mackinder, *Democratic Ideals and Reality: A Study in the Politics of Reconstruction* (New York: Henry Holt and Company, 1919), p. 186.

2. For some discussions about the origins of geopolitics and the relationship between Nazi strategists and theorists of geopolitics, see Ladis K. D. Kristof, "The Origins and

Evolution of Geopolitics," *The Journal of Conflict Resolution*, Vol. 4, No. 1 (Mar. 1960), pp. 15–51; Werner J. Cahnman, "Concepts of Geopolitics," *American Sociological Review*, Vol. 8, No. 1. (Feb. 1943), pp. 55–59; Phil Kelly, "A Critique of Critical Geopolitics," *Geopolitics*, Vol. 11 (2006), pp. 24–53; H. McD. Clokie, "Geopolitics—New Super-Science or Old Art?" *The Canadian Journal of Economics and Political Science/ Revue Canadienne d'Economique et de Science politique*, Vol. 10, No. 4 (Nov. 1944), pp. 492–502.

3. Germany's attempt to conquer Russia in 1941 has been described as one of history's strategic blunders, a story somewhat beyond the scope of this chapter.

4. The concept was first developed by Johan Rudolf Kjellén in the early 1900s from the earlier writings of Friedrich Ratzel on "political geography." Ratzel, not coincidentally, originated the theory of states seeking lebensraum (living space), which would in time become another of the idée fixes of Nazi Germany. Ratzel argued that history can be explained by states or *Völker* (peoples) fighting each other in order to gain geographic living space and natural resources. A parallel development was in the United States, where Admiral Alfred Thayer Mahan's writings, and in particular *The Influence of Sea Power Upon History, 1660–1783*, were the intellectual basis for the development of the United States as a great sea power at the turn of the 20th century. It is remarkable that the book was also influential in Japan, where the Japanese Imperial Navy used it as a manual during the 1920s. Mahan's contribution to geopolitics also includes the invention of the term "Middle East."

5. "Geopolitics is a war casualty; it has been used and misused by strategists and expansionists of all shades beginning with Mahan and Theodore Roosevelt and ending with Hitler and Tojo." Ladis K. D. Kristof, "The Origins and Evolution of Geopolitics," *The Journal of Conflict Resolution*, Vol. 4, No. 1 (Mar. 1960), p. 20.

6. Another definition of geopolitics is "Historic forces operating within a geographic framework are supposed to condition political action which, in turn, is to determine the course of economic development." See Werner J. Cahnman, "Concepts of Geopolitics," *American Sociological Review*, Vol. 8, No. 1 (Feb. 1943), p. 56.

7. Trading on the Amsterdam Bourse began in 1602, when the Dutch East India Company began to trade its shares there. It was the first exchange to formally and systematically trade in both stocks and bonds.

8. It is one of history's ironies that Amsterdam was supplanted by London, which was then overtaken by New York, which had been originally christened by its Dutch founders as New Amsterdam.

9. See Kathleen Burk, "The Diplomacy of Finance: British Financial Missions to the United States 1914–1918," *The Historical Journal*, Vol. 22, No. 2 (June 1979), pp. 351–372; William L. Silber, *When Washington Shut Down Wall Street* (Princeton, NJ: Princeton University Press, 2006).

10. William E. Gibson, Randall Hinshaw, Raymond F. Mikesell, and Carl H. Stem, "The Eurodollar Market and the Foreign Demand for Liquid Dollar Assets," *Journal of Money, Credit and Banking*, Vol. 4, No. 3 (Aug. 1972), pp. 643–703.

11. It was a contributing factor to the ending in 1971 of the Bretton Woods system that had managed international currency and financial markets for 27 years and underpinned many of the changes made to the international finance and banking system in the 1970s; see Stefano Battilossi, "Financial innovation and the golden ages of international banking: 1890–1931 and 1958–81," *Financial History Review*, Vol. 7 (2000), pp. 141–175.

12. The implication of a foreordained path of decline for any great power is belied by the late history of Byzantium. Between the Umayyad Siege of Constantinople (718) the Crusader sack of the city (1214), which signified its decline, The Byzantine Empire's fortunes ebbed and flowed. For instance, it recovered from its dramatic struggles with the Muslim powers during the 8th century and the loss of extensive territories in the Middle East and Africa. After the stabilization achieved by Basil I and the following Macedonian dynasty in the late 800s, the empire enjoyed a period of resurgence. While it was arguably somewhat in decline after the middle of the 11th century, this was only made evident by the Fourth Crusade sack of Constantinople in 1204 by Western knights and the Venetians. In other words the idea of an observable decline of a great power not possible, except arguably (and controversially) with 20/20 hindsight.

13. G. John Ikenberry, "Is American Multilateralism in Decline?" *Perspectives on Politics*, Vol. 1, No. 3 (Sept. 2003), p. 538.

14. We will treat many of these threats in separate chapters. In this instance, we look at geopolitics in the classical sense, as meaning simply the struggle between great powers for mastery and international wars.

15. Samuel P. Huntington, "The Clash of Civilizations?" *Foreign Affairs* (Summer 1993); *The Clash of Civilizations and the Remaking of World Order* (London: Simon & Schuster, 1996).

16. Samuel P. Huntington (ed.), *The Clash of Civilizations?: The Debate* (New York: Foreign Affairs, 1996).

17. In fact, some political philosophers, such as Carl Schmitt, argue that the essence of politics is distinguishing between friends and enemies, whether within a society or outside it. Therefore, using Schmitt's perspective, identifying risks (as posed by others) is the ultimate political act. See Carl Schmitt, *The Concept of the Political* (Chicago: University of Chicago Press, expanded ed., 2007).

18. Paul Ormerod and Shaun Riordan, "A New Approach to the Analysis of Geo-Political Risk," *Diplomacy & Statecraft*, Vol. 15, No. 4 (2004), p. 644.

19. In this book we typically separate risk identification (or risk mapping) and risk analysis, as they are theoretically distinct risk management stages. In reality, however, and

especially in terms of geopolitics, where so much of the risk identification is often driven by deductive (or a priori) analysis, we shall treat them together. For geopolitical risk in particular, the two are mutually interdependent and do not necessarily need to be performed in the "risk identification, then risk analysis" order.

20. Another tool for early warning, risk maps are used to give a broad geopolitical view of country risks over a short- to medium-term time frame. They usually depend on country analyst input and, unlike "grand" scenarios or cognitive maps, they tend to actually forecast a probability and impact (usually related to the exposures held by the client, whether government or corporate). Such tools are effective in giving corporate boards or policy makers a broad view of the ongoing political risks (at a macro level) faced by their respective entities.

Risk maps are often presented in a matrix with two dimensions: probability and impact. In a two-by-two matrix, there are then four rough categories of risk:

- "Severe risks": Those with high probability and high potential impact, those with potentially catastrophic outcomes
- "Long-tail risks": Those with high potential impact, but low probability
- Minor risks: Those with both low probability and low impact
- "Death by a thousand cuts": events that are almost certain to happen, but with relatively low impact. What is particularly dangerous about these kinds of risks is not the individual impact of any one event, but the cumulative impact of many.

21. Information primarily from Niall Ferguson, *The House of Rothschild: Money's Prophets, 1798–1848* (New York: Penguin, 1998).

22. For instance, in the War of 1812, Andrew Jackson's U.S. forces defeated the British at the Battle of New Orleans a few weeks *after* the United States and Britain signed a peace treaty (the Treaty of Ghent). News reached the combatants slowly, by courier and by boat, so neither of the combatants knew their countries had already signed a peace treaty.

23. Two classic texts are Robert Kaplan's *The Coming Anarchy: Shattering the Dreams of the Post Cold War* (Vintage, 2001), and Thomas F. Homer-Dixon, *Environment, Scarcity, and Violence* (Princeton, NJ: Princeton University Press, 2001).

24. Much of the writing in this vein, like Kaplan's and Homer-Dixon's, was inspired by water issues in the Middle East and by the anarchic conditions that plagued certain West African states during the 1990s, such as Liberia and Sierra Leone.

25. Thomas Malthus (1766–1834), an English political economist, is best known for writing *An Essay on the Principle of Population* (1798), which argued that global population increases geometrically, while global food supplies increase arithmetically. Therefore population growth would eventually far outstrip existing food supplies, leading to mass famine around the globe. Needless to say, Malthus's predictions have not come true. Among the many reasons why population growth has not outstripped

the global food supply have been technological advances, increased agricultural production, and higher industrial productivity and wages, as well as lower population growth than predicted by Malthus.

Neo-Malthusians are similar to Malthus in the sense that they assume that scarcities of natural resources, ranging from water to oil, will result in catastrophes ranging from famines and poverty to wars. For some basic critiques and refutations of neo-Malthusian arguments, see, for instance, David G. Victor, "What Resource Wars?" *National Interest online*, Nov. 12, 2007, http://www.nationalinterest.org/Article.aspx?id=16020 (accessed July 17, 2008), and Alex De Waal, "Anarchy Postponed," *Prospect* (Feb. 1997). For an argument that tests both the critics and the proponents of the war-resource scarcity link, see Henrik Urdal, "People vs. Malthus: Population Pressure, Environmental Degradation, and Armed Conflict Revisited," *Journal of Peace Research*, Vol. 42, No. 4 (2005), pp. 417–434.

26. Such as the fabled Northern Passage, sought by many early modern explorers, which is now a real possibility, given the unfreezing of large portions of the sea in the Canadian north.

27. In fact its intellectual antecedents are Thomas Hobbes and the diplomats of the 19th century, like Klemens von Metternich. It was formalized as a theory by Hans Morgenthau and Walter Lippmann in the 1940s and 1950s.

28. Doyle, Michael, *Ways of War and Peace: Realism, Liberalism, and Socialism* (London: W. W. Norton & Company, 1997); Gideon Rose, "Neoclassical Realism and Theories of Foreign Policy," *World Politics*, Vol. 51, No. 1 (Oct. 1998); Hedley Bull, *The Anarchical Society, A Study of Order in World Politics,* 2nd ed. (New York: Columbia University Press, 1977); Robert O. Keohane, *After Hegemony: Cooperation and Discord in the World Political Economy* (Princeton, NJ: Princeton University Press, 1984).

29. See, for instance, Robert Jervis, "Realism, Neoliberalism, and Cooperation: Understanding the Debate," *International Security*, Vol. 24, No. 1 (Summer 1999), pp. 42–63.

30. Robert O. Keohane and Lisa L. Martin, "The Promise of Institutionalist Theory," *International Security*, Vol. 20, No. 1 (Summer 1995), pp. 39–51.

31. The literature on institutionalism draws on the field of international political economy. See also Robert O. Keohane, "International Institutions: Can Interdependence Work?" *Foreign Policy*, No. 110 (Spring 1998), pp. 82–96, 194.

32. Admittedly a bit of a straw man, like all of our other hypothetical IR analysts.

33. See for instance Kimberly Hutchins, "Foucault and International Relations Theory," in *The Impact of Foucault on the Social Sciences and Humanities*, Moya Lloyd and Andrew Thacker, eds. (London: Macmillan, 1997), pp. 102–127.

34. Alexander Wendt, "Anarchy Is What States Make of It: The Social Construction of Power Politics." *International Organization*, Vol. 46, No. 2 (Spring 1992), pp. 419–420.

35. A mention should be made of an offshoot of constructivism, critical geopolitics. Critical geopolitics contends that geopolitical theories are often constructed to support

the goals of different international actors. One valuable contribution of this school of thought, which we briefly touched on at the beginning of this chapter, is that it raises the question of whether geopolitical thinking actually provides an objective view of future risks or whether it provides a series of self-fulfilling prophecies. This question is ultimately academic (and thus unanswerable), but it does provide analysts of geopolitical risks with a warning about the uses and misuses of political risk analysis.

36. Russia saw itself as the "Third Rome," the rightful successor to the Byzantine Empire (the Second Rome) and its imperial legacy. The title of the Russian Emperor, *Czar* or *Tsar*, is in fact a Russian borrowing of the word *Caesar*, one of the titles of the Roman emperors. This is also the origin of *Kaiser*, the German title of the Holy Roman Emperor, another potentate to claim the mantle of Imperial Rome.

37. This policy became famously enshrined as National Security Council Report 68, or NSC-68.

38. Kennan in fact warned against his analysis being used to justify the Vietnam war.

39. Mikkel Vedby Rasmussen, "Reflexive Security: NATO and International Risk Society," *Millennium: Journal of International Studies*, Vol. 30, No. 2 (2001), pp. 285–309; Yee-Kuang Heng, "The 'Transformation of War' Debate: Through the Looking Glass of Ulrich Beck's World Risk Society," *International Relations*, Vol. 20, No. 1 (2006), pp. 69–91.

40. Keith Spence, "World Risk Society and War Against Terror," *Political Studies*, Vol. 53 (2005), pp. 284–302.

41. Rasmussen, "Reflexive Security."

42. National Security Council, *The National Security Strategy of the United States*, Sept. 20, 2002, http://www.whitehouse.gov/nsc/nss.pdf (accessed September 12, 2007).

43. Heng, "The 'Transformation of War' Debate," p. 74.

44. Data from Peter Wallensteen and Margareta Sollenberg, "Armed Conflict 1989–1999," *Journal of Peace Research*, Vol. 37, No. 5 (2000), pp. 635–649.

45. Juliana Pilon, "Strategic Trade with Moscow: U.S. Leverage in the Polish Crisis," Heritage Foundation Backgrounder #160 (Jan. 2, 1982).

46. A. L. Müller, "Soviet Technology and the West, 1945–1985," *South African Journal of Economics*, Vol. 56, No. 4 (Dec. 1988), pp. 198–205.

47. Alan Dobson, "The Export-Import Bank and U.S. Foreign Economic Relations," *Diplomatic History*, Vol. 29, No. 2 (Apr. 2005), pp. 375–378.

48. Lionel S. Johns et al., *Technology and East-West Trade: An Update*, Office of Technology Assessment, U.S. Congress, May 1983.

49. Nathan Jensen, "Measuring Risk: Political Risk Insurance Premiums and Domestic Political Institutions," http://www.polisci.ucla.edu/cpworkshop/papers/Jensen.pdf (accessed September 12, 2007).

50. Although, as we have seen in our earlier example of the effect of the victory at Waterloo on the House of Rothschild's investments, one can also lose significant money from geopolitical bets.

51. See chronology of recent events in U.S.-Taiwan and U.S.-China relations at http:// www.taiwandc.org/hst-9596.htm (accessed July 17, 2008).

52. "Taiwan Stock Market Plunges in Wake of KMT Election Defeat," *Asian Economic News*, Mar. 27, 2000, http://findarticles.com/p/articles/mi_m0WDP/is_2000_March_27/ai_61543763 (accessed July 17, 2008).

53. Based on a March 2007 Eurasia Group survey of its financial clients, there was no agreement on exactly how much the Iran premium was—$2, $10, or $15 per barrel—but there was general agreement that there in fact was a premium.

54. The downside of Russia's geostrategic ambitions became more obvious to market participants in the wake of the Georgia-Russia conflict in August of 2008. Markets in a number of countries, including Russia, Georgia, and Ukraine, were down, at least in part as a result of the conflict and concerns about what the Russian government might do next.

## Chapter 4

1. Susan Strange, "The Dollar Crisis of 1971," *International Affairs*, Vol. 48, No. 2 (Apr. 1972), pp. 193–194.

2. Tim Golden, "The Fall Came Quickly for Mexico's Rising Star," *New York Times*, Dec. 30, 1994.

3. Joseph L. Klesner, "The End of Mexico's One-Party Regime," *PS: Political Science and Politics*, Vol. 34, No. 1 (Mar. 2001), p. 107.

4. John Ward Anderson and Baer Delal, "Mexican Standoff," *Foreign Policy*, No. 110 (Spring 1998), p. 191.

5. Jeffrey Sachs, Aaron Tornell, and Andrés Velasco, "The Collapse of the Mexican Peso: What Have We Learned?" *Economic Policy*, Apr. 1996, p. 16.

6. Sachs et al., "The Collapse of the Mexican Peso," p. 15.

7. Several surveys showed the opposition winning. However, during the vote count the computer system that counted national votes crashed. When it came back online, Salinas was declared president.

8. See Rudiger Dornbusch, Alejandro Werner, Guillermo Calvo, and Stanley Fischer, "Mexico: Stabilization, Reform, and No Growth," *Brookings Papers on Economic Activity*, Vol. 1994, No. 1 (1994), pp. 253–315. Also Sebastian Edwards, "The Mexican Peso Crisis: How Much Did We Know? When Did We Know It?" *The World Economy*, Vol. 21, No. 1 (Jan. 1998), for a discussion of what was known to economists before the crisis.

9. This may be one of the reasons for which some risk indices, like the Euromoney country risk index, were showing that Mexico's country risk actually decreased from March to September 1994. While the Euromoney index does admittedly include

a measure for political risk, this accounts for no more than 25% of the index's weight, with the rest being geared toward measures of credit and economic worthiness. See Edwards, "The Mexican Peso Crisis," p. 7.

10. Daniel l. Rubinfeld, Reference Guide on Multiple Regression, Federal Judicial Center, http://www.fjc.gov/public/pdf.nsf/lookup/sciman03.pdf/$file/sciman03.pdf (accessed August 28, 2008).

11. Martin Stone, "Managing Currency Inconvertibility and Exchange Transfer Risk: Identification, Assessment and Risk Transfer Issues," in Sam Wilkin, ed., *Country and Political Risk: Practical Insights for Global Finance* (London: Risk Books, 2004), pp. 327–328.

12. Generally, if markets perceive an event to have a potential impact this will change the market equilibrium and lead to a revaluation of an asset.

13. The Malaysian government was able to isolate itself from the global financial markets because of three primary characteristics: (1) the national bank (Bank Negara Malaysia) had a high level of foreign exchange reserves; (2) Malaysia had relatively low external debt; and (3) the links between the government and the financial system were deeply institutionalized, so that banks were heavily influenced by the government.

14. Stone, "Managing Currency Inconvertibility," 328–329.

15. Wayne Arnold, "Singaporeans Wait for a Stock Freeze in Malaysia to Melt," *New York Times,* July 9, 1999.

16. Thomas L. Brewer, "Political Sources of Risk in the International Money Markets: Conceptual, Methodological, and Interpretive Refinements," *Journal of International Business Studies,* Vol. 14, No. 1 (Spring–Summer 1983), p. 162.

17. *Dreaming with BRICs: The Path to 2050,* Global Economics Paper No. 99, Goldman Sachs, Oct. 2003.

18. Ian Bremmer, "Taking a Brick Out of a BRIC," *Fortune,* Feb. 7, 2006.

19. In a way, emerging markets are those states where economics are a subset of politics, but where economics are becoming increasingly autonomous from politics. Obviously this is a continuous process and, like ideal democracy, ideal economic autonomy is never fully achieved (which is why politics matter even in the G7 economies). This concept works, but only in a relative manner, and there are some glaring exceptions (e.g., *dirigisme* in France).

20. Arvid Lukauskas and Susan Minushkin, "Explaining Styles of Financial Market Opening in Chile, Mexico, South Korea, and Turkey," *International Studies Quarterly,* Vol. 44, No. 4 (Dec. 2000), p. 697.

21. The politicians who have ruled Turkey since its birth as a nation-state in 1923 have fiercely safeguarded its identity as a secular, "modern" country. Its military has several times imposed its will on politicians who challenged this idea. But many of the pressures and problems that have elevated Islamist voices elsewhere in the Muslim

world have reopened this potentially explosive issue in Turkey. If the country's progress toward membership in the European Union (a long-standing goal) falters, the
political reforms it has adopted to meet EU guidelines, the economic reforms needed
for both EU accession and access to funding from the International Monetary Fund,
and improved relations with Turkey's minority Kurds could all fall victim to populist
and nationalist political pressures.

22. Albert Fishlow, "Lessons from the Past: Capital Markets During the 19th Century
and the Interwar Period," *International Organization*, Vol. 39, No. 3 (Summer 1985),
p. 390.

23. Fishlow, "Lessons from the Past," p. 390.

24. Juan Martínez and Javier Santiso, "Financial Markets and Politics: The Confidence
Game in Latin American Emerging Economies," *International Political Science
Review/Revue internationale de science politique*, Vol. 24, No. 3 (2003), p. 369.

25. Enrique Hidalgo-Noriega, Vitali Meschoulam, Chris Garman.

26. Alina Mungiu-Pippidi and Sorin Ionita, "Interpreting an Electoral Setback—Romania 2000," *East European Constitutional Review*, Vol. 10, No. 1 (Winter 2001), http://
www.law.nyu.edu/eecr/vo110num1/features/interpreting.html (accessed on August
28, 2008).

27. Saul Estrin, "The Russian Default," *Business Strategy Review*, Vol. 9, No. 3 (Sept. 1998),
p. 2.

28. Estrin, "The Russian Default," p.1.

29. Padma Desai, "Why Did the Ruble Collapse in August 1998?" *The American Economic
Review*, Vol. 90, No. 2 (May 2000), pp. 48–49.

30. Preston Keat and Alexander Motyl, "Assessing State Stability and Political Risk in
Emerging Markets," in Wilkin (ed.), *Country and Political Risk*, p. 63.

31. Keat and Motyl, "Assessing State Stability," p. 66.

32. Christoph Moser, "The Impact of Political Risk on Sovereign Bond Spreads—Evidence
from Latin America," Proceedings of the German Development Economics Conference, Göttingen, 2007, No. 24, p. 3.

33. Jianping Mei, "Political Risk, Financial Crisis, and Market Volatility," New York University, Leonard N. Stern School Finance Department Working Paper Series No. 99-049,
Aug. 1999, p. 3.

34. Schamis and Way, 2001, as quoted in Martínez and Santiso, "Financial Markets and
Politics," 366.

35. Martínez and Santiso, "Financial Markets and Politics," 366.

36. In July 2008, the Turkish Constitutional Court only narrowly decided not to ban the
AKP for antisecular activities. The party was fined and received a warning instead.
Sabrina Tavernise and Sebnem Arsu, "Turkish Court Calls Ruling Party Constitu-
tional," *New York Times*, July 31, 2008; Owen Matthews, "Democracy in the Dock,"
*Newsweek*, Jul. 26, 2008.

37. Andrew Finkel, "The Many Battles for Turkey's Soul," *Le Monde diplomatique,* Sept. 2007, http://mondediplo.com/2007/09/04turkey (accessed August 27, 2008).

38. Eurasia Group analysts constructed an index for scoring government strength and cohesiveness (STGV). This index was scored monthly by analysts, and the index's results were correlated to sovereign bond spreads. A number of economic control measures were used, and the model was run for a set of emerging markets, including Brazil, Bulgaria, Colombia, Mexico, Philippines, Poland, Russia, Turkey, Ukraine, and Venezuela, using data from 2002–04. Without going into the statistics behind it, the higher STGV scores correspond to lower sovereign debt spreads. It seems that government fragmentation is a useful indicator of whether a country's risk profile will increase or not.

39. Cooking the books is a time-honored, albeit dubious, tradition. Governments as well as corporations engage in it with some regularity (see Enron or WorldCom). The governments of the Communist world were notorious for constantly trumpeting fictitious bumper crops of beets, record production of pig iron, and other stunning Stalinist achievements. The result was risible propaganda with significant, though grim, humor value.

40. Examples of this included using price agreement data related to tourism rather than actual price data, as well as placing suspected "ceilings" on data related to prices of certain products so that the government would say data was unavailable if the price of a product exceeded the ceiling. In order to try to bolster the credibility of the index, deflect criticism, and lower the controversy surrounding the release of monthly inflation figures, the government announced a new method for calculating CPI vaguely based on methods used in the United States and Spain. At the time of writing, expectations about the new method reducing manipulation were limited, given that the methodology will likely fail to live up to international standards. The government will be able to continue arbitrarily affecting reported amounts regardless of purported methodology.

41. Current and future hedging: For most portfolio investors, political risk remains an issue that is best dealt with through an understanding of the political environment and the political issues that can impact the value of investments. Unlike for other types of risks, such as credit and market risk, there is at the moment limited hedging possible for political risk in capital markets. Credit default swaps (CDS) are one mechanism. They are "credit-protection contracts whereby one party agrees, in exchange for a periodic premium, to make a contingent payment in the case of a defined credit event. For buyers of credit protection, the CDS market offers the opportunity to reduce credit concentration and regulatory capital while maintaining customer relationships. For sellers of protection, it offers the opportunity to take credit exposure over a customized term and earn income without having to fund the position" (Frank Packer and Chamaree Suthiphongchai, "The Expanding Market for Sovereign Credit Default Swaps," in Wilkin (ed.), *Country and Political Risk,* p. 340).

For some emerging market countries, sovereign debt CDS are commonly traded, ensuring that investors have some protection against sovereign debt default. Brazil, Mexico, Japan, the Philippines, South Africa, Colombia, and China account for about 50% of the traded sovereign CDS (Packer and Suthiphongchai, "The Expanding Market," p. 343). That said, the markets for political risk–based derivatives remain relatively small.

Even for currencies, the liquidity to ensure hedging is not always available, especially for large exposures. When it comes to Foreign Direct Investment (FDI), one way to deal with the risk of currency devaluation is to find local funding for the project, as a form of hedging. However, the availability of local currency may not exist. Often, multilateral agencies need to be involved in these kinds of processes. For instance, in the Philippines, the Asian Development Bank (ADB) created a currency swap with the Philippine government so that the ADB could then provide local currency loans to companies wanting to invest in the Philippines (Tomoko Matsukawa and Odo Habeck, *Review of Risk Mitigation Instruments for Infrastructure: Financing and Recent Trends and Development* [World Bank Publications, 2007], p. 7).

The development of more sophisticated political insurance derivatives in the future is likely. This would enable political risk insurance, a fairly small and illiquid part of the insurance industry, to be securitized and capital markets to trade on political risk exposures. This would be not dissimilar to catastrophe bonds, which already exist and are basically derivatives based on the disaster insurance industry. So, as there is a market for derivatives in bonds based on events like hurricanes and earthquakes, there is no reason why there could not be a derivative market developed around political risk insurance (see John D. Finnerty, "Securitizing Political Risk Investment Insurance," in Theodore H. Moran, ed., *International Political Risk Management: Exploring New Frontiers* [Washington, DC: World Bank Publications, 2001], p. 144). "There appears to be growing interest in the potential for securitizing political risk insurance. This interest is due at least in part to the dramatic rise in foreign direct investment in developing countries in the 1990s coupled with the 1997–98 Asian financial crises and the 1998 Russian debt moratorium, which heightened investor sensitivity to emerging market political risk. As the emerging markets continue to attract new overseas investment, foreign suppliers of capital are naturally concerned about hedging their exposure to the political risks inherent in such investing" (Finnerty, "Securitizing Political Risk Investment Insurance," p. 78).

The development of political risk futures is another possibility. To some extent this is already happening (on a very small scale) with companies like Intrade that allow bets by individuals on political events (such as the U.S. elections). However there is no reason why such a market for large and institutional investors could not be developed to cover specific classes of political risk.

Given that many if not most equities, bonds, commodities, and currencies are relatively liquid (i.e., easy to buy and sell), political risk in capital markets is perhaps best mitigated by knowing of a risk before the event happens. In this sense, political risk analysis is the best form of risk mitigation, to the extent that it allows investors to reallocate their assets before a political risk event occurs. Knowing that the risk of Russia defaulting on its debt was substantially greater than most other market participants thought it was during the summer of 1998 would have been not only enough to mitigate the risk, but actually a good opportunity to make money.

## Chapter 5

1. Teodor Shanin, *The Roots of Otherness: Russia's Turn of the Century*, vol. 2: *Russia, 1905–07: Revolution as a Moment of Truth* (New Haven, CT: Yale University Press, 1986), quoted in John Foran, *Taking Power: On the Origins of Third World Revolutions* (Cambridge, UK: Cambridge University Press, 2005), p. 13.
2. Michael J. Matheson, U.S. urges passage of Iran Claims Act—transcript, U.S. Department of State Bulletin, Aug. 1985.
3. See http://www.state.gov/p/us/rm/2008/106817.htm (accessed August 28, 2008).
4. Iranian Youth: Measures of Merit in the Islamic Republic, http://www.rand.org/international_programs/cmepp/imey/projects/students.html (accessed August 28, 2008).
5. In China's case, this of course may be tempered by the fact that the population is also falling again.
6. Eurasia Group, for instance, has developed two indexes that can be used to monitor the stability of urban areas. The City Stability Index (CSI) scores cities on a set of variables comparable to those used for country stability indices (things like youth disaffection and access to water).
7. Demographia World Urban Areas (World Agglomerations: 2007), 3, http://demographia.com/db-worldua.pdf (accessed June 16, 2008).
8. That said, there are exceptions to this rule, and especially if one begins to ask what is a democracy.
9. Samuel P. Huntington, *Political Order in Changing Societies* (New Haven, CT: Yale University Press, 1968), p. 264.
10. Linwood T. Geiger, "Expropriation and External Capital Flows," *Economic Development and Cultural Change*, Vol. 37, No. 3 (Apr. 1989), p. 537.
11. James D. Fearon, "Iraq's Civil War," *Foreign Affairs*, Vol. 86, No. 2 (March/April 2007), pp. 2–15.
12. Ibid. Quote from Joseph Wertheim, Tea Importers, Inc.
13. The facts of this case study are largely drawn from OPIC. See Project Profiles: Rwanda Tea Importers. Persistence and a long-term commitment make a differ-

ence in Rwanda, http://www.opic.gov/Insurance/projects/profile_rwanda_tea.asp (accessed June 16, 2008).

14. Ibid.

15. Ibid.

16. Martin Lindeberg and Staffan Morndal, Managing Political Risk—A Contextual Approach, Linköping University, January 17, 2002, pp. 64–65, 70, http://www.ep.liu.se/exjobb/eki/2002/iep/012/ (accessed June 24, 2008).

17. One caveat is that this kind of project-level strategy is better suited to a company that operates in a sector like construction that is relatively unregulated (compared to say, banking) and where the break-even point is relatively quick (compared to say, oil exploration). In regulated sectors or for companies that have to wait years between the initial investment and turning a profit, often country-level risk is a more important a predictor than project-level risks.

18. "Conflict diamonds" is a popular name given to diamonds taken from states undergoing violent conflict, the proceeds of which are used to purchase weapons, thus fueling the cycle of war. A popular awareness campaign was launched to get people to avoid purchasing these "blood diamonds."

19. Greg Campbell, "The Sordid History Behind Africa's Conflict Diamonds," *Christian Science Monitor*, Dec. 11, 2006.

20. Gary King and Langche Zeng, "Improving Forecasts of State Failure," *World Politics*, Vol. 53 (July 2001), p. 623.

21. Daniel C. Esty, Jack A. Goldstone, Ted Robert Gurr, Barbara Harff, Marc Levy, Geoffrey D. Dabelko, Pamela T. Surko, and Alan N. Unger, "State Failure Task Force: Report: Phase II Findings," *Environmental Change & Security Project Report*, Issue 5 (Summer 1999).

22. Rosemary H.T. O'Kane, *The Likelihood of Coups* (Aldershot, UK: Avebury, 1987).

23. "Industry Impacted by Attacks on America," Alabama Independent Insurance Agents, Inc., http://www.aiia.org/arcsep01.html (accessed August 28, 2008).

24. "Tongan Economy Still in Ruins a Year after Riots," *Marianas Variety*, Nov. 19, 2007.

25. See Roger Donnelly, Cambodia—Risk Assessment, February 2006, Export Finance and Insurance Corporation, http://www.efic.gov.au/static/efi/cra/cambodia.htm (accessed June 18, 2008).

26. James C. Leontiades, *Multinational Corporate Strategy: Planning for World Markets* (Lanham, Md.: Lexington Books, 1987), p. 162.

27. Yadong Luo, "Toward a Cooperative View of MNC-Host Government Relations: Building Blocks and Performance Implications," *Journal of International Business Studies*, Vol. 32, No. 3 (2001), p. 403.

28. Ibid.

29. See Jedrzej George Frynas, "Political Instability and Business: Focus on Shell in Nigeria," *Third World Quarterly*, Vol. 19, No. 3 (1998), pp. 457–478.

30. Basil Louvaris, "Protecting Corporate Balance Sheets against Political Uncertainty," *Business Credit* (Nov./Dec. 2002).

31. See OPIC Project Profiles—Rwanda Tea Importers at http://www.opic.gov/Insurance/projects/profile_rwanda_tea.asp (accessed August 28, 2008).

32. Satoshi Kambayashi, "Of Coups and Coverage: Political Turmoil Is Costly Unless You Are Fully Insured," *Economist*, April 4, 2007, http://www.economist.com/finance/displaystory.cfm?story_id=8967224 (accessed August 28, 2008).

33. As mentioned in Jasminka Udovicki and James Ridgeway, *Yugoslavia's Ethnic Nightmare. The Inside Story of Europe's Unfolding Ordeal* (New York: Lawrence Hill Books, 1995), pp. 102–103.

34. Warren Zimmerman, *Origins of a Catastrophe: Yugoslavia and Its Destroyers* (New York: Three Rivers Press, 1999), pp. 8, 248.

## Chapter 6

1. Who were oppressed at the time by the Protestant ruling classes.

2. The group itself called its assassins fida'in ("fedayeen").

3. It was an early form of suicide terrorism, for the assassin by killing with a dagger would know in advance that he would inevitably be caught and executed.

4. For a detailed history of this sect see Bernard Lewis, *The Assassins* (Basic Books, 2002).

5. Walter Laqueur, *Terrorism: A Study of National and International Violence* (Boston: Little, Brown and Company, 1977).

6. Alex P. Schmid, Albert J. Jongman, *Political Terrorism: A New Guide to Actors, Authors, Concepts, Data Bases, Theories, and Literature* (New Brunswick, N.J.: Transaction Books, 1988), pp. 5–6.

7. Department of Defense Dictionary of Military and Associated Terms, Washington, D.C.: Department of Defense, April 2001, p. 428. Also available online at http://www.dtic.mil/doctrine/jel/doddict/data/t/05488.html (accessed June 25, 2008).

8. Laqueur, *Terrorism*, pp. 4–5.

9. The English word *thug* comes from this sect of Indian highway robbers, which would ritually kill travelers as an offering to the goddess Kali.

10. Colombian drug lord Pablo Escobar protected his cocaine empire not only by bribing, controlling, and routinely assassinating Colombian politicians, but also by carrying out mass bombings in Bogotá and other Colombian cities in order to terrorize the population and force the government to stop its investigations of his activities. It is extremely likely that Escobar and his organization can to a large extent be labeled as political terrorists, although their ultimate goals were purely economic. This again underscores the difficulty of figuring out who is a terrorist and who is not. For an extended discussion of Pablo Escobar, see Mark Bowden, *Killing Pablo: The Hunt for the World's Greatest Outlaw* (Atlantic Monthly Press, 2001).

11. *The Life of Brian* is set in the Middle East of the 1st century A.D.

12. Governments may not be able to prevent a few disgruntled individuals or an increasingly disaffected fringe group from carrying out its first act of terrorism. However, they can prevent, disrupt, or stop sustained terrorist campaigns, which is why most analysts focus on understanding organizations involved in sustained acts of terror.

13. Richard Drake, "The Red and the Black: Terrorism in Contemporary Italy," *International Political Science Review,* Vol. 5, No. 3 (1980), p. 279. According to Drake, terrorist violence in Italy during this period, due to both right-wing and left-wing groups, resulted in a minimum of 351 deaths and 768 injuries.

14. Adding to the confusion, both the Red Brigades (Drake, "The Red and the Black," 284) and right-wing terrorist groups in Italy had alleged links to organized crime organizations such as the Nuova Camorra.

15. Antonio Negri and Alexander Stille, "'Apocalypse Soon': An Exchange," *The New York Review of Books,* Vol. 50, No. 3 (February 27, 2003), http://www.nybooks.com/articles/16090 (accessed June 25, 2008).

16. The Khmer Rouge was perhaps the clearest example of such a revolutionary party, which employed mass killings of urban bourgeoisie and landowners in an attempt to abolish traditional social and political relations and replace them with a "new" Maoist utopia.

17. Ethnic militias like the now defunct Moro National Liberation Front (MNLF) in the southern Philippines are closely tied to ethnic or clan interests and act in their defense. Status quo groups are organizationally difficult to eliminate, since they persist as long as the local interests and conditions that generate them persist.

18. They tend to operate within the existing social institutions but attempt to transform these while carrying out armed struggle. These groups typically establish front organizations—political parties, charities, trade unions—that are sometimes subservient to the armed campaign, but are often equal partners in the struggle. One of the strengths of the IRA was the successful coordination between its military and political wing (i.e., the Sinn Fein Party).

19. In January 2007, the latter group announced a formal change of name to Al Qaeda Organization in the Islamic Maghreb.

20. In certain cases, groups that straddle the line between terrorism and insurgency, like the Tamil Tigers (who seek to gain an ethnic Tamil state independent from Sri Lanka), can deploy large military units to conduct conventional warfare. More generally, though, terrorist groups engage in ambushes of government troops as well as attacks on military facilities and command centers, in classic guerrilla fashion. An example is Hizbullah's 1983 suicide bombing of the U.S. Marines barracks in Beirut, which left 241 Marines dead and resulted in the withdrawal of U.S. troops from Lebanon.

21. Although the latter were soldiers and not terrorists.

22. M.M. Hafez, "Rationality, Culture, and Structure in the Making of Suicide Bombers: A Preliminary Theoretical Synthesis and Illustrative Case Study," *Studies in Conflict and Terrorism* 29 (2006), pp. 165–185. See page 166.

23. Laqueur, *Terrorism,* 109.

24. For an overview of the costs of 9/11 see: Robert Looney, "The Economic Costs to the United States Stemming from the 9/11 Attacks," *Strategic Insights,* Vol. 1, No. 6 (August 2002), http://www.ccc.nps.navy.mil/si/aug02/homeland.asp (accessed June 24, 2008).

25. International Monetary Fund, "World economic outlook—the global economy after 11 September, December 2001: a survey by the staff of the international monetary fund," World Economic and Financial Surveys, http://www.imf.org/external/pubs/ft/weo/2001/03/index.htm (accessed June 25, 2008).

26. Jeffrey M. Lacker, "Payment System Disruptions and the Federal Reserve Following September 11, 2001," *Federal Reserve Bank of Richmond,* March 5, 2004, http://64.233.169.104/search?q=cache:T111dDzOYNQJ:www.frbatlanta.org/filelegacydocs/epconf_lacker.pdf+%22Bank+of+New+York%22+fines+%E2%80%9Cclearing+and+settlement%E2%80%9D+terrorist+%22World+Trade+Center%22&hl=en&ct=clnk&cd=9&gl=us (accessed June 25, 2008).

27. Paul Beckett and Jathon Sapsford, "Rebuilding Wall Street: How Wall Street's Nervous System Caused Pain," *Wall Street Journal,* September 21, 2001, p. C1.

28. Kenneth C. Loudon and Jane C. Loudon, "The World Trade Center Disaster: Who Was Prepared?" in *Essentials of Management Information Systems: Managing the Digital Firm* Companion Website, http://wps.prenhall.com/bp_laudon_essmis_6/0,9311,1423428-,00.utf8.html (accessed June 24, 2008).

29. Catherine Walsh, "Leadership on 9/11: Morgan Stanley's Challenge," *Harvard Business School,* December 17, 2001, http://hbswk.hbs.edu/archive/2690.html (accessed June 24, 2008).

30. Raymond Whitaker, Paul Lashmar, Sophie Goodchild, Severin Carrell, Justin Huggler, and Lauren Veevers, "The Fight against Terror: Surveillance UK," *The Independent,* August 20, 2006, http://www.independent.co.uk/news/uk/crime/the-fight-against-terror-surveillance-uk-412645.html (accessed June 24, 2006).

31. Ian Cobain, "The Mysterious Disappearance of an Alleged Terrorist Mastermind," *The Guardian,* January 28, 2008, http://www.guardian.co.uk/uk/2008/jan/28/pakistan.world1 (accessed June 24, 2008).

32. The 9–11 Commission Report: Final Report of the National Commission on Terrorist Attacks Upon the United States, Official Government Edition. Washington, DC: U.S. Government Printing Office (Internet download version: http://www.gpoaccess.gov/911/), p. 336.

33. In one interesting variation on this theme, in 1981 the Italian state decided to pay a ransom for an Italian politician kidnapped by the Red Brigades. However, the

exchange was negotiated by a Neapolitan organized crime family that also had to be paid, more than the actual ransom.

34. Nevertheless, Sinn Fein does not see its decision to participate in the political process as capitulation, nor does it see its electoral victories as representing the ultimate objectives of the party. Instead, it views the political process as a more productive means toward the realization of those objectives than was armed struggle.

## Chapter 7

1. For a detailed treatment of the events preceding the coup as well as CIA involvement, see Stephen Kinzer, *All the Shah's Men: An American Coup and the Roots of Middle East Terror* (Hoboken, NJ: Wiley, 2003).

2. Sunita Kikeri and Aishetu Kolo, "Privatization Trends: What's Been Done," The World Bank Group Private Sector Development Vice Presidency, Note 303, February 2006, p. 1, http://rru.worldbank.org/documents/publicpolicyjournal/303Kikeri_Kolo.pdf (accessed August 28, 2008).

3. Michael S. Minor, "The Demise of Expropriation as an Instrument of LDC Policy," *Journal of International Business Studies,* Vol. 25, No. 1 (1994), 182.

4. This is not that different than from the 1970s, when during the high tide of expropriations, expropriation claims amounted to about 96% of all claims OPIC paid out in political risk insurance. See Nathan Jensen, "Measuring Risk: Political Risk Insurance Premiums and Domestic Political Institutions," paper presented at 2005 Political Economy of Multinational Corporations and Foreign Direct Investment Conference, Washington University, p. 4.

5. What are expropriations? Expropriation is the involuntary deprivation of property rights by government policy or law. Governments, as sovereign actors, are well within their legal rights to expropriate. Under international law, all governments are allowed to take away private property (whether from domestic or foreign investors), as long as they provide the deprived owners with compensation that is "prompt, adequate and effective."

The range of what governments nationalize varies from a single company to a whole economy. For instance, governments can nationalize specific companies. One example is that of the nationalization of Olympic Airlines, which was bought in 1975 by the center-right Greek government from Aristotle Onassis's heirs. Another is the French expropriation of car-maker Renault in 1945, after Renault's collaboration with the Nazi occupation.

Governments sometimes nationalize whole industrial sectors. In Britain in the late 1940s, the Clement Attlee government nationalized the railroads and the mining and telecommunication industries. As we discussed in the introduction to this book, the nationalization of the Mexican oil industry in 1938, a seminal case of modern expropriation, was another wholesale nationalization of an industrial sector. That year, Mexican president Lázaro Cárdenas expropriated Mexico's petroleum industry, which, until then, had been owned primarily by U.S., British, and Dutch companies.

In other instances, nationalizations have involved all the private property within a country. Governments in Russia, China, Cuba, and Eastern Europe, after Communist takeovers, usually declared that most—from the largest factory to the smallest newsstand—belonged to the "people," as represented by the ruling Communist party. As expropriations of all property are usually tied to political ideology and require a significant amount of political repression, they have become increasingly rare.

That said, expropriations can still involve a show of force. On May 1, 2006, Bolivian leftist president Evo Morales sent troops to surround the facilities of the Brazilian company Petrobras as he launched the nationalization of Bolivia's hydrocarbon sector. On the other hand, some governments, such as the Russian one, have carried out expropriation simply by changing regulations and tax codes or by putting legal pressure on key shareholders. How expropriations can be carried out not only varies, but often is dependent on a government's interests. At least four broad categories of outright expropriations can be identified: formal expropriations, intervention (or direct seizure), forced sale, and contract renegotiations.

Formal expropriations occur when a government either uses existing laws and decrees or creates new ones to take over or reassign existing property rights. In Mexico's case, the government's order to nationalize the petroleum industry followed a Mexican Supreme Court decision that found the operating companies in defiance of a previous court order. In other cases, governments can create new laws or decrees to expropriate. Eastern Europe's Communist governments nationalized most of the private property in 1945–48 through a series of decrees.

Second, governments also often just intervene and seize existing properties, ignoring all legal niceties. Some governments simply send in the army or police and take over a piece of property without much legal cover. Sometimes, this is done by proxy, using government supporters or militants. In Zimbabwe in 2000, white-owned farms were occupied by government-backed "veterans," and later the properties were redistributed to government supporters. Similarly, in Chile, under Salvador Allende "workers" seized foreign-owned enterprises that were slated for expropriation by that government. In both cases, laws were later passed to make these takeovers legal, but this was done post facto; at the time of the seizures, the government willfully chose not to enforce existing laws protecting the properties in question.

Forced sales occur when governments coerce foreign companies to sell off their properties through threats of expropriations or through harassment. Recently, Russian authorities have pressured private investors, both foreign and Russian, to relinquish controlling stakes in the energy sector to the state. While in 2003 most Russian oil assets were in private hands, they are now overwhelmingly in state-controlled or state-friendly hands. State-owned Rosneft has gone from trailing private companies like Lukoil, TNK-BP, Yukos, and Surgutneftegaz to being the leading Russian oil producer. This was accomplished mostly through a series of forced sales that were backed by legal threats to the previous owners (some of whom ended in jail on spurious charges).

Lastly, government can simply force corporations to renegotiate the existing terms of a signed contract. To the extent that they interfere with ownership and operation rights, such renegotiations can amount to expropriation of existing property. In Ecuador, the government declared in October 2007 that all foreign oil companies will be required to hand over to the government all earnings over $24 per barrel, a significant divergence from the initial contracts the foreign oil operators signed, by which only 50% of earnings over $24 were to be handed over. The Ecuadorian government also gave the companies the choice to switch to new service contracts, whose terms were equally unfavorable. A similar process has happened recently in Venezuela, where the Chávez government has forced all private investors to switch to new joint venture contracts with the state-owned oil corporation PDVSA, which was given a controlling interest in the oil field concessions.

For some leaders, like Chávez in Venezuela, nationalization is something to celebrate openly and to be pointed to as a sign of progress or social justice. However, directly interfering with property rights of foreign or even domestic investors comes with costs, such as reduced access to international capital markets, lawsuits, and reduced amounts of foreign direct investment—investors generally tend to be wary of putting money into countries where their property is taken away.

Thus, for some governments, whose interest is more in gaining greater tax revenue and control of cash flows and less in the domestic political capital gained, "creeping expropriations" are a more common path to take. For instance, in 2004, China announced a set of regulatory policies in its domestic automotive sector. These policies banned "the sale and transfer of manufacturing licenses by bankrupt or failing manufacturers" to either domestic or foreign investors. Additionally, the policies required any new investors setting up new automotive plants to invest over a certain amount (over $240 million) and to invest in R&D that would become Chinese-owned intellectual property. In this case, by prohibiting automotive companies from selling their licenses and by imposing intellectual property requirements the Chinese government has effectively taken a significant part of the ability of foreign corporations in the automotive sector to viably operate as private enterprises in China.

Indirect or "creeping expropriations" are a way for governments to expropriate without severely damaging their international reputation. If a government interferes with taxation or the ability of a company to appoint its own management, or if a government uses existing regulations to target a specific corporation, that may effectively amount to an expropriation.

In contrast to Chávez's bombast, Russian officials at times appeared almost defensive about retaking control of the country's oil assets after 2003. Russia and Kazakhstan have been far more quiet about taking back assets, using legalistic approaches that often target one company or one project at a time rather than an entire industry. Both governments, for example, have used alleged environmental or accounting violations as a means to renegotiate investment agreements with foreign companies whose deals with the governments were once seen as inviolable. These nationalizations often involve some form of compensation for the investor, whether in the form of cash or future joint development work with state-backed companies.

Minimizing the legal claims of private investors can be an objective, as is ensuring that other investors will not flee from other sectors of the economy out of fear that their industry will be the next target. Selectively nationalizing specific companies or assets also can be a way to avoid scaring investors away from the sector that is the focus of attention. Russian officials have argued that their country's oil and gas assets are still more open to foreign investment than those in Saudi Arabia or Mexico; certainly, foreign oil operators remain eager to stay engaged in Russia. Regardless of how benign governments attempt to make this kind of creeping nationalization, existing players who face the brunt of the nationalization wave will still be vulnerable to moves by the state to seize assets. On the other hand, investors preparing to enter such a market after the wave has swept through may find that governments welcome them, albeit on the governments' terms.

6. When, for instance, in 1902 Venezuela defaulted on its foreign debt, the Italian, British, and German navies sent ships to blockade and bombard ports until all debts were settled.

7. Roderick Duncan, "Price or Politics? An Investigation of the Causes of Expropriation," *The Australian Journal of Agricultural and Resource Economics,* Vol. 50, No. 1 (March 2006), p. 87.

8. That said, there were exceptions, such as the 1956 Suez crisis, when Egypt's nationalization of the Suez Canal prompted a brief war with Britain, France, and Israel, and the CIA-sponsored coup d'état against the Iranian government after it expropriated the assets of the British-owned Anglo-Iranian Oil Company in 1953.

9. Amy L. Chua, "The Privatization-Nationalization Cycle: The Link between Markets and Ethnicity in Developing Countries," *Columbia Law Review,* Vol. 95, No. 2 (Mar. 1995), p. 256.

10. Despite the losses of WWI and the turmoil of the Bolshevik revolution and the civil war that followed, the Soviet Union was still a great power in the late 1910s and early 1920s, if for no other reasons than its size and the relative weakness of its Western opponents, which were also suffering from the exhaustions of the Great War.

11. This is also shown by the compensation issue surrounding expropriations carried out by Communist states. China, the Soviet Union, and their Eastern bloc Commu-

nist satellites (e.g., Poland, Hungary, Romania) paid no compensation for nationalizations.

12. Eurasia Group data/analysis.

13. Economic interdependence, among other variables, is found to be an aid in forecasting political risk in D. W. Bunn and M. M. Mustafaoglu, "Forecasting Political Risk," *Management Science,* Vol. 24, No. 15 (Nov. 1978), pp. 1559, 1565.

14. Eurasia Group data.

15. The nationalization of distressed bank assets in the United States and Britain in 2008 following the global financial crisis offers another excellent example. Distressed financial institutions like American International Group and Royal Bank of Scotland were seen as too important for the stability of the international financial system to fail. The U.S. and British governments respectively forced them to accept partial state control in exchange for recapitalization.

16. Jensen, "Measuring Risk," p. 22, quoting David A. Jodice, "Sources of Change in Third World Regimes for Foreign Direct Investment." *International Organization,* Vol. 34, No. 2 (1980), p. 192.

17. Duncan, "Price or Politics?" pp. 93–96.

18. Bunn and Mustafaoglu, "Forecasting Political Risk," pp. 1559 and 1564.

19. Michel Leonard, "Creeping Expropriation, Threats to Property Rights, and Rising Economic Risk: Remember Communism?" *Country Briefing,* June 7, 2004, AON Trade Credit, http://www.offshoregroup.com/newsfiles/chinabriefing.pdf (accessed June 18, 2008).

20. Chua, "The Privatization-Nationalization Cycle," p. 231.

21. Chua, "The Privatization-Nationalization Cycle," p. 225.

22. Marina Azzimonti and Pierre-Daniel G. Sarte, "Barriers to Foreign Direct Investment under Political Instability," *Economic Quarterly,* Vol. 93, No. 3 (Summer 2007), p. 296.

23. Jonathan Eaton and Mark Gersovitz, "A Theory of Expropriation and Deviations from Perfect Capital Mobility," *The Economic Journal,* Vol. 94, No. 373 (Mar. 1984), p. 17.

24. Michael Shafer, "Capturing the Mineral Multinationals: Advantage or Disadvantage," *International Organization,* Vol. 37, No. 1 (Winter 1983), p. 110.

25. Eurasia Group data.

26. Bunn and Mustafaoglu, "Forecasting Political Risk," pp. 1559, 1564.

27. Chua, "The Privatization-Nationalization Cycle," p. 270.

28. Chua, "The Privatization-Nationalization Cycle," pp. 256–262.

29. Minor, "The Demise of Expropriation," p. 185.

30. See Raymond Vernon, *Sovereignty at Bay: The Transnational Spread of U.S. Enterprises* (London: Longman, 1971); Ramamurti R., "The Obsolescing 'Bargaining Model'? MNC-Host Developing Country Relations Revisited "Source: Journal of International Business Studies, Vol. 32, No. 1 (Mar. 2001), pp. 23–39; Sushil Vachani, "Enhancing the Obsolescing Bargain Theory: A Longitudinal Study of Foreign

Ownership of U.S. and European Multinationals," *Journal of International Business Studies*, Vol. 26, No. 1 (1st Qtr., 1995), pp. 159–180 and J. M. Chermak, "Political Risk Analysis: Past and Present," *Resources Policy* (Sept. 1992).

31. M. G. Majd, "The 1951–1953 Oil Nationalization Dispute and the Iranian Economy: A Rejoinder," *Middle Eastern Studies*, Vol. 31, No. 3 (Jul. 1995), pp. 449–459.

32. The case comes from Theodore H. Moran, "Transnational Strategies of Protection and Defense by Multinational Corporations: Spreading the Risk and Raising the Cost for Nationalization in Natural Resources," *International Organization*, Vol. 27, No. 2 (Spring 1973), pp. 273–287.

33. Louis T. Wells, "God and Fair Competition: Does the Foreign Direct Investor Face Still Other Risks in Emerging Markets?" in Theodore H. Moran, *Managing International Political Risk* (Cambridge, MA: Blackwell, 1998), p. 37.

34. Rudolph Dolzer "Indirect Expropriations: New Developments?" *NYU Environmental Law Journal*, Vol. 11 (2002), pp. 64–65.

35. Helen Mountfield, "Regulatory Expropriations in Europe: The Approach of the European Court of Human Rights," *NYU Environmental Law Journal*, Vol. 11 (2002), pp. 144–145.

36. See Philippe Beaujard, "The Indian Ocean in Eurasian and African World-Systems before the Sixteenth Century," *Journal of World History*, Vol. 16, No. 4 (2005), p. 454. In Egypt, from 1429, the Burji Mamluks created a monopoly on the trade in spices, fixed market prices, and overburdened merchants through taxation and the strict restricting of their business, thereby killing "the goose that laid the golden egg in what was an already difficult international scene." See also John L. Meloy "Imperial Strategy and Political Exigency: The Red Sea Spice Trade and the Mamluk Sultanate in the Fifteenth Century," *Journal of the American Oriental Society*, Vol. 123, No. 1. (Jan.–Mar. 2003), pp. 1–19.

37. Walter J. Fischel, "The Spice Trade in Mamluk Egypt: A Contribution to the Economic History of Medieval Islam," *Journal of the Economic and Social History of the Orient*, Vol. 1, No. 2 (Apr. 1958), pp. 164, 174.

## Chapter 8

1. EIU, "Regulatory Risk: Trends and Strategies for CRO," *Economist*, July 2005.

2. In most developed countries, regulations govern virtually every aspect of a business transaction (in its simplest form, the term "regulation" refers to control over actions of private individuals and businesses over what they may do and sometimes how they may perform certain activities). Government has always exercised such control through the legal system, but regulations are different in that they are secondary statutes issued to implement the meaning of laws that prima facie can be quite abstract. Since laws cannot take into account every unique circumstance that businesses may face in compliance, government agencies issue regulations to address changing circumstances during implementation and break down laws into parameters, which

regulators can use to make decisions based on open-ended standards (D. J. Galligan, *Discretionary Powers: A Legal Study of Official Discretion* [Oxford: Clarendon Press, 1986]). Regulations can serve an extremely varied number of economic and societal benefits, ranging from rules governing neighborhood-level garbage disposal to rules dealing with the trading of financial derivative options. In this chapter we mostly discuss how regulations impact investments abroad. In markets, regulations are critical in dealing with failures and with prohibiting specific forms of "unfair" dealing, such as insider trading or price manipulations (Robert Musgrave, *The Theory of Public Finance: A Study in Political Economy* [New York: McGraw-Hill, 1959]).

3. A new, pro-market government was elected in late 2007, and these practices stopped immediately.

4. Chalmers Johnson, *MITI and the Japanese Miracle: The Growth of Industrial Policy, 1925–1975* (Stanford, CA.: Stanford University Press, 1982).

5. Margaret Pearson, "The Business of Governing Business in China: Institutions and Norms of the Emerging Regulatory State," *World Politics* 57 (Jan. 2005), pp. 296–322 (300–301). A classic statement on the developmental model is Johnson, *MITI and the Japanese Miracle*.

6. It can provide a good sense about a number of other possible political risks as well. In fact, monitoring elections and political agendas is one of the better indicators of potential political risks.

7. See http://web.worldbank.org/WBSITE/EXTERNAL/COUNTRIES/EASTASIAPACI-FICEXT/CHINAEXTN/0,,contentMDK:20680895~pagePK:1497618~piPK:217854~theSitePK:318950,00.html (accessed August 28, 2008).

8. See http://www.hhs.gov/news/speech/2007/sp20071025a.html (accessed August 28, 2008).

9. Data from the U.S. Census Bureau's "Trade in Goods (Imports, Exports and Trade Balance) with China," http://www.census.gov/foreign-trade/balance/c5700.html#2008 (accessed, August 28, 2008).

10. Boston Consulting Group, "The New Global Challengers: How 100 Top Companies from Rapidly Developing Economies Are Changing the World," BCG Report, May 2006, p. 10, http://iis-db.stanford.edu/evnts/4326/New_Global_Challengers_May06.pdf (accessed on June 16, 2008).

11. As U.S. lawmakers broaden their definition of national security and create barriers to entry against some foreign firms, the risk will grow that EM-based companies might draw their home governments into unexpected diplomatic conflicts with Washington. American companies may lose some access to certain foreign markets as the governments of these countries retaliate against new U.S. restrictions. In sum, FDI approvals in many countries may become more politicized and unpredictable.

12. George Stigler, "The Theory of Economic Regulations," *Bell Journal of Economics and Management Science*, Vol. 6, No. 2 (1971). A third vein in regulatory scholarship is the institutionalist approach: Terry Moe, "Interests, Institutions, and Positive Theory: The Politics of the NLRB," *Studies in American Political Development*, Vol. 2 (1987).

13. Pearson, "The Business of Governing Business."

14. Pearson, "The Business of Governing Business," pp. 309, 310.

15. Joel Kurtzman and Glenn Yago, *Global Edge: Using the Opacity Index to Manage the Risks of Cross-border Business* (Cambridge, MA.: Harvard Business School Press, 2007), p. 136.

16. As with most political analysis, there are no one-size-fits-all methods for figuring out whether a regulatory regime will be more or less risky. That said, figuring out whether regulatory institutions are weak is a relatively commonsensical, if time-intensive, task. The first thing is to look at whether the regulatory authority has institutions and a structure that would facilitate a fair business environment. There are quite a few key characteristics that have been identified for an effective regulatory regime (see Paul Correa et al., "Regulatory Governance in Infrastructure Industries: Assessment and Measurement of Brazilian Regulators," *Trend and Policy Options* 3 [Washington, DC: World Bank and PPIAF, 2006]; David Baron, "Design of Regulatory Mechanisms and Institutions," in Richard Schmalensee and Robert Willig, eds., *Hand Book of Industrial Organization,* Vol. 2, [Amsterdam: North-Holland, 1989]). These include:
    - autonomy from legislative and executive branch to avoid political interference
    - autonomy from the regulated industrial actors to prevent political "capture"
    - well-developed procedural requirements for regulators that minimize discretionary power, encourage systematic deliberations, strengthen coherence and predictability in the enforcement of laws and contracts, and reduce the likelihood that regulator decisions will be reversed later in court (see Jon Stern and Stuart Holder, "Criteria for Assessing the Performace of Regulatory Systems," *Utility Policy,* Vol. 8, No. 1 [1999], 33–50)
    - transparent decision-making procedures (see Warrick Smith, "Utility Regulators—The Independence Debate," in *Private Sector in Infrastructure: Strategy, Regulation, and Risk* [Washington, DC: World Bank and International Forum for Utility Regulation, 1997], 21–24)
    - access to adequate information and resources to make informed decisions
    - audit and oversight mechanism to hold regulators accountable (see Paul Correa, "What It Takes to Lower Regulatory Risk in Infrastructure Industries," *Gridlines* [September 2007], Washington, DC: PPIAF and World Bank.)

17. Raymond Vernon, *Sovereignty at Bay* (New York: Basic Books, 1971); Raymond Vernon, "The Obsolescing Bargain: A Key Factor in Political Risk," in Mark Winchester (ed.), *The International Essays for Business Decision Makers,* 5th ed. (Houston, TX: Center for International Business, 1980).

18. Stephen J. Kobrin, "Testing the Bargaining Hypothesis in the Manufacturing Sector in Developing Countries," *International Organization,* Vol. 41, No. 4 (1987), pp. 609–638.

19. Barbara Jenkins, "Reexamining the 'Obsolescing Bargain': A Study of Canada's National Energy Program," *International Organization,* Vol. 40, No. 1 (1986), pp. 139–165.

20. Kobrin, "Testing the Bargaining Hypothesis," pp. 609–648; Jenkins, "Re-examining the 'Obsolescing Bargain,'" pp. 139–145.

21. Kobrin, "Testing the Bargaining Hypothesis."

22. Kobrin, "Testing the Bargaining Hypothesis," p. 613.

23. Holly Brasher and David Lowery, "The Corporate Context of Lobbying Activity," *Business and Politics*, Vol. 8, No. 1 (2006), pp. 1–23; Gene Grossman and Elhanen Helpman, "Protection for Sale," *American Economic Review*, Vol. 84 (1994), pp. 833–850; Gene Grossman and Elhanen Helpman, *Interest Groups and Trade Policy* (Princeton, N.J.: Princeton University Press, 2002); Kishore Gawande and Usree Bandyyopadhyay, "Is Protection for Sale? A Test of the Grossman Helpman Theory of Endogenous Protection," *Review of Economics and Statistics*, Vol. 89 (2002), pp. 139–152.

24. Tarun Khanna and Krishna Palepu, "Why Focused Strategies May Be Wrong for Emerging Markets," *Harvard Business Review*, Vol. 75, No. 4 (Jul.–Aug. 1997), pp. 41–51.

25. Witold J. Henisz and Bennet A. Zelner, "Resistance to Illegitimate Multilateral Influence on Reform: The Political Backlash against Private Infrastructure Investments," September 25, 2004, http://www-management.wharton.upenn.edu/henisz/papers/hz_rimir.pdf (accessed on June 25, 2008).

26. Henisz and Zelner, "Resistance to Illegitimate Multilateral Influence."

## Chapter 9

1. The first siege took place in 1529, in the wake of the Ottoman conquest of most of Hungary. It was also unsuccessful.

2. John Stoye, *The Siege of Vienna: The Last Great Trial Between Cross & Crescent* (New York: Pegasus Books, 2006), p. 22.

3. Ibid., pp. 32–33.

4. Ibid., p. 67.

5. Ibid., p. 60.

6. Ibid., p. 60.

7. Ibid., p. 26.

8. Ibid., p. 26.

9. For a classic text on risk selection see Mary Douglas and Aaron Wildavsky, *Risk and Culture* (Berkeley: University of California Press, 1983).

10. This is an issue that touches about both communicating a threat, as well as understanding it—the two are intertwined.

11. J. Steven Ott and Jay M. Shafritz, "Toward a Definition of Organizational Incompetence: A Neglected Variable in Organization Theory," *Public Administration Review*, Vol. 54, No. 4 (Jul.–Aug. 1994), pp. 370–377.

12. See Max Weber, *Economy and Society,* eds. Guenther Roth and Claus Wittich (Berkeley: University of California Press, 1978), in particular the chapter on Bureaucracy, pp. 956–1007.

13. Weber, *Economy and Society,* p. 975.

14. George Ritzer, *The McDonaldization of Society* (Thousand Oaks, CA: Pine Forge Press, 1993), p. 99.

15. *The 9–11 Commission Report: Final Report of the National Commission on Terrorist Attacks Upon the United States, Official Government Edition.* Washington, DC: U.S. Government Printing Office (Internet download version: http://www.gpoaccess. gov/911/), p. 264.

16. Jeff Taylor, "How the FBI Let 9/11 Happen: The smoldering gun was right there all the time," *Reason Magazine,* June 2006, http://www.reason.com/news/show/36676.html (accessed August 28, 2008).

17. Anna Zarkada-Fraser and Campbell Fraser, "Risk Perceptions by UK Firms toward the Russian Market," *International Journal of Project Management,* Vol. 20, No. 2 (Feb. 2002), p. 102.

18. Ibid.

19. Ibid.

20. Ibid.

21. Barry Bozeman and Gordon Kingsley, "Risk Culture in Public and Private Organizations," *Public Administration Review,* Vol. 58, No. 2 (Mar./Apr. 1988).

22. Zarkada-Fraser and Fraser, "Risk Perceptions," pp. 102–103.

23. *9/11 Commission Report,* p. 345.

24. Steve Chan, "The Intelligence of Stupidity: Understanding Failures in Strategic Warning," *The American Political Science Review,* Vol. 73, No. 1 (Mar. 1979), p. 172.

25. CNN.com, "Key questions about the Dubai port deal," March 6, 2006, http://www. cnn.com/2006/POLITICS/03/06/dubai.ports.qa/index.html (accessed August 28, 2008).

26. For a general discussion of politicization of CFIUS after Dubai Ports in context of FINSA see Douglas Holtz-Eakin, "You Can't Be CFIUS," *Wall Street Journal,* July 13, 2006.

27. In the financial world, "Chinese Walls" between investment banks and brokerage firms were imposed following the 1929 stock market crash by the Glass-Steagall Act of 1933 in an effort to separate delivery of information from financial and organizational interests. But this wall, designed to eliminate conflicts of interest, has often been ineffective. Ultimately, separating organizational power from the ability to manipulate information is a fundamentally difficult task, one that will vary from organization to organization. It does pay, however, to try to design governance structures that avoid conflicts of interest.

28. Sheldon Appleton, "Systematic Bias in U.S. Foreign Affairs Reporting: A Critique and a Proposal," *International Studies Quarterly*, Vol. 16, No. 2. (Jun. 1972), p. 223.

29. For a general discussion of this, see Mary Douglas, *Risk and Blame* (London: Routledge, 2002).

30. Dan M. Kahan, "The Cognitively Illiberal State," *Stanford Law Review*, Vol. 60 (2007), p. 104.

31. Douglas and Wildavsky, *Risk and Culture,* pp. 7–8.

32. Kahan, "The Cognitively Illiberal State," p. 121.

33. As with the U.S.-supported coup in Guatemala in 1954, which brought down a leftist government that was planning to nationalize some arable land held by one U.S. company.

34. Frederick J. Philips-Patrick, "Political Risk and Organizational Form," *Journal of Law & Economics,* Vol. 24, No. 2 (Oct. 1992), pp. 681–682.

35. Philips-Patrick, "Political Risk and Organizational Form," p. 687.

36. Eurasia Group data/analysis.

37. Chris Isidore, "Airlines still in upheaval, 5 years after 9/11. Experts say 9/11 only sped up significant changes that were bound to shake airlines even without the attack," *CNN Money*, Sept. 8, 2006, http://money.cnn.com/2006/09/08/news/companies/airlines_sept11/index.htm?postversion=2006090813 (accessed June 20, 2008).

38. Howard Kunreuther, "Risk Analysis and Risk Management in an Uncertain World," Paper for Distinguished Achievement Award, Society for Risk Analysis Annual Meeting, Seattle, Wash., December 4, 2001, pp. 10–12.

39. Michael Sivak and Michael Flannagan, "Flying and Driving after the September 11 Attacks," *American Scientist,* Vol. 91, No. 1 (2003), http://www.americanscientist.org/issues/pub/flying-and-driving-after-the-september-11-attacks (accessed June 17, 2008).

40. Ibid.

41. Michael J. Sniffen, "No Deaths in 2007 Accidents on Scheduled U.S. Airlines," Yahoo News, April 17, 2008, http://news.yahoo.com/s/ap_travel/20080417/ap_tr_ge/travel_brief_air_accidents (accessed July 30, 2008).

42. Bryan Hubbard, "Civil Defense: More than Duck and Cover," Military.com, http://www.military.com/Content/MoreContent1/?file=cw_cd_story (accessed August 28, 2008).

43. Kunreuther, "Risk Analysis and Risk Management," pp. 20–21.

44. Richards J. Heuer Jr., *Psychology of Intelligence Analysis,* Center for the Study of Intelligence, Central Intelligence Agency, 1999, p. 112, https://www.cia.gov/library/center-for-the-study-of-intelligence/csi-publications/books-and-monographs/psychology-of-intelligence-analysis/PsychofIntelNew.pdf (accessed August 28, 2008).

45. When it came to persuading the Bush administration to order the invasion of Iraq, the hedgehogs may have had a built-in advantage, as the administration was favorable to that line of argument.

46. Heuer, *Psychology of Intelligence Analysis,* pp. 70–71.
47. Amos Tversky and Daniel Kahneman, "Extensional versus Intuitive Reasoning: The Conjunction Fallacy in Probability Judgment." *Psychological Review,* Vol. 90, No. 4 (Oct. 1983), pp. 307–308.
48. See Nicholas Nassim Taleb's *The Black Swan,* p. 76, for a similar discussion of this bias.
49. Richard Betts, for instance, discusses the ways in which organizations can begin to explain away information that does not confirm the data they want to believe. See Richard Betts, "Surprise Despite Warning: Why Sudden Attacks Succeed," *Political Science Quarterly,* Vol. 95, No. 4 (Winter 1980–1981), p. 563.
50. Bremmer, "Managing Risk," p. 51.
51. For discussions of the chronology and causes of the Latin American debt crisis, see Jeffrey Sachs, "Recent Studies of the Latin American Debt Crisis," *Latin American Research Review,* Vol. 23, No. 3 (1988), pp. 170–179; Barbara Stallings, "The Reluctant Giant: Japan and the Latin American Debt Crisis," *Journal of Latin American Studies,* Vol. 22, No. 1 (Feb. 1990), pp. 1–30; Stephen Golub, "The Political Economy of the Latin American Debt Crisis," *Latin American Research Review,* Vol. 26, No. 1 (1991), pp. 175–215.
52. Chan, "The Intelligence of Stupidity," p. 177.
53. Betts, "Surprise Despite Warning," p. 560.
54. See Taleb, *The Black Swan.*
55. See Betts, "Surprise Despite Warning."
56. See Philip M. Linsley and Michael J. Lawrence, "Risk Reporting by the Largest UK Companies: Readability and Lack of Obfuscation," *Accounting, Auditing & Accountability Journal,* Vol. 20, No. 4 (2007), pp. 620–627.
57. Greenpeace press release, "Credit Suisse Bank—Swiss Guarantee of Destruction of Sakhalin's Ecosystem?" June 27, 2005, http://www.greenpeace.org/russia/en/press/releases/credit-suisse-bank-swiss-gua (accessed February 26, 2008).
58. Ibid.
59. René P. Buholzer and Manuel Rybach, "Political Risk and Public Policy Management at Credit Suisse," in Bengt Sundelius, Beat Habegger et al., eds., *International Handbook on Risk Analysis and Management: Professional Experiences* (Zurich: Center for Security Studies, 2008), p. 185.
60. Organizations have found that one way to ensure that conflicts of interest in reporting are minimized and that reporting is performed accurately is through the creation of proper incentives. Incentives are very important to effective risk management. In their absence, an organization's employees may simply go through the motions and not really implement the risk-reporting rules specified in the organizational structure. For instance, a common complaint of risk managers in financial institutions is that traders often provide useless data and information. Unless a culture of risk

management is effectively implemented, risk management and reporting, no matter how sophisticated the tools and methodologies used, will suffer from a garbage in–garbage out problem.

61. Buholzer and Rybach, "Political Risk," p. 197.

62. Ibid, p. 199.

63. Bracken, p. 21.

64. Eric Banfield, "Creating Incentives for Proper Data and Risk Reporting and Disclosure," http://www.riskcenter.com/story.php?id=7922 (accessed August 28, 2008).

65. The guidelines and recommendations of the Basel Committee are nonbinding and must be legally implemented by the authorities within individual nation-states. In the United States, the Basel II guidelines will enter into force April 1, 2008. See *Federal Register,* Vol. 72, No. 235 (Dec. 7, 2007), Rules and Regulations, Department of the Treasury, Office of Thrift Supervision, Risk-Based Capital Standards: Advanced Capital Adequacy Framework—Basel II, Docket No. OTS 2007–0021.

66. Ibid., p. 137.

67. *International Convergence of Capital Measurement and Capital Standards: A Revised Framework,* Basel Committee on Banking Supervision, Bank for International Settlements, June 2004, p. 160, http://www.bis.org/publ/bcbs107.pdf (accessed Jan. 25, 2008).

68. Claudio Borio and Kostas Tsatsaronis, "Risk in Financial Reporting: Status, Challenges and Suggested Directions," BIS Working Papers No. 213, Monetary and Economic Department, Bank for International Settlements (Aug. 2006), p. 3.

69. Paul Bracken, Ian Bremmer, and David Gordon, *Managing Strategic Surprise: Lessons from Risk Management and Risk Assessment* (Cambridge, UK: Cambridge University Press, 2008), p. 19.

70. Lou Cannon, *President Reagan: The Role of a Lifetime* (New York: Simon & Schuster, 1991), as cited in Richard Rhodes, *Arsenals of Folly: The Making of the Nuclear Arms Race* (New York: Alfred A. Knopf, 2007), p. 169.

71. Yuval Rottenstreich and Christopher K. Hsee, "Money, Kisses, and Electric Shocks: On the Affective Psychology of Risk," *Psychological Science,* Vol. 12, No. 3 (May 2001), p. 186.

72. Ibid.

### Conclusion

1. Lawrence James, *The Rise and Fall of the British Empire* (London: Abacus, 1998), p. 128 and pp. 122–138. See also H. V. Bowen, "Investment and Empire in the Later Eighteenth Century: East India Stockholding, 1756–1791," *The Economic History Review,* New Series, Vol. 42, No. 2 (May 1989), p. 187.

2. However, the HEIC was closely tied and regulated by the English state and, after the 1707 Anglo-Scottish Acts of Union, by the British state. In particular, British legislative acts in 1773 and 1784 increased British governmental supervision and involvement in the company's affairs and began to transfer sovereignty from the company to the British state, although the HEIC would technically still rule India as a corporate entity until after the Indian Mutiny of 1857, when the British state assumed formal control over most of India. See Bowen, "Investment and Empire." Similarly some of the troops that fought at Plassey belonged directly to the company's army, while some were British troops "loaned" to the company. In any case, the troops at Plassey were there as agents of a corporation.

3. James, *Rise and Fall*, p. 25.

4. Ibid., p. 123.

5. Ibid.

6. Alfred Manes, "Outlines of a General Economic History of Insurance," *The Journal of Business of the University of Chicago*, Vol. 15, No. 1. (Jan. 1942), p. 33.

7. W. R. Vance, "The Early History of Insurance Law," *Columbia Law Review*, Vol. 8, No. 1 (Jan. 1908), p. 5.

8. Interestingly, the process of mitigating the risks of sea trade led to the creation of another set of potential problems, including credit default risk.

9. Jan de Vries and Ad van der Woude, *The First Modern Economy: Success, Failure, and Perseverance of the Dutch Economy, 1500–1815* (Cambridge, U.K.: Cambridge University Press, 1997).

10. See Peter L. Bernstein, *Against the Gods: The Remarkable Story of Risk* (New York: John Wiley and Sons, 1998). Peter Bernstein points out that chance was seen as an attribute of the gods. We can say that even in warfare, perhaps the earliest of human activities to display truly strategic behavior (Sun Tzu in China and Tacitus in Rome wrote manuals of war over 2,000 years ago), success was seen as being decided by the favor of gods, to be appeased or manipulated through sacrifices and rituals.

11. This is where there is a big difference between the past and the present. Before 1945, political risks faced by corporations were often met by the threat of force. A threat to foreign investment and trade was considered a legitimate casus belli. As we discussed, "gunboat diplomacy" was used significantly in the 19th and early 20th centuries, when a great power would enforce commercial terms for its enterprises abroad by sending its navy to threaten or attack the offending country. For instance, the Opium War (1839–42), which pitted Britain versus China and resulted in the British gaining control of Hong Kong, was caused by a Chinese ban on the opium trade. This essentially amounted to a regulatory change that significantly impacted the Honourable East India Company's opium trade with China. In the early 19th century the HEIC had monopolized the opium trade from China, which it would trade in exchange for tea or silver. This was a significant source of income for the HEIC, but it

was something of a problem for the Chinese imperial government, which rightly saw opium as leading to a number of addiction-related social ills and to a loss of bullion. In 1839, when the Chinese banned the trade, the result was war.

12. See: Kenneth Hansen, Robert C. O'Sullivan and W. Geoffrey Anderson, "The Dabhol Power Project Settlement: What Happened and How?" *Infrastructure Journal,* December 2005, http://www.chadbourne.com/files/Publication/a5aa1e52–4285–4bb5–87e6–7201123895a0/Presentation/PublicationAttachment/352f8f09-ae96–40fc-a293–720d0b8f0ca8/Dabhol_InfrastructureJournal12_2005.pdf (assessed on August 24, 2008); also Jyoti P. Gupta and Anil K. Sravat, "Development and Project Financing of Private Power Projects in Developing Countries: A Case Study of India," *International Journal of Project Management,* Vol. 16, No. 2 (1998), pp. 99–105.

13. Chadbourne & Parke Press Release: *Chadbourne Represented OPIC in Settlement over Dabhol Power Plant—Four-Year Dispute Resolved Over $3 Billion Indian Project Once Owned by Enron,* July 19, 2005, http://www.chadbourne.com/newsevents/NewsDetail.aspx?news=240 (accessed August 24, 2008).

14. Anil Sasi, "Dabhol's domestic lenders to buy out offshore debt—SPV to float bonds to raise funds," *The Hindu Business Line,* Apr. 14, 2005, http://www.thehindubusinessline.com/2005/04/14/stories/2005041401790100.htm (accessed August 24, 2008).

15. Lynn Drennan and Allan McConnell, *Risk and Crisis Management in the Public Sector* (Abingdon, U.K.: Routledge, 2007), pp. 154–155.

16. See Jedrzej George Frynas, "Political Instability and Business: Focus on Shell in Nigeria," *Third World Quarterly,* Vol. 19, No. 3 (1998), 457–478.

17. One of the largest problems facing Shell is delays by the Nigerian government in meeting its funding obligations in joint ventures. In joint ventures, the operator and partners must make available at regular intervals the resources to pay for operating costs. With the government-owned firm Nigerian National Petroleum Corporation (NNPC) owning 55% of petroleum joint ventures with Western oil companies, the government must provide a majority of the expenditures for oil production. But the state firm frequently fails to pay its share because of government mismanagement. Consequently, the joint venture has scaled down exploration and production on a number of occasions. To address this challenge, Shell has tried establishing escrow accounts in the U.K. responsible for collecting the oil revenues and disbursing operating costs and profits. Shell has also attempted to use production sharing agreements rather than joint venture agreements when cooperating with the government. This contract structure puts all operation cost responsibilities and production risk on Shell, but in return the corporation takes a larger cut of the revenues.

A second major risk is political-military instability. Ethnic, sectarian, and tribal conflict has been endemic to the Nigerian political scene for years. Many of Shell's onshore oil wells and facilities are located in unstable regions, such as the Niger

Delta. Gangs and militants have sabotaged pipelines, kidnapped workers, attacked and vandalized facilities, and illegally siphoned fuel from Shell's production. Most recently, the Movement for the Emancipation of the Niger Delta (MEND) has kidnapped employees and threatened installations, leading to reduced production. In addition to these violent and illicit activities, locals have protested against the environmental pollution and perceived political-economic exploitation caused by infrastructure degradation, corruption, and political negligence.

To address these dangers, Shell has invested heavily in both security and public relations. Shell not only receives police support from the Nigerian government, but also has hired well-paid Nigerian security forces (known as "spy police") to protect oil facilities and personnel. Shell has also hired leading international security consulting companies with experience in Iraq and other volatile areas to develop strategic security measures. And they have banned the paying of local gangs for protection.

In addition to these security measures, Shell adopted the principle of corporate social responsibility to improve environmental and human rights conditions in the various locales where the company does business in Nigeria. On the environmental front, Shell has invested billions of dollars to repair and replace aging infrastructure and pipelines that have been the cause of oil spills, gas fires, and other forms of pollution that have impacted the local quality of life. They have also channeled millions of dollars into community development, including building hospitals and schools and establishing microcredit financial institutions. The corporation has developed regional development councils in local communities to work with the Nigerian government and local community leaders to develop community projects. The purpose of this initiative is to increase grassroots ownership of local projects, improve relations between the oil businesses and people, and provide transparency in the decision-making process of these developmental efforts. Shell has also collaborated with international NGOs and the United Nations Development Programme to implement developmental programs.

Finally, a major risk for Shell is instability at the regional and federal government levels, which has contributed to delayed decision making. Despite frequent changes in leadership, the governments have been relatively consistent in their support to ensure that Nigerian oil development continues. Shell has invested in and built up a vast network of personal contacts within the Nigerian government. Shell managers have become Nigerian bureaucrats, local governors, and ministers, and vice versa. In 1993 a former Shell director, Ernest Shonekan, even became the Nigerian head of state. Shell has repeatedly used these connections to lobby the government to resolve government funding problems and any regulatory issues that have hampered its oil business. Source: Jedrzej George Frynas, "Political Instability and Business: Focus on Shell in Nigeria" *Third World Quarterly,* Vol. 19, No. 3 (1998), pp. 457–478.

18. Similarly, in times of financial crises, central banks often act to prevent the spread of contagion. For instance, the U.S. Federal Reserve (and JPMorgan Chase) bailout of Bear Stearns following the U.S. mortgage crisis (2008) was enacted specifically to prevent a liquidity crisis and contagion to other U.S. banks. Quarantines and curfews are used to mitigate anything from riots to the spread of disease to currency or credit crises.

19. Sandy Markwick, "Trends in Political Risk for Corporate Investors," in Theodore H. Moran, ed., *Managing International Political Risk,* p. 48.

20. Drennan and McConnell, *Risk and Crisis Management,* pp. 154–155.

21. For the Peru example, see Chapter 5 that discusses domestic strife and instability.

22. Firms operating in one country sometimes choose to become directly involved in lobbying efforts, thereby becoming interest groups themselves, and thus part of the political process. This happens with some regularity, and it holds significant risks for a firm, such as being seen as interfering in the politics of a foreign country. That said, for some companies this can be a successful endeavor.

    Increased lobbying is in fact part of an increasing trend toward corporate diplomacy. In an interconnected world, corporations have to interact with governments, NGOs, media, and shareholders on an almost 24-hour basis. Senior executives increasingly have to act as negotiators and diplomats, creating dynamic alliances that protect the company and further its interests. This is in part driven by regulations, such as Sarbanes-Oxley, that force executives to become much more accessible, by an increase in mergers and acquisitions that require executives to be increasingly involved in negotiations, and particularly by "an increasing realization by business executives that they have to play an active role in influencing governmental rule making and in shaping public perceptions" (Michael Watkins, "The Rise of Corporate Diplomacy (Finally!)," *Harvard Business On-line,* May 18, 2007, http://discussionleader. hbsp.com/watkins/2007/05/the_rise_of_corporate_diplomac.html [accessed on August 24, 2008]).

    On the other hand, strategic alliances, joint ventures, and joint financing are also classic ways of spreading risk around when investing abroad. It is good practice to have local partners, lenders, and suppliers that have an active interest in the success of the investment. However, things are not always that simple. For instance, while joint ownership can help reduce political risks, it is important to know who the local partners are.

23. Ulrich Bech, *Risk Society: Towards a New Modernity* (London: Sage, 1992).

24. "Despite all of the talk about ERM in the trade press, evidence indicates that it is still not widely practiced. For example, a 2001 study by the Economist Intelligence Unit (EIU, 2001) found that 41 percent of companies in Europe, North America, and Asia had implemented some form of ERM, but when looking at just North America, the number drops to 34 percent. Why is ERM not more common in practice? Some

reasons may include organizational structures that are not conducive to ERM, individuals who do not want to give up their specific responsibilities, a lack of understanding regarding how to effectively implement ERM and measure its benefits, and difficulties in measuring risk and correlations across risks in the company." Anne E. Kleffner, Ryan B. Lee, and Bill McGannon, "The Effect of Corporate Governance on the Use of Enterprise Risk Management: Evidence from Canada," *Risk Management & Insurance Review* Vol. 6, No. 1 (Feb. 2003), p. 54.

25. Carl Mortished, "Gazprom to Raise Its Own Private Army to Protect Oil Installations," *The Times (London)*, July 5, 2007.

26. Kimberly Hefling, "Report: Iraq Contracts Have Cost at Least $85B," Associated Press, August 13, 2008.

# Index

Note: page numbers followed by *f* and *t* indicate figures and tables, respectively.